BAZIL'S BUSH

THE
FAMOUS
5

Bountyhunter
Publications

BAZIL'S BUSH

THE STORY OF A MAN AND HIS OBSESSION
BY
ROB MAYLIN AND FRIENDS

Bountyhunter
Publications

ANGLING TITLES BY ROB MAYLIN

TIGER BAY
First published in 1988 by
Beekay Publishers
Withy Pool
Bedford Road
Henlow Camp
Bedfordshire
SG16 6EA
England

FOX POOL
First published in 1989 by
Bountyhunter Publications
The Acorns
Woburn Close
Flitwick
Bedfordshire
MK45 1TE

BAZIL'S BUSH
First published in 1993 by
Bountyhunter Publications
The Acorns
Woburn Close
Flitwick
Bedfordshire
MK45 1TE

ISBN 0 9515127 2 2

Produced by Print Solutions, London, W4

CONTENTS

Front Cover: 'Bazil' in her September splendour

Rear Cover: I just didn't want to let her go

INTRODUCTION

The story you are about to read not only concerns the fishing of myself, Rob Maylin, from the years 1989 to 1993 but also the story of a man and a fish. A story that brings together heartache, sorrow, jealousy and finally happiness. Happiness beyond words.

When trying to think of a title for this book, all sorts of names went through my head. The lakes that I'd been fishing were all very hard, not only were you trying to catch a fish from these lakes but you were also trying to catch the biggest fish from these venues. Names like 'Pursuit of the Biggest', 'Land of the Giants' all came to mind but in the end, when only *Bazil* really mattered to me, it just had to be *Bazil's Bush*.

But don't be misled into thinking that this whole book is about *Bazil*, it isn't. It's about the fishing of myself, some of my friends, including the Famous Five, on some of the hardest venues in the country. You find the fishing on Fox Pool in its last year, and the incredible things which happened there. The sad netting of Longfield. The Famous Five then went to Johnson's, that extremely difficult Railway Lake with its huge leather carp and the adventures they had there. Yateley, Stanstead Abbots, Harefield, truly some of the greatest names in carp fishing history.

Whilst I and my friends had been fishing on these difficult lakes, other friends of ours had been tackling different waters and you'll find stories by some of those anglers, Peter Springate and his struggles on Wraysbury and the final pleasure of landing one of the biggest brace of carp in British history. And of course Dave Lane and his fantastic seasons on the Church Pool at Horton. Seasons that have never been equalled by any carp angler.

There are individual articles by Steve Allcott - the last fish ever to be taken from Longfield. Tony Moore and his fantastic brace of Yateley fish. Ritchie McDonald - the brace of forties at the end of the season which brought a three year wait to an incredible climax, and of course my good friend Stuart Gillham, probably the most successful angler ever on Harefield, his tally of thirty pounders in one season was mind-blowing.

So there you have it. A book of stories, a continuation from my previous two books, *Tiger Bay* and *Fox Pool. Bazil's Bush* was written entirely on the bank, written from the bivvy as things occurred. The writing may be slightly different to my other books but it's truly from the heart. These are the events as they happened, the successes and the failures and the times when you just want to reach your arms up to the sky and shout at the top of your voice because you have conquered the biggest fish in the lake.

Chapter 1

GOD SAVE THE KING

W e left Fox Pool at the end of the 1988/89 season with mixed feelings. We'd had tremendous results there in the short time we'd spent on the water. I personally felt that I hadn't done as well as I should have done. Looking back over the fish that we caught, we'd taken all the big fish that were in the lake between us, other than one, *The Koi*. *The Koi*, a 35 pound fish, made only one appearance that season and fell to the rods of Clive Williams of Horsham in Sussex. That story is well documented in *Fox Pool*.

I knew at the end of this season that it just wouldn't be the same going back there now that some of the lads I was fishing with had received a suspension from Leisure Sport Angling. Looking ahead to the new season, we didn't really know where we were going to fish, one thing about which we *had* made up our minds was that we'd be fishing some new waters this season. We'd been fortunate at Fox Pool in meeting two lads from Brighton, Peter Jones and Dave Brown - Pete the Burglar and John Travolta as they were affectionately known. They told us about a lake in Kent which they had been fishing on and off for the last couple of years that held some real whackers. The lake was known as Johnson's or the Railway Lake and I would guess it was around ten acres, and wedge-shaped. The fish were by no means easy, I think this was mainly due to the nature of the lake - very, very deep, a lot of the water was 18 to 20 feet deep in the margins, and extremely weedy.

If we were to fish there in the coming season, we would obviously have to get down there as often as we could in the close season, do some plumbing and try and sort out the water a little bit before we made our assault at the start of the season.

We went down a couple of times, probably not as many times as we should have, in the May of that year and it's funny how you conjure up a picture of a water in your mind from information received from other people. When I eventually found myself on Johnson's, it was entirely different from what I'd expected. I seemed to have this picture in my mind of overhanging trees and fishing in the margins as I'd done on another deep lake that I'd fished before. Johnson's was nothing like this, it was more or less a hole in the ground with very little cover close to the banks. Dave Whibley, Steve Allcott and I parked our cars on the road bank and made our way down the causeway between Leisure Sport's Larkfield and Johnson's Lake.

Situated halfway down this bank is a wooden bridge which goes across a small bay. We stood on the bridge and looked into the large bed of lily pads to the left hand side of the swim. We could make out about 20 very large fish moving around amongst the pads. We fired out some mixers and eventually got most of the fish taking them close in. These fish looked very big to me but I must admit to overestimating their size, as later on in the season when we began catching, some of the fish that we had seen in the close season which we estimated at 30 pounds were only in the mid-twenties.

Peter Jones had told us that in the past the lake contained about six thirties: a lovely leather, probably the best fish in the lake, was the one that he had taken and you can find his story in *Fox Pool*; other than that, the fish known as the *Spotty Fish* coming out around 34 pounds; another fish, a real old battle-scarred warrior known as *The Dinosaur* or *Prehistoric* again was around 32 to 34 pounds; but there was one big one, a fish very distinctive because of a bullet-shaped hole through its tail. This fish hadn't been caught for a couple of seasons, last time out it was over 36 pounds and we were hoping that this fish could do the forty. Obviously we like to fish lakes that have 40 pound fish in if possible. Steve Allcott and I had not taken a 40 pounder and this was what we wanted to catch so we were really hoping that this fish would be big.

During our close season visits to the lake, we became very knowledgeable about the fish and could recognise several of them very easily in the water. The leather was particularly distinctive because of its sandy coloured appearance. This fish looked big to me - I estimated its size at 35 pounds, due to its enormous length, almost 36 inches long.

Although the lake was different to what I expected, I certainly wasn't disappointed with what I saw. It was a fantastic looking water and really spelt carp. I looked forward with eager anticipation to the forthcoming season. I decided to do a little bit of prebaiting at this time, it's not something I put much faith in normally, I just thought as I was using a new bait I would introduce some to the water. I was using one of the Tandoori Spice baits that I market for Catchum, with an Indian spiced bait and some fish oil.

I put in several mixes during the close season. The fish wasted no time in getting their heads down so I thought I was obviously on to a winner with the bait. Another thing I wanted to do this season was some serious floater-fishing and this water also offered

Johnson's, open and windswept, a formidable challenge

Dave Whibley, first to catch a Johnson's carp

opportunities for fishing on the top. Peter Jones had taken the leather on the top the season before. As with most of these very deep lakes, surface fishing can be a better proposition than fishing on the bottom a lot of the time, especially early in the year when the weather is very warm. Anyway, after a lot of deliberation in the pub later that day, we'd made our minds up to do the first week of the season at Johnson's Railway Lake.

We arrived on the water three days before the start, we'd been told that the lake gets very busy and that if we were to get sorted out in a reasonable swim, we'd be best to get down there fairly early - we were the first anglers on the water. Dave Whibley and Trotter went in *The Bridge* swim, I went in *The Pads* on the causeway, Steve Allcott went in the *Secret* swim just to my left. Other than that Peter Jones was to the right of Dave Whibley and John Travolta just to the left of Steve.

In the two days leading up to the start of the season, we had an enormous amount of fish in front of us and the bait that we were putting out was obviously turning them on, as they rolled and crashed continually. The wind at this time was almost nonexistent, and conditions looked good for a reasonable start to the season. As is always the case, things change - as the lake became more and more crowded and the wind got up, blowing onto the road bank, most of the fish moved down to this area. On opening night, I can honestly say that we didn't have a fish in front of us, they were all rolling and crashing off the road bank side. Opening night was a disappointment again to us all, but it came as no surprise to learn that several good fish had been taken off the road bank, four twenties - the biggest being 29 pounds. These fish again fell to Derek, the chap who had taken the 36 pound fish two years before.

Unfortunately there were no free swims on that bank and I couldn't move in, however I knew that people would be going home after the first weekend and I decided to make plenty of bait in preparation for a move as soon as a swim became available. It was probably the worst move I'd ever made, I must have passed the fish on my way down to the road bank with my tackle. The wind had died off by this time and as I walked down to the road bank, the fish passed me and moved - guess where? - In front of *The Bridge* swim. Knowing what good anglers I fish with you can imagine that they soon closed up the gaps and there was no room for me to move back.

I moved back round to *The Pads* swim, where a few fish were showing on the top - I took a stalking rod with me and finally managed to get about three fish coming up, one of which was the leather. It looked absolutely gorgeous and it was having them. I tried my hardest to catch the fish but every time I cast to it it would move to another bunch of mixers. As I said, the wind was blowing on to the road bank which was pushing the mixers from left to right across the swim in front of me, that meant that the mixers were heading down towards Trotter and Dave Whibley and I knew they both had floater rods set up just in case anything came up.

It wasn't long before the leather was in front of Dave who presented a single floating boilie on a size six Kamasan hook and a home-made controller. There was an almighty swirl, the rod bent double and the fish screamed across the lake. We knew that it was the leather, the fish that we had come down here for. The fight was absolutely incredible! It made several runs, and this is no exaggeration, of 40 yards or more. This really was a fighter - in fact, it seemed to be fighting *too* much, we wondered if the fish could be foul-hooked. When Dave eventually got it to the net, there was the hook embedded in the side of the fish. It's no wonder that it fought so hard, Dave was unable to get a direct line to the fish, he was absolutely gutted as you would be. He put it on the scales anyway just to see how heavy it was, surprisingly it was only 32 pounds. I say only (I mean 32 pounds is a good fish) but we were thinking that it could well be in the 35 pound class.

That put an end to all the action on the top. I moved back round into *The Road Bank* swim, putting out three pounds of bait during the first night in the swim. The fish had well and truly moved out in front of *The Bridge* and over the next of couple of days, Dave Whibley, Trotter and Peter Jones had intense action. Dave Whibley had two fish, both twenties, 21 and 22 pounds, one a leather, and lost two other fish. Peter Jones had a 19 and a 21 along with other smaller fish and lost one as well.

There was nothing I could do other than sit and wait, and hope that the wind got up again. The forecast told me that it was due to come back on to the road bank and I hoped it would get up to the force it was at the start of the season. I kept putting the bait out and hoped the fish would return.

Action on the causeway ceased and I thought to myself the fish could well be on the move. That night the wind picked up again,

The 'Bent Tail' at 25lb 4oz, check the hairstyle

Kent carp no. 2 at 24lb 4oz

blowing straight into the bivvy door. I thought to myself at the time, if I'm going to get any action, tonight's going to be the night. That night, I went to bed full of anticipation. There was a howling gale blowing straight at me and I had loads of bait out there, conditions were perfect.

One thing that had happened at this time that I didn't realise, was the buzzer on my right hand rod had packed up. I don't know what roused me but I woke up about one o'clock in the morning and noticed that the right hand rod had come off the rest. The wind was extremely strong that night. I got up and pulled the line but couldn't feel anything on the end, so I replaced the rod on the buzzer and thought the wind must just have pulled it off. Back off to sleep again, but awake at about five o'clock in the morning, again not knowing why. I looked down at the rods - nothing had moved - the rods were still perfectly positioned, indicators in the same place at the top of the pin, all three rods on Baitrunner. As I sat and listened, I heard a click, click, click. I looked down again and it was the right hand rod. Something was definitely amiss. I ran down the bank and picked that same rod up, the one that had been off the rest at one o'clock in the morning, all I felt was a solid weight. I'd obviously had a pick-up in the early hours of the morning, the buzzer had not registered and the fish had just laid doggo, completely dormant in the weed. I kept heaving and pulling, hoping that the fish was still on. Suddenly I felt a tug on the end, and when the fish was in the margins I recognised it as a fish I had seen many times in the close season, very distinctive because of its bent-over tail. I estimated the fish in the close season at around 28 pounds but when I eventually got it on the bank, it weighed 25lb 4oz. I was pleased that my first Kent carp was my first Johnson's fish.

I was just taking the photographs when the middle rod hammered off. I was down the bank in a second and soon had another fish of similar size on the bank, this one 24lb 4oz. Right, I thought to myself, I'm really going to stack them up now, so I put some more bait out and waited for the early hours again, but that was it. The fish moved through my swim and carried on down to my right despite large quantities of bait remaining in the area.

Phil Harper had been down on the Snake Pit for the start of the season, it had been very quiet down there, he'd done the first week. We'd phoned him at regular intervals to tell him of our successes on the water and he soon became keen to come down and get in on the action. He arrived on the morning I'd caught the two fish and moved in to my right, immediately putting out a large bed of bait. I don't know whether it was the bait or just the fact that the fish were on the move, but they moved out in front of Phil and over the next two days he took three fish, 21, 23 and a small double. We were all willing Phil to catch a good fish, he'd had a disastrous season the year before on Fox Pool, he hadn't landed a single fish. So we ended our first week at Johnson's Lake, a fantastic session really, quite a few 20 pound fish on the bank, the best being the fish I took, *Bent Tail* at 25lb 4oz. We'd certainly be back for some more of this.

I'd made up my mind in the close season that I wouldn't be fishing Fox Pool seriously this season. The fishing was very, very hard, harder than I wanted it to be. I'd waited a long time to take my first fish from the water the previous season and although as I said we'd had the results, there was no way I was going to spend the amount of time that I'd spent on the water previously. However, I did want to go down mid-week just for evening sessions after work if conditions looked favourable.

It had been a long-standing ambition of mine to take a big fish from the surface, and past results, from people like Jan Wenzcka, Chris Ball and John Allen, had proved it was possible to take a 30 pound fish from the surface on this particular lake and I wanted some of that sort of action.

I went down there on the first Wednesday after my week at Johnson's. It was overcast, a slight wind coming off the bungalow bank blowing down towards the car park. Previous years had told me that these were ideal conditions although most of the action we'd had at this time of year had been first thing in the morning and this was the evening. I didn't intend to do the night down there though I did have my equipment with me just in case I fancied staying. I walked round into the *Noddy* swim, there were several anglers on the water, none of whom I recognised, though I knew that some very good anglers were seriously fishing the lake this year, among them Terry Dempsey, Bernard Loftus and Dave Moore.

As I stood in the *Noddy* swim talking to one of the bailiffs, I saw a fish pop its head out of the water, off the bungalow. I thought 'right that'll do for me'. So saying nothing more I moved round with my tackle. As I stood in the middle of that bank another fish came out, I recognised this one as being *Shoulders*, a big chestnut brown

Phil and the bream-shaped carp

700 hours? No - ten minutes

fish I'd seen on the bank a couple of times before. I knew this fish to be around the 35 pound mark. Just after I set my rod up, I was ready to cast out when the same fish jumped out again to the right of where I was standing. I picked the rod up and moved down in to that swim, almost ready to cast out again and it jumped again to my right. The game was cat and mouse, the fish obviously knew that I was there and I knew that the fish was there. No way were they going to let me get on top of them. What I decided to do in the end was cast a rod where I first saw the fish and put that on the Baitrunner, then take a rod to where I'd last seen the fish and put a rod out there on the Baitrunner, then stand in the middle and hope. Unbelievably, 15 minutes later, the line screamed from the right hand rod - I couldn't believe my luck. The season before I'd waited 700 hours for my first take, yet here I was 20 minutes into the session and already into a fish. I really hoped that it was *Shoulders* as it was a fish I really wanted to catch. Closer in, I could see that it wasn't but it was still a fish in the mid-twenties. On the bank it proved to be 25lb 8oz. I was well pleased with the fish though - a tremendous result, unbelievable in such a short space of time. I took a few pictures, packed my gear up and went home a happy man. That's the sort of fishing I like to do, a 25 pound fish and I'm not on the water any longer than an hour, but I knew that kind of fishing was just too good to be true and that I would have to put the time in for consistent results.

We were back up at Johnson's the following weekend. Fishing was very slow due to the heat, I didn't expect to catch anything off the bottom but hoped there might be some action on the top. I was proved wrong as John Travolta was into a very good fish, it was very long, scaly, very handsome - 26lb 8oz. When I looked at the fish I noticed that it had a small hole in it's tail. I hadn't seen the bullet-tailed 36 on the bank before and I said to Dave that I suspected that this was indeed the 36 and that it had shed spawn or lost weight dramatically.

He couldn't believe it could possibly be the same fish, but at a later date we compared photos with those of Derek's and sure enough, this was the 36 dropped an incredible ten pounds in three seasons. This was an absolute gutter for me. It probably meant that the largest fish we were fishing for were only in the low thirties now, possibly the leather being the biggest at 32. It certainly changed my outlook on the water and I must admit I lost a lot of enthusiasm.

We continued fishing the water on and off for the next few weeks. Dave Whibley again was the next one with action, he took *The Spotty Fish* at 32 pounds. This fish turned out to be quite friendly and was caught the following week by Clive Williams from the surface, again at the same weight. Next weekend we were down again, Phil Harper fishing on the road bank had a take around 6am and I immediately went round with my camera. The way the fish was fighting we knew that it was going to be a big one, we couldn't believe it when we got it in the net and saw that it was *The Spotty Fish* again. Unfortunately for Phil it was foulhooked, his luck just wasn't running. We all felt really sorry for him, his first thirty for quite a while - very disappointing.

I'd had enough of Johnson's by now and fancied a change of scenery, so the next week Phil and I planned to do a weekend on the Snake Pit. Quite a daunting prospect as there are only four carp in the lake, one however was a 40 pound common. This was another lake that made the fishing very difficult, half of the lake was filled with submerged trees and this was where the fish could be found. In fact, you could see the fish on most days down in one area of the snags - impossible to fish for. I was tempted and went round there with a floater rod and I had the 40 pound common taking mixers. It was as much as I could do to restrain myself from casting. I knew that there was no chance of me landing that fish if I hooked it, and decided I would rather cause the fish no damage than attempt to catch it. All sorts of thoughts were going through my mind, I'd jump in, I'd swim under the branches, I'd even try and cast a line over the top and let it go through the snags. After a lot of careful thought I decided against it, fate has a funny way of kicking you in the balls sometimes. Six o'clock the next morning I heard someone coming down into my swim, my head wasn't quite together and I wondered who the bloody hell could be walking around at this time of the morning, knowing Phil gets his beauty sleep until at least 11.30! It was Phil with a great big smile on his face: "I've had it, I've had it!" They were the only words he could say and, "it's bloody big." I couldn't believe it, yes six o'clock that morning he'd caught the big common. Quite incredible, we'd gone out that night to the pub, had our usual quota of beer and on returning to the lake, he'd given a 'Holsten-cast' into the middle of nowhere and at six o'clock in the morning it had roared off. The

Travolta with 'Bullet-Tail' drastically down in weight

Clive Williams with 'Spotty' the friendly carp

Longfield, the King of carp waters

common went 41lb 4oz and it was an absolutely incredible sight, huge length, dark gold, it looked like a pile of gold sovereigns lying on the floor. It absolutely took my breath away, I could feel goose pimples standing up on my back and the hair standing up on the back of my head. Phil was in another world, it was his second forty, his first forty being the Silver End fish that he'd taken several years before. It was absolutely brilliant to see a fish like this on the bank and I couldn't have been more pleased. Well, I could have been a little bit more pleased if I'd caught it but I was well pleased for Phil. It was celebration after celebration after the capture of that fish! A memory that will stay with me for ever, an absolutely fantastic common.

We were now into the middle of the summer and I hadn't taken anything since that last fish at Longfield. I'd been working for Vauxhall Motors for the last 15 years, when a brilliant job opportunity came up for me to work down in London for another car company, designing Swedish vehicles, and I decided to leave Vauxhall. It so happened that after I finished at Vauxhall, I had four days before the start of my new appointment and I decided to utilise this time to the full with a bit of floater-fishing down at Fox Pool.

Weather conditions were perfect for floater-fishing down at Staines and I decided this is what I would do. I didn't want to night fish, night fishing in these sort of conditions had proved futile the season before. It was very, very hot and flat calm. Not only were the weather conditions perfect but so were other requirements. None of the big fish, other than the forty, had been taken so far from Staines, that meant there were possibly six thirties which hadn't been caught so far this season, and I knew that most of them were suckers for a floater on the surface.

I'd kept in touch with what was going on down there, Terry Dempsey was spending a tremendous amount of time there, as was Bernard Loftus. I packed my gear up and roared off down the motorway, heading for what is, or was, my favourite lake. It may sound a bit sentimental but when I drove into the car park, the feeling that swept over me was absolutely tremendous. Never has another water had this sort of effect on me. The lake contained about 30 fish, ten of which at any one time could be over 30 pounds in weight, with half of those possibly going over 35 pounds. That meant that I had a one-in-three chance of a 30 pound fish if I had a take. When you did get a take on there, you never knew how big the fish was going to be. Chances were it was going to be a big boy.

Taking my floater rod, net, a small box of bits and pieces and a bag of mixers sprayed with Tandoori bait soak, I walked round to the pier behind the car park. I found Bernard in a haze of purple smoke, half-asleep on his bedchair. A strange aroma filled the air. I then walked round to Terry Dempsey in the *Secret* swim, he too was out for the count, this meant I had the lake to myself, something I had hoped would happen.

One thing I do try when I'm floater fishing is to fish with the wind over my shoulder, that way you can drift the mixers out into the lake - this saves unnecessary commotion caused by spodding. I walked around the lake a couple of times and eventually I found three fish out in front of the *Middle* swim. Climbing up the large climbing tree by the side of the swim I could see that two of the fish were very large, one of them was *The Parrot*, a fish I had taken the season before at 35lb 4oz. I sat down quietly in the swim and began to feed in a few mixers. These fish were ultra-wary, no way do they go mad on the mixers, only taking a few and then moving off. I sat there for about an hour, putting out a few mixers every now and again and they began to slowly snake out across the lake. Out of the corner of my left eye I saw a fish coming up taking a couple of mixers, I quickly went back up the climbing tree - it was *The Parrot*. My nerve totally broke then, a fish of that size taking close in on mixers is one of the most exciting sights in carp fishing. I couldn't get a mixer on in my hurry and then I got a hook in my trousers. In the end, I had to re-tackle the lot, panic set in, no way am I a floater fisherman of the same quality as Jan Wenzcka, that is their sort of fishing, continually walking round the lake with one rod, float fishing in the snags, freelining boilies and floater fishing on the top. My sort of fishing is more suited to sitting behind a pair of static rods working on a swim, learning about the topography of the bottom and hoping that I'd done it right. Eventually I managed to get set up. I knew that the cast had to be perfect, cast beyond the fish and draw back. The last floater fishing I'd done had been on Arlesey Lake in 1983 which was quite a long time ago. I swept the rod back and crash, straight on top of its head, I had frightened the life out of it. Well that was the end of that, I sat there with my head in my hands - I'd missed my chance. No... to my right there it was again, sucking at a small group of mixers that had floated off to the right. I quickly reeled in, this time the cast was perfect, about 20 feet beyond the mixers. I

The 'Snake Pit', the most difficult water in Essex

A pile of gold sovereigns

'Heart-tail' not Shoulders

drew the float slowly back into the path of the fish. He had other ideas - he then moved back to where he was in the first place. I kept thinking to myself, don't keep casting, you're only going to frighten it in the end. When a fish is taking mixers to your left and your float's the farthest to the right you can put it, it's very hard to sit still. I picked the rod up and recast again to the left, then the fish was to the right. This is when everything went wrong, I turned into a demented fly fisherman, thrashing the water to a foam, trying to get the float on top of the fish. Of course, a fish like this wasn't going to stand for that for very long, soon it was gone.

Another fish then made an appearance but further out, I tried casting at that and managed to frighten that one off as well. Two or three chances blown in a short space of time, was I ever going to get a fish on the bank on a floater? And then, right on the horizon I saw another big back coming out of the water taking a few of the mixers that had gone right out. This fish looked like *Shoulders*. Using the weighted controller that I had it was possible to cast over 90 yards, even with the ten pound line that I was using. Luckily this swim didn't have too much cover over the top and the 13 foot rod I was using was perfect for the job of punching the floater out long range. The float landed right on top of the fish and I cursed myself that I couldn't just get those extra few feet. Everything was quiet, the lake was still and I sat there looking out at my float. I could see my mixer drifting just behind it, then out of the depth came that huge back which will stay forever in my mind. I saw it crash down right next to the float and before I could lift the rod, the line was tight to the tip. I screamed across the lake: "Bernard, Bernard." I needed help with the netting due to the weed and the fact that I was only using the light line hooklink. "Bernard, you lazy bastard, get up." He was in the land of the dead mate, no way was he going to get up. In the end Terry heard me shouting and came round. "I think it's *Shoulders*," I said. Eventually we got the fish close in and I could see it down there under the rod tip plunging around, the mixer just hanging by its lips, this huge white mouth. "It is *Shoulders*." Terry netted it and hoisted it ashore. This fish has got to be 35 pounds. On the scales, 31lb 12oz - I wasn't disappointed, it was a fish I really had wanted to catch but I couldn't believe the weight was so low.

Everyone cursed my golden anatomy. I packed up and went home very, very pleased that I'd caught the fish. My wife was also delighted that I'd caught it. When I got home I was in a very good mood indeed and come the morning she was keen for me to go out and catch another one. I got to the lake again about ten o'clock in the morning and wandered round. No sign of any fish in the swims they had occupied yesterday. I sat in the *Middle* swim for a while but nothing could be seen. After about an hour on the water I made my mind up that I might as well go home, perhaps come back later that evening. I walked down and found Dave Moore with the kettle on and decided to sit down with him and have a cup of tea before I went. Jan Wenzcka then appeared, he had come down to do some float fishing in the *Corner* and asked me if I'd seen any fish on the top at all and I told him that I hadn't. He already knew that I'd taken the big fish the day before, I asked him if he'd seen any fish and he said: "It so happens that I have seen a couple of small fish on the *Out-of-Bounds*, probably only about 15 pounds."

I sat with Dave and finished my tea and then turned to him and said "I think I might as well go for a 15 pounder, I'd rather catch a 15 than nothing." I walked round to the *Out-of-Bounds* swim, there were about three or four fish there. Jan was right, they were small. I put a few mixers out and gradually one or two started to be taken. I waited until the fish were confident and then cast my mixer out amongst them. Jan noticed that I'd got some fish feeding and came down and set up in the swim to my left. Jan had some great big mixers with him, like dog biscuits, I think they were used for Bull Terriers or something. He was firing his out with a Wrist Rocket and they were going about three times as far as I could fire my mixers, he put about 30 of these out and they soon drifted well out, slightly in front of me. Chris Ball then turned up, he was having a walk round and he too had heard of the fish I'd taken the day before. He'd just come down with a pair of binoculars to have a look around the lake.

If any of you have ever fished with Chris Ball in the past, you will know that he is the most excitable angler you could ever have on the bank, not only in his own fishing but if anyone else is in with a chance, he's equally as bad. Chris could see that several fish were now taking, a couple of them now better fish and his old nerves started to go. He got in a panic which eventually got me in a panic. He was up and down the trees with binoculars, running along the margins, standing at the next swim. "You're going to get one boy, I haven't seen them like this since last summer." Now unfortunately my nerves were getting as bad as Chris's. As soon as he started

The 'Parrot' at 37lb 8oz, it's nice to meet old friends

'Shoulders' for certain this time – 34lb 12oz

going on, I couldn't stop my hands shaking. I couldn't get a mixer on, then I had to tie another hook on - same old story. Eventually, I managed to get my float out there, nothing happening though. Those big mixers that Jan had fired out had now drifted right out in front of me, about 90 yards range. As we stared out onto the horizon we could see several fish moving towards them. Chris went up the tree with his binoculars and called down: "It's the A-Team." (The A-Team was a name that we'd given to the largest fish in the lake that tend to stick together.) He could make out that out there was *The Forty, The Parrot, The Koi* and *Shoulders* and they were going for them. Absolutely incredible to see these fish in action, ploughing through the water towards each one of these big mixers. They had thrown all caution to the wind and the mixers, which had now spread out so that there was about 15 feet in between each one, were being taken voraciously. The fish then turned round to see the next mixer, ploughing through the water with a huge bow-wave behind them, with their backs coming right out of the water. I put a fresh mixer on and gave it my best cast and landed out there amongst the big dog biscuits. I looked through Chris's binoculars and I could see my float, the mixer however had done the worst thing it could do, because the line had sunk between the mixer and the float, the mixer had drifted to within an inch of the float. Absolutely the worst presentation for floater fishing, I cursed my luck but knew that I couldn't better that cast, I would have to leave it there. Gradually they cleared up all the big biscuits until there was only mine out there. I could see my little mixer floating against the side of the controller. Chris looked through his binoculars again, we could see the fish had shoaled up into a 'V' formation, suddenly they spied my little mixer and began to head for it. "They've seen it boy, they're heading straight for it." I grasped the rod in my hand, praying, wishing, hoping, they certainly were heading straight towards it. "They're only about 12 feet away, ten feet away, eight feet away, six feet away, three feet away." Crash, there was an almighty explosion out in the middle of the lake and I struck like a madman up into the air. The line got tangled round the tree, round my arm, round the rear handle, there was nothing on the end. I sat there shaking, the blood had totally left my body. Chris turned to me and his immortal words will stay with me evermore: "I really thought you were going to get one then, I'll leave you for a minute to get your nerves back together," and he walked off. I just sat there shaking, I couldn't believe what had happened, a really good chance and I'd messed it up.

Chris then proceeded to go round the lake and tell everyone what a prat I was. All having a good laugh at how I'd balls'd up the chance of a massive fish. The other anglers wasted no time in coming round to tell me what a fool I was. "Chris said you really should have caught one." "Yes I know," I kept saying as the next one arrived. In the end about six anglers stood in my swim, all taking the piss out of me.

I looked down and in the edge where a few mixers had dropped from the pouch, a tiny mouth was coming up sucking in one after another. As there was a glare on the water I couldn't see the fish, I could just make out a very small mouth gradually devouring the mixers. An underarm flick and I had my mixer out there amongst them. We all stood there looking down into the water, the mouth came up again and took yet another. My mixer, I thought, but nothing had moved, not the line or the float. I turned round to Chris and said "that was mine wasn't it?" He said: "Well, that's the one I've been looking at." I looked at Dave Moore, he hunched his shoulders and said "I thought that one was yours." Then I detected the slightest motion on the float, it seemed to be moving from side to side. Christ, these cagey fish. The fish had taken the mixer, realised that it had done something wrong and sat just a couple of feet below the surface with the mixer in its mouth, shaking its head from side to side. I had a 13 foot rod in my hand and I decided to give it everything that it was worth. I heaved into it and the water exploded like a food mixer at my feet as the fish headed off to my left through Jan's swim. "It's only a little one Chris," I said to him. Jan came round. It was a dogged fight and when I saw the fish in the edge, it was a lot bigger than I'd thought. As soon as we got it in the net, I knew which fish it was - *The Parrot*. "You're looking at a 35 pound fish there," said Chris. We put it on the scales, 37lb 8oz. I couldn't believe my luck, a personal best for me and a fish that I had been very attached to since I had first seen it caught last year. I couldn't be more pleased, I packed my gear away and went off home. Two thirties off the top in two days. Fantastic!

The next day I got down there about dinner time. Whereas I had the floater fishing to myself on the previous two days, everything had now changed. The word had got out and every swim was taken by a carp angler, all floater fishing, and there in the middle of the

Don Orriss with 'Heather' at 40lb 4oz, time to smile

My first meeting with 'Bazil', this time she went forty-three

lake was the biggest sea of mixers I have ever seen. There had to
a hundredweight of mixers floating on the top and every now and
then, you could see a little red dot in the middle of them as
everyone's controllers were bobbing around. There was no way
anyone was going to catch a thing, just too much disturbance. When
you've got floater fishing to yourself on a water like this you've got
a chance but when you've got 20 people doing it, and all those
mixers out there, no-one's got a prayer.

I walked around the lake about three or four times and couldn't
see any fish. Eventually I climbed the climbing tree in the *Middle*
swim, although the 'pest' was already set up with his tackle. The
'pest' is one of the regulars down there, you can guess how he gets
his name! As I got to the top of the climbing tree, I stared out into
the centre of the lake. Nothing moved on the surface but out there
I could see, about two feet down, a shoal of very large fish. Yes,
they were out in the *Middle* swim. I made my mind up that probably
the only way to get one would be to critically weight a mixer with
a small piece of anglers putty so that the mixer slowly sank in front
of the fish. Even a mixer fished at three feet under the surface under
a float can be effective at times. Yes, this is what I was going to have
to do but how could I get on the fish with the 'pest' firmly installed
in the *Middle* swim? I even thought about offering him a fiver to let
me fish his swim for half an hour. In the end I changed my mind and
moved into a very small swim to his right, a swim which
unfortunately has a lot of branches over the top of it and made
casting very difficult with a 13 foot rod, especially considering I had
a fair distance to get to the fish. I laid down flat on my stomach and
tried to punch the controller out as far as it would go, the float
dropped about 30 feet from the bank and I knew that this was no
good at all. I just sat there with the float bobbing around in front of
me, wondering how on earth I could manage to get out to the fish
with all the swims taken.

From my left came three bow-waves, three fish and heading
straight towards my float. I couldn't believe it. Surely they couldn't
see that single mixer with five million of them floating out in the
middle and only one in the edge? They got closer and closer and
closer and then a great back again came out of the water and I was
in. Everyone came round, cursing and swearing at my luck. The net
was under - it was *Shoulders*. I wasn't going to weigh it as I'd only
had it two days before, but decided to put it on the scales just the

same - 34lb 12oz. I just couldn't believe it, surely the first fish must have been weighed wrong? When I eventually got the pictures back the first fish wasn't *Shoulders* at all, it was a fish called the *Heart-tailed Mirror*, very similar to *Shoulders* as you will see from the pictures. It is not really that similar but when you are on the bank it is easy to make that sort of mistake, especially considering I had never seen the *Heart-tail* on the bank before and it had only been caught once in all the sessions I had been down there. So, that was *Shoulders*, 34lb 12oz. Three thirties in three days, all off the top. Absolutely brilliant!

Time moved on quickly and we soon found ourselves in my favourite month of the year - October. I had a week's annual leave left and I decided to spend it on one of my favourite waters, Yateley in Surrey. At the time the complex held two 40 pound fish, a large scaly mirror in the North Lake which had reached a weight of 45 pounds in previous years and a large leather in the Car Park Lake known as *Heather*, which had been around 42 pounds, although just recently some of the fish had been coming out a lot lighter. Either of those fish were worth fishing for and I hadn't made any plans as to what lake I was going to go on until I went to the complex. I'd have a look and see which lake looked best or what had been caught and then make my mind up which I was going to fish.

I drove into the car park, opened the door and I heard a loud 'Ya-Hoo' from the Car Park Lake, someone had got a fish on the bank. I quickly picked up my camera and went down the path. On the causeway between the Lily Lake and the Car Park Lake, half way down I could see a huge fish laying on the bank - it was *Heather the Leather*, 40lb 4oz. Unbelievable, I had seen two forties in a couple of weeks, a common and a leather. I wondered if the big North Lake mirror would make an appearance and make it three for me to see. I hoped it would be on the end of my line.

My mind had now been made up for me, it had to be the North Lake. I went and got my gear and made my way up to the lake. I had a quick look around and decided that *The Point* swim offered me the best choice as it gives you access to a small bay which runs behind it. The fish often get in this area at this time of the year but it also gives you the chance to fish out in the main lake or the edge of the islands. For those of you that haven't seen Yateley North Lake, it is approximately eight acres in size, about four acres of it are lines of islands, the other half is open water with this small back channel running behind the point as I said. There are about eight fish in the North Lake; there's *The Forty*, there's a mirror of around thirty and a few smaller fish. This made the fishing very difficult, such a small number of fish and the fact that there were so many islands and overhanging trees where they could take refuge, it was very hard to get yourself on them, the only way really is by sighting the fish or by pure luck.

Terry Pethybridge was fishing opposite me in the *OK Corral*, he was fishing out into the open water and had been baiting the lake heavily with a fishmeal bait. I decided to fish out into the open water as well, I put one on the edge of the islands. Over the next couple of days I spent a lot of time walking around the lake looking for fish and eventually located two fish in the back bay, one a common and one a mirror. The mirror was quite long and after thinking about it, after I'd left the water, I now think this fish must have been *The Forty*. Luckily from the position I was in, I could swing my rods around behind the bivvy and fish into this channel and that's what I decided to do on the next night.

I was lying in bed at seven o'clock in the morning when I heard

Nice and quiet down at Stanstead Abbots

Terry shout from opposite me, another 'Ya-Hoo'. Oh no, not *The Forty*! I went round and he'd got the other mirror on the bank at 34lb 12oz. This fish had certainly put on a lot of weight since the last time it was caught. I was relieved in a way that it wasn't *The Forty* because that would have meant the end of my holiday. I'd obviously done it wrong by fishing in the back channel and the fish had moved out and gone into the main part of the lake. So the next night I swung my rods round again fishing back out into the open water. Another angler then arrived on the water and he went and fished in the back channel. Unbelievably at seven o'clock the next morning, I heard a shout from behind me. Oh no! "Have you got any big scales Mister?" Came the shout, "I've got the big 'un." I couldn't believe it, not out of the back channel, I'd only just moved my rods out of there. I went round and there it was, what a fish! 43lb. An absolutely brilliant looking fish.

Well that just about ended the holiday as far as I was concerned. There was nothing left to fish for on the complex, I decided to go up to the cafe and give some careful thought to what I should do next. Another friend of mine had turned up, he suggested that perhaps we should go to Stanstead Abbots as he'd spent some time

A 35lb 12oz dream

down there over the last couple of weeks.

We knew it held a 40 pounder that hadn't been caught this season but that the stocks were very low again and this lake is very large, between 30 and 40 acres in size. I don't like going on to new waters this late in the year, normally I like to have a look at them first in the close season and then make a proper assault on the water as the season begins, but after careful thought there seemed no other choice. The Staines fish, *The Forty*, had come out to Terry Dempsey so there was nothing else in the forty bracket to fish for other than this one. It was lovely and quiet down there, you won't see another soul, you can relax. I needed to relax, my nerves had gone seeing all these big fish on the bank, three forties had done me in. When I got down there however, things were not quite as people had told me. For a start, the Transatlantic Yacht Race was in the middle of my swim with about 30 yachts going round and round over my baited area, I just cast them out as far as I could and climbed into the bag. My other friend who turned up then did a rather silly thing, he cast over my line with his marker float. I didn't know he'd done it but as he began to reel in so my Baitrunner began to go and the buzzer began to bleep. Being the evil sod that he is, he decided to play a trick on me. He began to reel in madly, sending my rod flying off the rod rest and the line screaming off the Baitrunner. I flew out of the bed, struck into whatever it was and saw a float bob to the surface. I struck so hard I cut his line off and the float came up in front of me. My friend then came along the bank, "you're up and about early. I don't know what's happened here, I had a tremendous take, struck, and that float came bobbing up, so it must have been a pike towing tackle that had gone through my lines." "God," I said, "I've had enough of this, look at all these bloody yachts." I picked the rod up and slung it out, God knows where, probably about 50 yards out just in the middle, set the rod down on the rest and jumped back in the bag. The bait had only been out there ten minutes when it absolutely flew. Now, this is no exaggeration when I say that this was the most incredible fight I've had from a big fish, I think probably due to the fact that this fish had never been caught before, or if it had, certainly not many times. Its huge rudder sent this fish screaming across the lake on a 70 yard run, absolutely mind-blowing. On the bank, the fish weighed 35lb 12oz and was an immaculate silver mirror.

To say I was pleased would be the understatement of the year.

After all the heartache that this week had brought me, seeing all those big fish on the bank, my turn had come - the one with *my* name on it.

As winter approached, I decided to go back on to one of my favourite waters for a couple of months, Fox Pool. Steve Allcott decided to join me down there, we fished the water on and off for the next few weeks. We knew that the big fish was due to come out and if the water fished as it had done in the previous seasons, it would be at least Christmas week before it made its appearance again. This time it could be very big, as it had been 42 pounds in the summer. Going by previous years, if it maintained or gained weight as it had done, you were talking about a fish in the 44 pound class. Also one of the other fish in there, *The Parrot,* had been out at 39lb 12oz so there was a chance of two possible forty pounders. After Christmas we had a full week's holiday on the water, this was going to be it! This was the week that the big fish normally showed up. Steve went in the *Middle* swim as he was there a day before me, I moved round on to the bungalow bank, both fishing similar areas. I decided only to fish single hookbaits and not put any free offerings out as previously this had been a better alternative than fishing with a large bed of bait. Nothing had been caught for the last few months but we were anticipating that this could be the week.

A couple of days into the holiday, I was round with Steve having a cup of tea, just along the bank from his swim and a couple of other anglers. Steve received a single bleep on his right hand rod, we walked down and looked at his rod but the line hadn't moved. We then walked back and finished our tea and biscuits, 15 minutes later he had another bleep on the same rod. It was strange because he wasn't receiving any other bleeps at any other time and the wind was not affecting his lines. We walked back down again to have a look, I said to Steve: "You never know with these sort of fish, there could be one on the end just sitting there trying to rid itself of the hook." Steve picked the rod up and swept it over his shoulder, yes a big lump on the end. Not much of a fight, fairly typical with these fish and soon we had the fish in the net. It was *The Parrot,* could it be forty? We put it on the scales, it was 37lb 12oz - only four ounces up on the catch when I had it earlier in the year yet it had been out at 39 pounds, strange!

That certainly made the two years that Steve had spent on the water without success worthwhile, a fish of this size and a new personal best for Steve. We celebrated in true Famous Five tradition that night. On returning to the lake, Steve cast out in the same area and early in the morning had a screaming take from the same rod, I was quickly at his side with a net. The fish was certainly doing the business! We thought it must be a small fish from the way it was fighting, it was very, very powerful, long surging runs along the margins. As soon as it came to the net, I shouted up the bank to him: "I don't know what you've got here but it's bigger than the last one!" Steve was beside himself, I had to weigh the fish for him - 44lb 4oz. An absolutely unbelievable fish in immaculate winter condition, bright orange with the sun shining off its huge scales. A fantastic carp and as it turned out, the last carp ever to be caught in Fox Pool.

This brings us to a rather sad tale and a desperately sad ending. Fox Pool, as I said was my favourite water, a water that had meant a great deal to me over the last couple of years, so much so that I had fallen in love with it. Leisure Sport Angling decided to sell the venue in the close season of this year which meant that the lakes had to be drained and the fish taken away and put into a new fishery. My heart was absolutely broken when I visited the water in the close season and saw the trees and the banks torn to pieces as

Pad Lake 'Pole Position'. A daunting prospect in the depths of winter

Ritchie with 'the thirty' at 36lb, a good result on this testing venue

they had tried to get down with their equipment and pumps.

The lake was drained dry over a two month period and all the fish, bar a couple of small ones, were taken and moved to their new home, Church Pool at Horton. A very, very sad day for carp fishing. The lake was raped, destroyed, ruined and a piece of carp angling history removed from the surface of the earth forever. In my opinion, there will never be a water like that again in my lifetime. I thank God that I was fortunate enough to fish it when I did. God Save Longfield.

With the Fox Pool fish now out of the way, there seemed little point in me staying on the venue. However at this time a remarkable thing happened, Jock White of the Yateley Ya-Hoo Crew landed a new forty from the Yateley complex from the Lily Lake venue, an immaculate looking fish in brilliant condition, an absolutely stunning carp. Ritchie McDonald, Kevin Maddocks and I all had the same idea to get on the venue and fish it to the end of the season and hope that the big fish made another appearance.

I fished it right up until the end of the season and had no success whatsoever. Kevin Maddocks and Ritchie McDonald however both had action... Kevin taking one fish at 25 pounds and Ritchie taking three fish, Kevin's 25 again, a 29 and a 36. (However Ritchie had put a considerable time down on the venue.) Another two fish, a 28 and a 27 were taken over this three month period. Quite why I never received any action I don't know, probably just due to the length of time spent, I only fished for three or four weekends whereas most of the others were there full-time for that period. You just cannot compete with people who are spending that amount of time at the venue.

Ritchie McDonald's fish of 36 pounds was lovely, I'd been with him all weekend spending most of my time in his swim chatting and talking about old times. Ritchie and I hadn't seen eye to eye in the past but now found ourselves good friends. Both of us have come under fire from certain factions in the angling world and we had both 'weathered the storm' to coin a phrase. Ritchie hadn't received much action over the last couple of years and it was nice to see him with a big fish on the bank again. I was actually sitting in his swim by the side of his rods, saw his right hand rod tip spring round, called to him in the bivvy, he struck it immediately and it was the 36 pounder.

So ended the season for me, probably one of the best that I've ever had. Three thirty pounders off the top, some new fish from Johnson's and that incredible 35lb 12oz mirror from Stanstead Abbots, it truly remains one of the best fish I've ever caught.

The close season was upon us and I decided that this would be the close season I would fish Farlows Lake as much as I could. Farlows is on the William Boyer ticket and was run by that amiable man, John Stent. I really got on well with John and his attitude towards carp fishing and carp anglers is that he takes them as he finds them. He doesn't rely on other people's opinions, he accepted us with open arms down there, made us feel like royalty all the time we fished there and we had incredible action while we were down at that excellent fishery.

We took about eight 20 pounders throughout the close season between us, five of which were 20 pound commons, two 20 pound commons to me. My first 20 pound commons I might add, although obviously in the close season they don't count, same as foreign fish.

We found it best to put large beds of baits out there, fishing around the island areas and along with those 20 pounders we had a great number of double and single figure fish. The action was really fast and furious, sometimes if you were on the fish, you could have up to a dozen fish in a few hours fishing.

I have to thank William Boyers and Mr John Stent for letting us fish down there and for the excellent fishing he has provided for everyone. Albert fished with us one weekend and caught a 26lb 8oz and a 19 pounder. There were also a 27 pound common and 33 pound mirror taken out whilst we were there.

More on Farlows anyway in its own special chapter on close season fishing.

Farlows in winter. The most popular swim on the lake, 3ft from the bar!

Sometimes its just nice to put a bend in the rod

Chapter 2

THE NETTING OF FOX POOL

*This large aluminium boat was used to bring the carp back to the car
park corner once they had been netted*

*The sheer sides of Fox Pool leave you in no doubt as to why it was so
difficult. Notice the figure sitting on the outcrop. That was a good place
to position your bait once upon a time*

*These central plateaux were hardly ever fishable because of the vast
amount of Canadian Pondweed, but what a spot!*

*The main 'Bar' swim, but who could have possibly dreamt there was an
undercut like that on the side of this Jurassic lump of gravel*

Many of the fish hid in the snaggy corner at the top of the lake. Here they were trapped by 20ft. nets until the water was low enough to scoop them out

An old car, upside down in the 'Goose Pool'. I wonder how many people actually plumbed this area and found the smooth bar which was four feet off the bottom, as I did in 1988!

Chapter 3

THE RAILWAY

This was to be our second season on Johnson's Railway Lake and we intended to fish it from the start, right through the summer and maybe even do the winter, although the prospect was very daunting. The main lesson we had learned from the year before was that early season was definitely the time to catch these elusive fish. The first two weeks of the season normally gave ten per cent of the whole year's worth of fishing.

I arrived at the lake about four days before the start. This was the first time that I'd ever arrived so early for the start of the season. The reason was that I knew there were only two or three very good swims on the lake and I had to be assured of getting one of those, because this was to be my season to catch that beautiful leather that so far had eluded everyone we knew who fished there.

The wind was blowing across the lake towards the line of willow trees. I had decided that this *End of Willows* swim would be the best place for me to start, it was the spot where Phil Harper had taken three twenty-plus carp at the start of the previous season and it commanded an excellent view of 90 per cent of the lake and also gave you a variety of places to cast. The left hand rod was close in along the dangling fronds of willow stems which danced merrily in the water on those first few days of the season. I didn't see any fish at all moving about in front of me, the only place that I did see carp during those few days before the start was down in the pads, once again thinking about spawning at this time of year. It was obvious that these pads would give somebody a chance of catching a floater-caught carp some time during the season. The bait I was using at the time is the now extinct range of Obsession baits that I had formulated with Kevin Nash the season before. I'd settled on a Tandoori bait dip as the flavour and the soak for the pop-ups. This particular bait soak was going to be an outstanding captor during the coming season, as many of the fish, especially the thirties from Withy Pool and several other hard waters were to fall to this excellent flavour. Unfortunately this is no longer available, as it was discontinued at the end of this year.

I decided to use six rods on this start of the season session, which was to be two weeks duration - two weeks of my hard-earned annual vacation. I decided on fishing three long range rods to fish centrally any clear areas that I could find in the weed at a distance (this had produced fish for Dave Whibley the year before) and three close in rods, no more than 30 yards out, possibly the majority of the time, one rod fished along the edge of the willow trees. I decided on baiting two areas and positioning two rods on each of these, baiting another area heavily and fishing one rod on that and the other would be fished with single hookbaits on and around similar areas so that those that had visited the baited patch, on leaving, might come across one more and just couldn't resist.

Those few days before the start of the season passed very slowly. There were about half a dozen anglers that had taken the same initiative and arrived early for the start, but I still managed to get the swim that I wanted so at least luck was with me that far. I felt very weary come the start of the season, having spent most of the time since I'd arrived there either in the pub, or drinking beer on the lake and anyone who knows about drinking for long periods will know that it takes it out of you in the end. Anyway all the gang were here, Travolta, Peter Jones and Steve Briggs spaced out along the road bank (this had been where it had taken off at the start of the season the year before). Steve Allcott and Colin Martin took up the bridge area, so between us we had most of the lake covered and we could fish centrally if required.

There was a peculiar algae bloom on the lake that season at the start, but it was only just beginning to grow. We could never have foreseen the devastating effect that this algae was going to have on the lake in a month or so's time and how all our plans for fishing the full year on Johnson's would be thwarted.

Seven o'clock opening morning, I was to see my first Johnson's carp of the year. A chap fishing down to my right had got a few fish taking floaters the night before and capitalised on that as soon as it got light on the 16th. He took a fine 26lb 8oz mirror. The looks of these fish were so striking, old battle-scarred warriors, dark in colour but each one a beautiful fish and well worth the time spent putting in for them.

Travolta and Peter Jones were the next two to take fish but quite a few of the fish were moving off the road bank as they did in the opening two days in the previous season. They took a fish each off the bottom, both were 25 pounders.

This was very encouraging, at least the fish were feeding on the bottom this year. Many of the takes on the bottom ceased after July the previous season, about 60 per cent of the carp caught after that time were taken on floaters, and those were very few and far between.

I think I had the area covered!

Immaculate. The leatber at 32lb 4oz

Halfway through the session I was getting bored, I always do on these long sessions. All I'd had so far were three tench, two eights and one of 9lb 12oz. The tench in Johnson's were in huge proportions and they especially like the carp anglers' tactics and baits. I kept myself busy during this session, as I normally do, looking at the wildlife, the birds, the insects, whatever else comes creeping and crawling along. I noticed there were quite a lot of snakes at the back of my swim, I'd seen them slithering by during the course of the day and decided that I would spend the afternoon trying to catch one of these elusive 'critters'. I suppose I'd wandered about 20 yards away from the swim when two young fellows came walking along the path. "What you up to mate?" they said to me. "Oh, I saw some snakes here earlier and I'm trying to catch one." "Christ", he says, "you must be mad. Oh, by the way are they your fishing rods down there?" "Yes." "Oh, one of them's just fallen off the buzzer, I can see the spool turning round. Looks like you've got a big fish on there mate." That was an understatement!

I flew across the path, down the bank and into my swim and sure enough, there was the right hand rod laying on the floor. I pulled into it and found that the fish had swum underneath the weeds and down to my right. I shouted for Steve Briggs who I'd seen coming round the corner earlier with a floater rod. Steve came legging it down the path: "Have you got one mate?" "Yeah, yeah." I told him the story about the snakes etc. The fish moved right down the right hand margin and weeded itself up, there was a tree directly to my right and we had to get the rod over the top of this to enable me to walk down the bank and try and play the fish on a tighter line. Steve Briggs climbed up the tree taking my rod with him and handed it to me on the other side and I legged it along the path towards the place where the fish was weeded up.

When I got there, it was only about ten feet out from the bank and I could see huge boils and bubbles coming up in the strong Canadian stems. I decided the best thing to do was wade out and try and pull it through the weed. I was just thinking of doing this when the fish broke surface. We looked in amazement at each other, it was the leather, the sun was glistening on its golden shoulders, I just couldn't believe it. I was straight in the water with a landing net, charging up and down on the shallow gravel shelf after this huge leather. A leather that hadn't been out for over a year and could well be 35-plus. Eventually, he came to the net and I hoisted my prize ashore letting out a cry across the lake, dropping my trousers and showing the cheeks of my bottom to Colin and Steve on the other side, who didn't think it was very funny at all. I shouted across that it was the leather but they didn't believe me, they still thought I'd got a tench or something and they never even came round to see it whilst I was doing the photographs. They were still convinced it was only a small one. This fish was to be the front cover shot of a magazine I was to do in the future - an absolutely immaculate leather. I'd spent a lot of hours, summer and winter, chasing this very difficult fish and finally, she was in my arms. Needless to say we all ended up that night slightly the worse for wear. That was the last take of the session for me, the one and only take.

The algae seemed to be getting worse and worse and by the end of the first two weeks it was now thick and green all over most of the lake, we were already picking out strands of weed which were dying due to lack of sunlight.

We were back the following weekend and couldn't believe the change in the lake when we arrived, it had turned an inky black colour and all around the lake, signs were posted 'Poisonous - Blue Green Algae. Do not swim or drink this water'. We had no intention of doing either anyway, but the prospect of even fishing in it didn't look too good. Steve decided that he would just try floaters and patrol the left hand side of the lake. I plumped for the road bank area as it was an easy walk, you could park your car directly behind your tackle and everything is to hand. When the lake looked as it did, with no wind on it at all, inky black with this algae all over the top, it was not a very good prospect anyway and I almost packed up before I'd even got the rods out of the car.

It was however to be a red letter day for Steve, he'd found several fish taking floaters down in the corner including the old *Prehistoric* who'd only come up and taken two but was still half-interested. He quickly ran down and got his float gear, he was thwarted several times by the small commons that seemed intent on eating every mixer that was going out, not giving the big boy a chance to take it. After about half an hour, the big fella disappeared into the lake, he'd obviously had enough of the commons as well. Steve thrashed the water with a handful of mixers and left the commons to their greedy lunchtime snack. On walking back down the bank, he stopped at the pads and noticed a couple of dark shapes moving

Colin and 'Spotty' taking a bath

This is what it's all about!

'I belong in Johnson's'

The Victory Cry

beneath the lily pads. He fired out a couple of pouches of mixers three feet past the pads in an attempt to draw the fish out from under the pads, it didn't have that effect. Instead it brought in two or three previously unseen fish hiding out in the ripples, just beyond the pads anyway, and they soon began taking the free offerings ravenously.

I was watching all this through binoculars from the top bank and I could see Steve jumping up and down. He obviously thought he was in with a chance. After about half an hour of patiently trying for one of the bigger fish that he could see, he finally got one to take. I ran down to give him a hand but Colin was already there, wading out into the pads with the landing net, as the fish had already gone straight through many of the stems. It was about 15 feet deep under those pads and Colin was treading water in the middle of them with a landing net in his hand. Suddenly the fish swirled in front of him and Colin thrashed at it with the net, this made the fish dive down past him and disappear deep into the stems. Suddenly Colin disappeared as well, the fish then came back to the surface followed by Colin's head all shiny in the sun with the water on top of it. The prey dived again and Colin plunged under the water, still in hot pursuit. It seemed as though the two of them were bobbing about between the pads like two marshmallows. All of a sudden there was an almighty crack and Colin had broken one of the arms of the landing net. Now he was in trouble! The line was going here, there and everywhere - a spider's web around Colin's legs but the fish was getting closer. We could see it was one of the big ones and thought that perhaps, with luck, it could be *Spotty*. This fish was very distinctive when in the water and you could usually recognise it by it's colouring and shape. After a long, hard struggle the fish was finally in the net and everyone let out a cheer and clapped their hands as Colin bowed in the water, disappeared under the stems again and came up with a bit of bullrush in his mouth. He reckoned he'd seen a couple of good eels underneath the pads and intended presenting a lobworm to them that night. I'd forgotten to tell you that during the opening week Colin had caught his best ever eel of 3lb 4oz and was well pleased with the catch. Ha ha!

It was indeed *Spotty* and Steve jumped with joy as we got him on the bank, fantastic fish, lovely condition, very, very distinctive and one that I would love to have caught. We put it up on the scales and it was just over 33 pounds, he was well pleased.

There's a rather bizarre finish to this story because the same fish was caught a couple of weeks later in the same area on floaters and the character who caught it decided that he'd put it back in his lake, the other side of the path in Leisure Sports' Larkfield and that's where the fish resides now. There was a rumour spread that the fish had died, but I know that it's been caught several times from its new home. Whether it's dead or alive, no one in Johnson's Railway Lake will ever be catching it again. This is a shame as Johnson's has only two or three fish of that size, whilst Leisure Sports' Larkfield has fish fast approaching the 35 pound mark anyway. It was a shame to lose such a fish and I hope perhaps one day justice will be done and if the fish is caught in Leisure Sports' Larkfield it will be put back into the Railway Lake where it properly belongs.

Floater fishing was definitely the answer and I decided that for the rest of the summer at this venue that would be the main type of fishing I'd be using. I decided on two methods, one an anchored floater fished at 18 feet off the bottom in 20 feet of water. This put me above all the rotting, stinking slime, which had now killed all the weed in the lake, and was lying down on the bottom. If you cast a hooklink out in it, it turned black and smelt of foul, dead vegetation.

Bottom fishing was now totally out and after mid-July nobody caught a single fish off the bottom that year. It was an unbelievable change in the lake and one that was to affect it for years to come. The algae killed the weed and prevented it from growing properly for the next few years which enabled much bigger captures. Unfortunately, this didn't benefit us as this was to be our last summer on Johnson's. Around the corner Harefield was waiting for us, although we didn't know that at this time.

I fished with floaters for several weekends down there, although chances were few and far between. I ended up with just one more fish, a fish known as the small leather, around 24 pounds. Well pleased with it though. I'd had a few of the Johnson's fish, not a tremendous amount I admit, but I'd had the one that counted, the leather - a fantastic fish and a memory that will stay with me till the day I die.

With Johnson's now finished, because of the blue/green algae, we were a bit lost as to where to go for the rest of the summer. We'd been looking at another relatively unfished water in the Colne Valley that it was possible to get a ticket for, in fact Dave Whibley

The Little Leather

Pete Jones with a superb 24lb 8oz mirror

Phil and the 'Bent-Tail' now up to 28lbs

and Steve Allcott had both got tickets and they could take me as a guest if we decided to fish it. We'd also been looking at some of the waters around the Reading area, Burghfield where several of the anglers that we knew, including Peter Springate and Kenny Hodder, had done fairly well. Sonning Eye, again another huge water with a few big fish in it. Englefield Lagoon and Tarmac were two pits either side of the road on the Reading Angling Club ticket, Englefield is now a syndicate however. This was the water where Jock Downes caught that fantastic long 39 pounder which appeared in the Cotswold Bait adverts several years ago, a fantastic fish which we know has now reached 40 pounds. Steve and Dave decided that the lake in the Colne Valley was our best bet as it was closer to home. We also knew that there was a fair head of carp in there. Although the best we knew of was 29 pounds, fish much larger than that had been seen. They had booked several weeks annual summer holidays around this time, while I only had one week.

For the first two weeks that they fished on this lake in the Colne Valley, Dave took a fish of 24 pounds, then Steve lost a very big fish which came off at the net. Dave finished it up with a 28, previously uncaught as far as we know, a fantastic fish, and Steve caught a 24. I didn't really fancy this water and preferred Englefield, knowing that it had at least one huge fish in it. It's always a safer bet if you know for certain that the fish are there. It's nice catching these uncaught monsters, but give me one that I *know* is there and at least I think I'm in with a chance.

They decided to move down to Englefield on the last week of this holiday, that was my week as well and we'd do it properly. There was no night fishing allowed at the time but it was possible to leave tackle hidden in the bushes, so we had a good walk round the water, blew up the dinghy and went out and searched for some clear spots. It was very, very weedy. We selected the point area in the middle of the lake which covered a huge amount of water. So far, we hadn't seen any fish at all but by going out in the boat we saw two commons just to the right of where we were fishing, so at least we knew we were in the right area. The clear spots were few and far between and certainly very small when you did find them, you could just make out a gravel area the size of a bivvy here and there amongst the huge patches of weed. Steve sorted out his bait first and I went out in the dinghy, the wind was just starting to get up a bit, I knew that I didn't have very long before I wouldn't be able to see down to the bottom and distinguish the clear patches of gravel. I positioned two small black polyball marker floats on two areas about 80 yards out into the lake. It was going to be a hell of a cast to get there but I thought I might just be able to manage it. I then put in about ten kilos of boilies in each area, if anything did move in there I wanted that weed opening out so that there would be a larger area in which to cast.

I went back to the bank and after three hours of casting, yes, that's how long it took me, I managed to get both baits smack in the right areas. I could feel the bump, bump of the gravel and I dragged my lead and anti-tangle tube back in to the weed so that it was hidden, just leaving the hooklength and boilie hopefully out in the open. It was the master trap, something had to happen and I intended leaving my baits there in the right spot, the wind had now got up, it was impossible to go back out in the boat and I'd never find these spots again, plus I had put out a fair bit of my bait when I originally went out there. Twenty minutes later, the yachts came out, it was on with big black leads, pulling the line deep down into the margins. No way did I want to pick up a yacht, I laughed when the first half a dozen went over my rods. The lines didn't even flicker, yes I'd got away with it. Those centre boards weren't going to catch my line, then I saw one very close to my marker floats, going quite fast. A hand slipped over the side of the boat, scoop, scoop, both marker floats were picked up, he dragged them about 30 feet along and dropped them down out of the area. Very nice I thought! Now I've got no chance of recasting.

It didn't seem to be our week and unfortunately that was how it continued for the rest of the few days we were there. I tried the small lake behind me and hooked a carp in there although it only looked double figures. I actually lost that in the weed and decided that was the final straw. We all agreed that we'd go back and fish the lake in the Colne Valley, they would arrange to get me guest tickets. Back at the Horse and Barge, we arrived the night before we intended to fish, and all the lads from Savay and Harefield were in there, enjoying a drink and telling tales of the fish they'd had. Harefield was turning up some nice fish now, since the new fish from Rodney Meadow had gone in, and *Nelson* had been out a couple of times already at around 35 pounds. Oh, how we fancied fishing over at Harefield! It had never even interested us before but now these big fish were there, it was a different proposition

Have you been caught before?

Holiday 28 for Dave Whibley

Harefield, the Road Bank island, causeway and point. Photographed by a remote-controlled duck

entirely. Dougal was running the fishing over there as John Stent's fishery manager and doing a very good job of it as well, I might add.

We got to chat with Dougal about the good times at Savay and said how much we fancied having a go at Harefield. "How many days have you got left?" He said. "Three," we answered. "Well, I'll arrange for you to have three days on Harefield if you like. At least you'll be able to bivvy up over there." Fantastic, three days on Harefield. Oh, we couldn't wait to get over there. Of course wait we did, until closing time and then the Indian, and by the time we'd finished with all that, we were far too tired to set up that night. So first thing in the morning we were over there. We didn't know anything about the lake at all although Dave and Steve, I believe, had fished it on a couple of occasions in the past before the newer fish were put in.

This was the first time I'd been fishing with Essex Jon. Essex was doing very well on Harefield and I got chatting with him about areas and different places and he suggested that we might go up to the *stick bar* area on the road bank, as he'd seen several fish there. That sounded good enough for us, we could sit out in the sun, bivvy up. Fantastic! We were really looking forward to it. We had a walk round, saw a few fish jumping out in the open water and yes, there was one fish up by the *stick bar*. Not knowing the lake at all, we relied on what other people had told us and this was certainly the area that everyone was pointing towards. That had to be the place to go, surely?

We walked round the top bays and cruising around in the shallow water we saw about 30 fish. We just didn't know what we were looking at, we thought well there's so many fish in here this is just a small proportion of them. I'm sure there's a thirty everywhere you look. What fools we were, if only we'd set up in the bays then, because the majority of the fish in the lake must have been up in that area. I actually watched the huge *Fully-Scaled* feeding in the weed about three feet from the bank, although I didn't recognise it at that time, having had no previous experience of which fish were in the lake anyway. So we set up in the *stick bar*, three of us in a line. The three wise monkeys! Essex Jon came down and had a walk round, saw the fish in the bays, dropped in there and that night he had four, including *Nelson* at 33 pounds. It was obvious, why didn't we go there? We just thought there must carp all over the place.

I did manage to catch one fish that session on a floater from a swim behind the Barge. This is the area where I was later to make the video *Harefield Haulin'* and I saw several small fish, doubles, and possibly a few low twenties, one of them moving around behind the barge. I fired out some floaters and within a quarter of an hour I caught an 18 pound common - I was well pleased. There were still several fish taking there when Dougal arrived on his evening stroll, I told him about a wasps' nest just a little bit along the bank and how everyone had to be really quiet because I wanted to fish here for the whole evening, I'd got several fish taking floaters. Dougal said: "It's time for the pub." "Oh, I'm not going up the pub tonight Dougal. I've got a few fish taking floaters here and I want to make the most of it." With that Dougal picked up a huge lump of wood and poked it down into the mouth of the wasp nest, running the stake in and out of their home until the air was filled with millions of angry wasps, all landing on me and crawling up my rods. I had to drop my rod in the water and quickly reel the float in. Dougal had got his way - it was indeed time for the pub!

This was the only fish of the session but we'd certainly got the Harefield bug and I was quickly down to Farlows to have a word with Mr Stent to see whether he could sort us out some tickets for the rest of the winter. This was the place that I wanted to fish, there were some lovely carp in there and I liked the water very much. I knew one thing for certain though, after being there for that first session, the anglers that were already fishing there had far more sophisticated long-range tackle than we had seen for a number of years.

Having fished small waters for quite a while, we were totally out of touch with what had been happening on the tackle scene. Rods had become much larger, although I had my Extreme Pursuits, which could certainly outcast anything then or now on Harefield. These rods are no longer available, but they were the best casting tools ever brought out on the market and I have tried them all. The reels have also increased in size. Daiwa have brought out two reels, an absolute Rolls Royce of a long-range reel called the SS3000 and a larger model, I think it was the 7000 or 8000 with a huge spool. The spools looked to us like bulk spools of Sylcast, just poked on the end of the reels. They made our silly little Shimanos look like toys when compared to the reels that we saw as we were walking round. I made my mind up that should I be lucky enough to get a ticket for the winter through John Stent, I'd have to go out and

My first Harefield carp, and its off to the pub

'The Original' 27lb 4oz common, slow and deep she came to the net

invest in three new reels, some new line and some much heavier leads.

John, true to form, came through with the goods. We were all allowed a half-season ticket on there. We were in Harefield! One of the top waters in the country, we'd left it until the last minute and we were allowed in. Nice one John, thanks very much.

The next session down there was the first time I had met the infamous Frogger and Care Bear, two lads that had been taking the lake apart. These two lads could certainly catch them at Harefield, and I am sure would catch them on any other waters should they venture that far, although they have been content to fish just this water for a number of years. They weren't into long range fishing at all, they were fishing close range and told us that they didn't like fishing at distance. I couldn't quite understand this, a lot of the fish were caught at long range, why didn't they try? They taught me a hard lesson over the next couple of seasons. Their method was certainly the way to catch the big bags of fish.

I fished next to Frogger on the next session there. He was in the *Climbing Tree* swim and I was out in front of the road bank island to his left. There were several fish jumping at around the 140-yard mark and I could easily reach them with my new tackle. I was just sitting there in the sunlight, the rods tossed out into the distance. The first bit of long range fishing that I'd done for a number of years since I left Savay. Then one huge fish jumped directly over my right hand bait, everyone looked up to the bank. I was certainly going to catch something any minute. I just sat there watching the rod tips, then out of the blue, the right hand rod tip nodded. It hadn't pulled from the clip but just pulled down about three inches. I let out a huge cry across the lake "Haulin'" and everyone looked over. So far, I hadn't had a bleep and then the whole lot ripped from the clip and flew through the rings. Everyone laughed, the fish was on for a second or two before it pulled from the clip enabling me to shout before the take.

I had to walk down to Frogger to land this fish as the bar running from the island is only about six inches deep for about 15 yards out from the island itself. This made playing the fish very difficult. You had to pull the line across the bar, bringing them through a gap down in the next swim. The fish was slow and sluggish and came across the bar with its back out of the water, it looked around about 25 pounds. I didn't want to lose this fish, it would be my first decent one from the water. Slow and deep it ran along the margins, down in 15 feet of water, directly below our feet. Gradually the line pulled up and we could see the anti-tangle tube. When it finally came up, it was a huge common, the biggest I had ever caught.

Peter Jones netted the fish for me and I let out another cry. On the scales it was 27lb 4oz, a really fantastic bream-shaped common, one of the original fish left in Harefield and probably the only decent common that's left there now from the original stocking. I was well pleased.

The fish were still jumping over the area but I had to go and celebrate, a couple of beers were definitely in order. When I returned later that night, I hurled them both out in the same spot and climbed into bed. I liked Harefield I thought to myself, nice fish, you can bivvy up close to the pub, what more could you want?

A little after midnight I had a take on the left hand rod but couldn't get the line across the bar to bring it down through the gap and eventually the line parted. This too felt like a very good fish, I thought for a moment that I had definitely got the place sussed out. A long cast with a single pop-up onto a small hook was going to be the way that I would take Harefield apart. I was certainly catching as much as any of the other anglers on the lake at that time.

I continued with this approach to my fishing for the next few months at Harefield, right through until the end of November. I had action on almost every session that I fished, and of course these were only weekends at the time, as I was still employed full-time.

I would arrive on Friday night, get somewhere that had got a long chuck out in front and hurl two small pop-ups out into the middle. The next fish I caught was another 20 pound common, I thought Harefield was full of 20 pounders. I'd hardly had a 20 pound common before these, having not fished waters holding them, but it was obvious I was going to get quite a few from this prolific water. It was a lovely long fish, 23lb 8oz, one of the old Rodney fish and was recognised by anglers who had fished there in previous years as a fish that used to be about 18 or 19 pounds, so it was obvious that the fish were doing well here, better than they were doing in Rodney.

My old mate, Andy Khakoo from Country Pursuits Clothing, was with me on the next session. He'd had a ticket for a couple of seasons although he hadn't done a great deal of fishing on there, and I don't think he'd caught a fish, or maybe he'd had just one. He

'Maurice the Mirror' carp at 27lb 8oz

Autumn fruits

A hasty retreat for Briggsy and I, neither of us fancying a bath

was fishing up to my left and I was back in the road bank island swim, from where I'd taken the 27 pound common, hurling it over that bar from the island out into the gaps which were only about three feet deep directly behind the island area. This was a spot where you could always see fish.

Andy was standing in my swim, and I was just about to recast. He'd heard about my casting and wanted to see if what he'd heard was true. Suddenly, at about the 160-yard mark, a huge mirror jumped out to my right. I quickly changed my stance and hurled the lead like an animal across the lake. The line streaked out into the air, it must have gone almost as far up as it went out. Andy Kahoo stood there in amazement with his mouth open, as the lead dropped straight in the centre of the hole where the fish had just gone down. "Christ almighty," he said. "That's got to be 160 yards out to there." "Yeah," I said "it did drop short didn't it?" I put the rod down on the rest and turned round to him and said "I don't think I need to turn the buzzer on, it's not going to be out there long enough." With that the rod pulled round and I was in again. It felt like a big old fish and when I got it on the bank, I was sure that it was around 30 pounds. On the scales however it proved us wrong, it was 27lb 8oz and was recognised as a fish they called *Maurice. Maurice* the friendly carp, he was one of the regulars that came out, he'd a poor old mouth on him. However he was a big fish, he had a nice width to him and I was sure that in a couple of years he'd make 30 pounds. Disaster struck on the next couple of sessions down and the next two fish were lost.

Withy Pool had produced its first forty pounder this season and I'd been talking to Kevin Maddocks about the chance of having a syndicate ticket on it, as it's only about ten minutes from where I live. He didn't seem to think there'd be a problem although I'd have to go on the waiting list for a season or two. He did say however that we could pop down and have a week on there as his guests if we wanted to. None of us had any holiday left, we were sorry to turn that down, we did however say that we could come down for a weekend if that would be alright. So Steve, Dave and I decided to do the weekend down there. This was to be a pleasure for me, being only just down the road I could pop home for my tea if I wanted to, or anything else that took my fancy for that matter, God willing.

I was first down on the Thursday night and had a good walk

round the water. I managed to get Friday off work by saying I was sick again, but I think they were getting a bit fed up with that excuse, this was the thirtieth Friday in a row I'd had off for various things, from colds to a bad back - you know the score.

As I was saying, I had a walk round and stood over by the snag tree on the far side. Apparently there were always fish underneath this tree but as there were three of us fishing and we couldn't all fish there, I decided to have a look along the front, near Kevin's house. As I stood there on the front, the area where I'd caught a fish a couple of years before, a good fish broke the surface about 30 yards out, just past the large bomb-hole out in front of the *Open* swim. That'll do for me I thought and quickly got my gear together and set up. Dave was next down, he went to my left and Steve finally turned out the next morning and went to Dave's left, so we were all in a line. We could have a social, I'd brought the barbecue with me and plenty of steak and chops, we were going to have a nice little holiday at Withy Pool.

The next day we were fortunate enough to see one of the elusive Withy Pool carp caught, it was the small common that was in there, 24lb 8oz I believe it came out at on the Saturday. It was a long fish and, although not one of the big fish of the lake, it was a nice one and I fancied catching it. They were talking at the time of removing this fish and growing some of the other fish on to take its place, but I thought it would be a bit of a shame to get rid of it before I'd caught it. Anyway, I wasn't about to catch that one now, it had come out on the Saturday.

I fished the same tactics here as I had at Harefield, I'd done well there with the Crustacean-based pop-ups, small orange ones fished on the small hook, and 15 pound line straight through. I positioned both rods out on the shallow shelf to the side of the bomb hole at about 16 feet depth.

On Sunday afternoon we were sitting there all in a line, we'd had a fantastic time down there, loads and loads to eat and drink and really enjoyed ourselves. A simple bleep on one of my rods made us look round, I could see one of the back-leads coming up out of the water as the fish slowly moved off. "Haulin'" I cried out across the lake. I picked the rod up and jumped up on top of the wooden bench by the swim, holding the rod up high because I knew that there were roots and stumps sticking out along the rim of the bomb-hole. The fish came in slowly and I was sure it was one of the big

Winter in Withy Pool

The long common, twice in a weekend

What a state, 'Maurice' again at 27lb 12oz

ones when the back broke the surface. We could see it was a common, but there are only two commons in Withy Pool, both about the same size. In the net, we recognised it as the one that had been out the day before. That fish only came out twice that year, on the Saturday and Sunday of that week in November. It's unbelievable how these fish think, it just goes to show that catching them really doesn't make any difference to their attitude at all. They can easily be caught the next day if they are feeding.

I was the most confident person that you could possibly speak to, confident in the bait to the 'nth degree. I was certain that I'd have a few more fish out of Harefield that winter. How wrong I was. As soon as it got cold, and it did get cold that winter as Harefield froze on three occasions, the fish went totally off the feed. For all that time, right through the winter, there were only four more takes until the end of the season. These were taken from margin spots in deep water, a different place entirely to where the fish were caught in the summer. I'm sure if somebody took an echo sounder on the water and put in a little bit of homework, they'd find where those fish are holed up in the winter and could certainly capitalise with some big bags of fish. However winter fishing on Harefield was, and still is, very slow. In January the lake froze completely on a couple of occasions. I tried to break it with a boat and in the end only succeeded in breaking the boat and narrowly escaped being drowned in a frozen lake.

I decided to pop down to Farlows and see if I could do any good down there. I'd heard that the fish still came out regularly through even the coldest weather, and I knew that Dougal was going out each morning in the aluminium powerboat to break the ice, so at least we'd be able to get a lead in the water. I arranged to go down there and meet Steve Briggs and Johnny Allen, we all fancied having a go and perhaps knocking out a double. It had been slow fishing for us all on the lakes on which we were concentrating. John Stent let us fish outside on the front of Herons Point, right by the patio doors that go into the bar, so we could sit there in the warmth and see the rods only a couple of feet away. It was absolute heaven.

We were only going to fish the weekend and by Sunday afternoon, we'd had not so much as a sniff. Then all of a sudden, the fish turned on and we could see them jumping out on the right hand side of the swim, Steve Briggs was fishing on the right and at four o'clock on the Sunday afternoon he caught a fish. It was so nice to see one on the bank after such a long period of time that John and I decided that we'd stay for another day, and that I would move across into Briggsy's swim and he would move next to me. Steve went home and we settled in for the night.

No action that night but in the morning the fish were out there again. Over the next ten hours I had 14 fish, the majority of them single figures but with four going over 15 pounds, 17lb 8oz the biggest. It just went to show that the bait and rig were working but the fish in Harefield just weren't co-operating. Anyway, it was a confidence booster and put me in a better frame of mind to tackle Harefield for the next couple of months before the end of the season, when hopefully it would warm up and a few fish would come out.

The only winter fish I'd caught were a tench and two bream, fish that I hadn't even caught in the summer. The carp definitely were either not there, or not co-operating. It was a different story however once March arrived, the weather warmed up and temperatures soared, the temperature of the lake must have risen as well because the fish suddenly came alive.

Hampshire Chris, a nice young fellow who fishes there, was first in with a fish of 30lb 10oz. A fish with a split tail which I was later to catch in the *Harefield Haulin'* video (it's another one of the original fish) and then Chris had a 24 and his mate had a 25. Yes, the Harefield carp were going to have it. I moved in along the causeway and had a feel around with a lead in the swim called the *Tate Gallery*. I hadn't fished here before but I'd seen a couple of fish caught there by other anglers in the summer. I found a nice bar, about 120 yards out to the left of it, by plumbing this area I found a much shallower point. I was certain that the fish would be moving up into the upper layers now that the sun was warming those top two feet of the water. Nothing for the last few days of the season and then, on the last morning, I was lying in bed and had a one inch drop-back on the left hand rod. I looked at it and thought 'must be a bream', I shut my eyes again and prayed that it would get off the hook. Bleep again. I looked and the bobbin had gone up an inch, then it was down an inch, then it was up an inch. This was definitely a bream. My head was thumping, something must have happened the night before but I couldn't remember what it was. Eventually I thought 'it's not going to come off, I'll have to get up and hit it'. I picked the rod up and it was wrenched down as the fish disappeared over the back of the bar. The line must have been trapped and it must have been pulling backwards and forwards on a short line, for as I picked the rod up, it freed it from the rocks and enabled it to disappear over the back of the bar. This was definitely a good fish and I did not want to lose it at any cost. Slow and deep again along these deep margins on the causeway. I was looking down into the water hoping that it might be *Nelson*. This fish could well have been 40 pounds that winter and it would certainly have made a nice end to my season. When it appeared at the net, I recognised it immediately as *Maurice the Friendly Carp*. He'd come back to visit me again, the only mirror that I'd taken from Harefield that year and I'd caught it twice. On the scales 27lb 12oz, it had put on four ounces since I'd caught it three months ago.

And that was to be the end of Harefield for that season. It certainly left us in good stead for the following season though, we couldn't wait to get on there in the summer, when the big bags of fish came out. We were on the waiting list for the next season and almost certainly were going to get a place because we were near the top, having had a half-season ticket the year before. Next season would be our season on Harefield and hopefully in our search for the biggest, *Nelson* would fall to one of us.

Chapter 4

FRIENDS

UNBELIEVABLE!
Peter Springate

I had booked a couple of days off work (Thursday and Friday) so was hoping to go Wednesday night but didn't finish work until it was too late. That evening it started to pour with rain and the wind got up very strongly. As I was going to bed I knew that the north wind was blowing harder than before and I thought maybe it would push the fish down into the area I fished. I had an early morning call at 5am, but was so exhausted after work and getting everything ready, that I just turned over, went back to sleep and finally got up at 8.30am.

By the time I arrived at the lake it was 12.30pm. I spoke to a couple of guys fishing, "still nothing's been out," they said... and told me how grim it was looking. In spite of this I still felt confident. I made my way round to where I was going to fish. It was a swim I'd first fancied and fished a couple of years ago, but I enountered so many problems with the boats on there that I had decided to leave it alone. Last November I decided to give it another try and had to cut out some bushes to get in. The only other occasion I'd been here was for two nights during the first week of the season when I'd neither seen or heard any carp.

Now I was back, I set up my two 12 foot two and three-quarter pound Harrison rods with Aero Baitrunners, 20 pound ABU test line because of the thick weed and the gravel bars, with size 13 Kinryu hooks. The first rod I cast out to a clear spot 12 feet deep, just off the small island straight out in front of me at about 20 yards, baited with 14mm new Richworth Condensed Milk boilies and a pop-up. I put out about 100 baits around the hookbait. On the second rod I just had a Condensed Milk pop-up two inches off the bottom, cast to a bar running between two islands about 100 yards out to my right in six feet of water. I sat up until 11pm, watching the water for any signs but saw nothing, not even a tench so I got my head down.

At 5am I woke to a bleep... bleep... from my new Fox buzzer and immediately jumped up as the bobbin on the first rod had dropped back a couple of inches. Then another bleep and, as I struck, the rod arched over into what I knew was a big carp, which then started to move off into deep water. I flicked the anti-reverse off and had to start back-winding. Slowly at first, then faster and faster; so fast that I had a job to keep up with it. The rod was bent right round, so much so that I thought it was going to break. The reel was also groaning under the strain and I prayed that the handle wouldn't snap off in my hand. After taking about 80 yards of line, it went deep and tried to get into some weed. I kept the pressure on and managed to bring it out after a few moments and kept pumping it back. Then off it went again and there was nothing I could do about it. Eventually, I managed to get her in, so I waded out to the small island to net her.

It was the hardest fight I've ever had with a fish and I thought it might be one of the uncaught commons around the 35 pound mark from the way it was fighting. Then I saw it rolling in front of the net, a big mirror. The job I had to try and pull her over the net was unreal, it was like trying to pull a dead weight... inch by inch, until eventually she was in. I dropped the rod, grabbed the landing net arms and tried to lift it out, it was so heavy I had to get a better grip and just managed to struggle up the bank.

I laid her down on the unhooking mat and couldn't believe my eyes... she looked huge. I was glad I had solid glass landing net arms otherwise I think they would have broken under the strain. I quickly unhooked and weighed her, just over 47 pounds. I settled for 47 pounds as my scales only weigh in half-pound increments and put her into the sack.

I sat down and put the kettle on in a daze. Was she the 45 or a different fish? I thought she looked much deeper. Should I reel the other rod in and go and phone Bob Baker and Richard Skidmore? I thought, it's only 5.15am... a bit early, I'll wait until 8am, might as well cast back out. So I rebaited and cast back out to the same spot and kept thinking it over in my mind, drinking lots of coffee. The time seemed to take ages to pass, I was just finishing my last cup of coffee and a cigarette when the second Fox buzzer bleeped. I was on it like lightning , another bleep, I looked out to the gap to see if any coots were out there... no, I looked at the line, saw it start to tighten up, grabbed the rod and struck.

I felt the fish was on and remembered that (the other side of) the bar was very sharp, so I just held it tight and boiled the fish on top and began to pump it back. It started to kite at a 45 degree angle to my left and I had a job to keep up with it. I knew by the way she was going that it was making for the gap behind the small island on my left and I had to turn her. I managed to keep her on my side, but only just, as she made for the overhanging bushes. She then went

Peter Springate with 'Mary' the first time

Dave Cumpstone and a 50lb English carp

through the gap on my side and into the bay behind me. I knew then she would be mine. I got the landing net, waded out onto the bar to play her in from there but she didn't want to go into the net, then she nearly got tangled up with the one already sacked up. I could see it was another big mirror.

Eventually I managed to net her, laid her on the unhooking mat and had to use the forceps to get the hook out. I quickly sacked her then reeled the other rod in. I just couldn't believe my luck.

A Wraysbury Brace, A Dream Come True
Friday, July 3rd 1992
Bleep... Bleep... Buzz... Buzz... out of the blue
It's 5am, there's rain in the clouds,
my rod is arching, I'm cursing out loud.

Once on the bank, I can't believe what I see,
a beautiful carp, over 40 she must be.

My hands are shaking, my mind's in a whirl,
she weighs 47lb.. You're a beauty my girl.

A kiss, then safely in the sack,
in a daze, I just sit back.

Hands shaking, I light a ciggy,
Oh my, what a biggy.

Kettle on, I have a cuppa,
pondering, my heart a flutter.

Rods back in the water, baits on the hook,
Bleep... Bleep... Buzz... Buzz. I can't believe my luck.

Hands shaking, I strike with might,
she's hooked, now begins the fight.

It's 8am... I stand and stare...
She's 37lb 8oz... what a pair!

If you were there and read my face,
man was never so proud to have caught such a brace.

'LIFE BEGINS AT FORTY'
Steve Allcott

A new gallon of water sitting next to my humble bedsit mysteriously became empty, "Curly must be here," said Harper the Carper. Our area was a long walk from the car park and a heavy water bottle is an item you can do without. I moaned at Phil, accusing him of washing and shaving with it, for he looked his new pin ready-for-the-evening self as usual. His defence made sense, I knew Curly of old and what despicable tricks he was capable of. He was an old hand from the days when anglers were anglers, those that are know what I mean! I was up a tree looking one time and I saw him go into my bivvy, tip out my Gold Blend coffee and replace it with his Tesco Economy. I have known him swap his week-old milk for someone's fresh. I caught a couple of fish once next to him, next day he caught one, when I unhooked it guess whose bait - yep, mine! Get the picture of this unscrupulous hooligan carper? A long line cast from the right through my swim landing in Phil's confirmed our suspicions - he was here. We strolled along and this giant, frizzy-haired man stood amongst the tree tops laughing to himself. "How do you do," he said, "thought I had the lake to myself." Indeed we thought. "Didn't see your cars" (trying to make us think they had been nicked). "Have you had my water?" "No not me," he answered straight away, as though he knew I was going to ask. He had one of those, roll up, 'squash together' 'stuff anywhere' jobs, it sat full and fresh next to his shithouse. I pointed and he said "Oh, I've just filled that up out of the lake." I was "welcome to half of it as a friend" he said. Phil laughed his head off and walked away, I followed in disbelief and disgust. Later Curly crept round with rock salmon and chips for me: "Feeling guilty are we?" "Never gave it a thought." They were very nice, I'd never had rock before. As usual he talked and talked and I just listened, he told me of a not so far away place and what some of his friends had caught there over the years. What he told me was special - not his usual drivel, it left me numb and was on my mind for a long time. I am glad our paths crossed. If only there were more like you - heaven forbid!

I went for a look, you have heard the saying 'love at first sight'. But why here? I now wanted to catch a 40 pound carp. I had set myself a new goal, something that would be incredibly tough to achieve. Many anglers had caught a 40 pounder, only a few had single-mindedly set out to catch a forty. The right lake, a run from a carp and bang go the scales and onto the list of fame. Many have taken one without effort or much angling ability, such is life. Kerry caught one while with Phil who was after another one. The time was right, my sole ambition became apparent, nothing else would matter any more.

The first time I fished there I went alone and knew no one. The anglers on the water made me welcome, my eyes and ears could not believe it. So much beauty in one small place. Small it was indeed compared to what I was used to. You could not have found clearer water in a Perrier bottle, it was deep and mesmerising. The anglers were very good and the fish had the finest education mankind could give. Doctor Psychopath, one of the regulars, told me "they were the greatest carp in all the world." "Why?" I said. "They just are, ask anyone. That's the way it is, you will come to understand one day."

It was a one-off weekend in the depths of winter, I was with Rob. I don't know whether he liked his first impressions, given time I knew he would. We were going through a funny phase and our mates left us to it for a while, it was par for the course and we learned from it. The lake was fairly busy for the time of year, we felt like intruders, nevertheless we were made welcome. Standing looking out into the darkness, wondering why in all the lakes in the all the world we were here. Little did we know we had found somewhere to belong to again. We all belong somewhere some time. Everyone left for the Percy pub for a bottle of beer, a basket meal and a little socialising. Rob and I joined them, we ate, drank and listened. Like strangers sat on the end of the table hoping to hear something useful, for we thought they might know something we needed to know. One of the few anglers we both admire handed us a couple of pictures he though we might like to see. Indeed we did! Even now we both still recollect that moment. Three big fish, one season's hard-earned success brought about by years of learning. Without a doubt we were taken aback. We knew what we wanted. When no one was looking we smiled at each other. 'Thanks mate', you will never know what you did. We chanced our way here and there through the rest of the winter, making plans for the new term ahead. This was Longfield, and it's reputation would make that fish mean more than the other forties in achievement terms. We remember saying 'we wanted one too badly' and would probably only ever get one when they were everywhere. We were enjoying

Steve and the 'Parrot'

it, we had ambition.

The close season came but just didn't want to go. Odd days we would visit our Longfield and look at the carp, nothing like we had ever seen before. They were all so big, a shoal of low to upper thirties, that sight could not have been equalled anywhere at that time. Later we found out they were called the A-Team, big carp, a few tench and a couple of chub that cruised in formation together, the lords of the manor of Longfield. We got to know their names, anxiously we awaited a more intimate meeting.

The season started and the Famous Five caught the forty in the first week. Dave Whibley had it next to me. Over the season we made a few new friends and 'the Famous Five' grew to around a dozen. We caught all the fish that season. I never came near the big one... it was caught a couple of times when I was not on the water. The season ended, I had spent many hours fishing, next year I would try again. The season started and we moved onto another water for the summer to get a bit of peace, and the brief spell away cleared my mind. I wanted it more than ever, I was totally obsessed. It was the first thing I thought of every morning when I awoke, working all day with it turning over in my mind and finally falling asleep dreaming the impossible dream. Those that have not spent hour after hour staring at the still lake, watching it's changing moods, studying it's surface for carp activity, won't be able to fully understand the obsession, many others however will no doubt identify strongly with it.

We returned, the leaves lay upon the ground, the shadows and reflections seemed more alive than ever. Anglers had changed that year, bringing forth a new breed and a new gang of friends. We felt we knew the water from winters old, an advantage over the others. The carp were lying low, so to speak. Over the next couple of months the only one caught was by Geoff, a common of unlucky double figures, he deserved more for his effort. Time was to run out on him, we became friends and had a good laugh winding one another up into the early hours. He was there for the rest of my time there along with Rob, Terry 'D', and Tony 'M', Ginger Steve, Steve Nine/One, The Veg, Mad Mick the Arsonist, Nodd, The Wedge, Dodgey Moore and a few 'now and agains'. I will never forget the curry porridge Terry 'D' and Tony 'M' cooked me one night, cheap and warm they said!

It's a few weeks away from Christmas and I have left a little bit out, it is irrelevant and only for my memories. The winter hot spots on the bungalow bank were covered in dead weed, the fish must have chosen a new area this year. We were throwing leads everywhere, no spots seemed clean enough for them to have been active. Odd fish showed a week before Christmas. I told no one, it was not selfish, just angling, I knew the spot and begged for the swim to be free during my holiday session. Time drew nearer, the dreaded weed had a hole and the bottom was as hard as concrete, it reminded me of casting onto a square paving slab, the conditions just got better and better... mild nights, not too damp, only slight breezes.

Martin and Dave called in just before the festivities began, to say Happy Christmas, they were off to sunny Tenerife for two weeks, I envied them, Phil was joining them for the second week. So it was just me and Rob, brothers in arms. The forty had been out in the same week for two years now and anticipation was fierce. We were all getting more excited by the hour, I felt on top form. Christmas was very merry as it should be. I arrived on Boxing Day, the day before Rob, three or four anglers were already there, they had spent Christmas as they wished. As I waded through the mud with a can of beer and a rod bag I could hear Geoff singing the song we had been singing for months "all we can do is sit and wait, sit and wait". How true, it befitted us. As I walked past *The Corner* destiny started to lend a hand, the swim had been ignored, my friends had chosen the swims we'd caught from last winter. "Roach were very active at dusk," were the first words said. It may sound irrelevant, to us it was neat, my rod bag reserved the swim while I chatted the day away. There was no rush, later in the afternoon five and a half inch round leads were thudding down on the hard patch. Dawn was perfect, no recasts were needed, they would still be perfect and would only have to go back there anyway. Presentation, presented perfectly. We ate bacon and drank Irish coffee and Rob arrived. He chose one of his favourite swims round on the bungalow bank, a flock of ring-neck parakeets crossed by. Rob sang "early bird, early bird, early bird" - I don't know what he meant. Later I made a turkey curry with chick peas and rice, it was so hot I could not breathe, Rob and Geoff said it was like oxtail soup, I am sure they must have sneaked something in. Geoff said no one would catch unless it was on their bait. Rob winked and just said: "Look a barn owl." Everyone looked, it had gone through of course.

One bleep came totally out of the blue in mid-afternoon, Mick said: "A Robin." Wisely I stood by the rods, 15 minutes had passed, the lines were fished down from the tip very slack and along the weedy bottom. A bleep, a lift, then a fall, only a fraction, winding down, I struck as hard as I could, Rob said: "Christ what was that for?" "I'm in mate." It kited right, a small patch of weed surfaced and the spell was broken, Geoff appeared during mid-battle, just powerful lunges of a big winter carp. Rob netted it and said it was *The Parrot*, I totally didn't expect him to say those words, last time out it weighed just under forty, it felt heavy, cross your fingers someone said, "this time it will do it" someone else said. No, 37lb 12oz, it had lost a bit but I was really pleased. It was a character I wanted to catch. If it had been forty I might have packed up and gone home. Everyone was pleased for me, John Allan arrived, he knew of old and said the weather was perfect, the big one would be out, someone's turn is up. I felt then that I'd had my turn. Colin arrived and everyone got fishing. My baits were cast perfectly.

In the darkness of night a buzzer screamed into life, I was in a deep sleep and didn't know where I was. Striking without thinking, a skill the years give you, I was in and the fish made for the snags. I pulled it towards me and it fought away, Rob appeared and netted it in the darkness, big carp I knew. It was lifted ashore, I will never forget Rob's words: "I don't know which one you have caught but it's bigger than the last one." The torch shone and a cluster of scales I knew so well hit my eyes, it was over... 44lb 4oz. I packed away as everyone slept, and watched the night away. Fish jumped on the spot, I had no interest. I said farewell to the swims, thankful for the memory. Morning came and my life began at forty, for the cameras, what a pair, bad luck someone said, nearly two forties. Celebrations were planned around me, I left them to it, John and Rob both said "you ain't coming back are you?"

"No." I stopped at the phone and caught Phil just before he left for the airport. They were so happy for me on New Year's Eve they drank Tequila and Champagne slammers at midnight on the beach. Rob was happy for me, as I will be for him when his turn comes.

That was the last fish ever from Longfield, the lake record, it will never be beaten, it has gone. We don't know why no one did anything with the lake. I share the memory, we will always toast Longfield and what we had. Wherever we go, nothing will ever compare to what we had, when we were there.

The last fish from Fox Pool

A TALE OF TWO FORTIES
Ritchie McDonald

I do love a happy ending... you know how it goes in the films - geezer meets girl, geezer loses girl, geezer gets girl and they both live happily ever after. Magic! If it doesn't bring a lump to your throat, you're never normal. That's how it was last season with me and two lovely creatures called *Heather the Leather* and *The Pad Lake Big 'un.*

Not that it was *supposed* to have been an epic tale of heartache and sleepless nights. It should have been over in ten days. I remember telling Yvonne, as I left the house on 15th June, that I wouldn't be long. But it wasn't to be. The best laid plans of mice and men - and all that.

The fish I was after was the biggest in the Pad Lake of Leisure Sport's Yateley complex, in Surrey, and there was every chance that she might weigh over 40 pounds. The reason I was so confident was that between January and March of the previous season I'd caught three fish from the lake - 25lb, 29lb and 36lb 8oz - and I thought I'd got it sussed.

But June slipped by without success. Never mind, I thought, Rome wasn't built in ten days! I'll give it a couple more weekends, I'm bound to get a result. It was at the end of these that Tony Moore hooked something special, and when the fish rolled over his landing net it was the big 'un.

Now, some of you may expect me to be gutted when the fish I'm after is drawn over the rim of someone else's landing net, but it's not so. I was after a forty, and when the scales stopped short of the magic number I had a feeling that I wasn't meant to catch it. Not yet, anyway. My main chance would be at the back-end of the season.

So what should I do? The fish I wanted was weighing in at less than 40 pounds and was holed up somewhere, recovering from the fight and vowing never to touch another boilie. When this has happened before, I've packed my bags and legged it back indoors for a few weeks to enjoy a few home comforts while the big 'un gets its appetite back. However, at the back end of the previous season when I'd been fishing the Pad Lake, I'd heard walloping great crashes on the lake behind me and I'd nipped across and noted the spots.

Those of you who know this part of the Yateley complex will be aware that the Pad Lake and Car Park Lake are separated by just a narrow strip of land. They are so close that it would be possible, if you were daft enough, to cast a bait in each water and fish with rods pointing in opposite directions, though every passer-by would have to climb over you to get past. I hadn't anticipated fishing the Car Park Lake for *Heather the Leather* until later in the season, but things being what they were, this seemed an ideal time to start.

When I got a glimpse of *Heather*, I knew I'd made the right decision. She was huge, maybe over 45 pounds.

The weather was glorious, ideal for fish-spotting, and I must admit I thought she was there for the taking. Perhaps I was overconfident, but whatever the reason, I ended up spending the rest of the summer up and down trees more often than I want to be at my age, watching *Heather* - which is always good news because you should learn something every time you see the fish you are after - hearing *Heather*, casting to *Heather*, in fact doing everything short of putting her on the bank.

I dropped baits in her path and saw here ignore them, and I even bumped into her when clearing some weed, which was worse this year than I've known it, but still she refused to be caught. I watched her after I'd spooked her, and when she thought I'd gone she came straight back, which told me that the spot she'd returned to was rather special. Perhaps this was one of the larders that the fish visit, rich sources of bloodworm or snails, testing them to see which ones are ripe for harvesting.

I didn't mind spooking her. I believe you have to be where the fish are to learn about them, and there are going to be times when you overstep the mark and are spotted. I'm sure they know we are there 90 per cent of the time. It's their home and they know everything that goes on in it. Having said that, I reckon it's harder to put feeding fish off their food than we think. If I was hungry and I'd just sat down to dinner it would take a lot of disturbance to make me leave my grub. However, I couldn't understand why I hadn't had a chance at her yet. It wasn't like her to be so anti-social. The previous season she paid a visit to the lads on the bank in October at 40lb 10oz, 39lb in September of that year and three times in 1988 at 34lb 13oz, 38lb 4oz and 39lb. So what was I doing wrong? I made a cup of tea and had a ponder.

The more I look back on my fishing, the more I realise that success, for me at least, comes when I'm in tune with the water and its inhabitants. It may sound a bit strange to some, but it's a question of getting your head together. I can hear some of the lads laughing and shaking their heads saying: "Old Ritchie will be lighting jos-sticks and sitting cross-legged in front of his bivvy soon, chanting mantras and raising the palms of his hands to the sky. What is occurring?" But, they say that wisdom comes with age, and I think I'm getting more philosophical in my approach to fishing these days than when I couldn't get my bait in the water quick enough.

I want to feel in tune, because when I'm on form and everything's just right, I don't miss a thing. When I'm feeling right, if I see a bubble that looks out of place I'm on to it, the cast accurate and the strike and the fight perfectly controlled. If anyone could achieve that state of mind all the time, the fish wouldn't stand a chance, but it's just not possible to keep that sort of awareness going indefinitely. All you can do is realise it's happening and make the most of the situation.

I just needed to be patient and try to blend in, but things were destined to go very wrong before they finally came right.

The first set-back came when I got another look at *Heather* (we can't keep meeting like this) and she looked much smaller. Fish this big vary so much in size. In June they can be huge with one or two years' spawn inside them, then in July they can be down to their lowest weight. I think September to March is the best time for the genuine weight. There was no mistaking *Heather's* drop in size.

Then there was the problem of the tench. Don't get me wrong, I like tench. I've spent many a long session fishing for a big 'un and a hefty male can give you the sort of scrap that you won't forget in a hurry, but the sort I was catching were females of about four pounds. Every time the buzzer went my heart gave a jump, and every time there was a short, plucky fight and another green-flanked baby got lost in the folds of the carp-sized landing net.

Not that catching tench is a bad thing when you're after carp. They are far more finicky feeders than carp and if you're catching them, there can't be much wrong with your baits and rigs. Also, when you get them going, they create an attractive feeding area. The tench will stir up clouds from the bottom of the lake as they pick up the free offerings and this in turn will attract more carp. I would be much more confident of catching a carp if four or five tench were milling around the baits than if the fish I was after came across them alone.

As for hooked fish spooking the shoal and so scaring the carp, I learned a long time ago from a matchman that if you strike sideways you pull the fish through the shoal, not up above it, and provided you lead it carefully, without applying too much pressure (the harder you pull, the harder they pull back) they will come along without disturbing the others.

Then there was the fact that I'd told them at work at Hounslow Angling Centre how close I was coming to catching *Heather*, and begged a couple of extra days off because I thought it was going to happen at any moment. It seemed like it was, too, but despite everything pointing towards action, the moment I was waiting for just wouldn't come, and it looked like I'd have to face them without the capture I'd predicted.

Then I began to lose it with the tench. I missed a run, and I lost

Ritchie and the Pad Lake forty

a fish when it ran through weed and the hook pulled. I had been using a rig shown to me by Tony Moore, who used it to catch his fish of 45 and 38 pounds, and I couldn't resist giving it a try. He went out and freed the line, but the fish had gone. I'd broken one of my golden rules, not to try things for the first time on hard waters. But the rig's excellent, and when I've put it through its paces on smaller fish I think I'll be bringing it into the front line for my serious fishing.

To cap it all, after a sleepless night stalking *Heather*, I went to bed at dawn, and had been asleep for half an hour when I had a steaming run. I felt like Arnold Schwarzenegger in Total Recall. I was awake and sitting bolt upright on my bed but my brain was missing. For what seemed like ages I didn't know where I was, and by the time I'd got my head together, my slippers on and the rod in my hand, the line was lying limp on the surface. Looking back now, I've got a sneaking feeling that a swan was responsible. There was one skulking around not far away, looking sheepish - if that's possible - and that was the only screaming run I had, from carp or tench.

It's not unusual for me to be mooching around at night and asleep during the day. I swop information with the other lads on the lake, so if I've got my eyes and ears open at night and they're on the look out during the day, we've got a round-the-clock watch going. If you're asleep and you hear a crash, you'll never know if it was a fish jumping to clear its gills of silt and giving away its whereabouts, or a goose trying to get onto an island. However, if you're in tune you'll know straight away when it's a carp.

One disadvantage at this time was the number of anglers on the lake. A few years ago you could have gone down to Yateley in mid-week and almost had the place to yourself, but not now. Sometimes it feels like the world and his wife are down there, which makes the fishing that much harder. Add to that the fact that *Heather* was now making herself scarce during my regular visits and you begin to get the picture.

Never mind, though. There was a storm forecast - that would be sure to stir things up. I've usually found that if there's a storm while fish are active it can bring things to a halt, but if things have gone quiet, as they certainly had at this time, it will liven the fish up. However, this would have been all well and good if the weathermen hadn't got it round their necks. Every day they said it was on its way, but for all we saw of a storm, it may as well have been Scotch mist.

In August I spotted six fish feeding in a bay into which the wind was blowing. With just a gentle ripple the conditions were ideal for getting them going on floater, but anyone who's ever tried the method on Yateley will know it's a waste of time and energy. You only have to whisper the word floater and every coot, swan, tufty, goose and seagull - in fact anything with wings and a beak - will make your swim look like a corner of Trafalgar Square. You name it, they're there, squawking, flapping and fighting to mop up your free offerings.

You can hold some of them back by stretching a line across the mouth of a quiet bay. Swans and geese, for instance, won't go through line intentionally but seagulls don't give a damn. In fact, they seem to take a particular pleasure in getting where they are not wanted (I know a few human beings who behave like that). If it wasn't for the birdlife, catching fish at Yateley would be easy. As it is, we'll have to wait until the seagulls go back to the sea, where they belong, before we can expect some good floater fishing. What I would say, though, is that however much birdlife frustrates me, there's no way I would kill one, or put up with anyone else doing so, because they have more right to be there than we do.

Anyway, I tried my luck with the six fish in the bay, casting as far away from them as I could and reeling back in, to avoid spooking them. I watched them drift around for a while, just asking for a bit of floater, and then swim slowly out of the bay and away. And as if all this wasn't enough, one week later I finally found *Heather*, mooching about over a clear patch with another fish. I fetched the rod, cast in a little way along and straight away she came across to the bait. The float slid under, but I could see she was in mid-water and had touched the line. I sat there all night, gazing at the isotope - I always have one on the float in case daylight fishing turns into night fishing - and six times the float bobbed under and back up as she gave me line bites just a rod-length out.

What did I have to do? I told you this was a tear-jerker. Forget *Gone with the Wind*, you could set this to music and there wouldn't be a dry eye in the house. I found out later she was taking fry and pond-skaters which covered the surface in thousands, and in their pre-occupation the fish wouldn't look at my floater I'd rigged up with a worm wriggling enticingly in the middle.

The following week I was back again, and the first two captures were tufties (what was I telling you about the birdlife?) But this time I was determined to succeed. That fish had my name on it and I'd get her in the landing net or go mad trying. I gave it all I had. I stayed awake all night, I changed my rigs, I changed my bait. I even waded in and cleared out some weed to improve my chances. What was the result? The Heavens opened and down came the rain, making me cold, wet, frustrated and fed-up. The last straw came in October. I found a couple of her mates rolling in the weed, so I nipped around with my float rod, which I always have at the ready, set up with a waggler, and put out a bait. Keith Sullivan was behind me while I was fishing and it was just as I turned to speak to him that his eyes bulged and he said: "Your float's gone under." I turned back and struck, and there was a big fish on the end, but I knew almost at once that something wasn't right, and when she came towards me belly first, I knew what it was. She was foulhooked. I netted the fish, gave the rod and landing net to Keith and said: "Sort that out for me, I'm gutted," and walked away. One by one the lads came around to my swim that afternoon to offer me their condolences. I felt that they were genuinely very sorry that I had foulhooked a big carp.

When the weather turned cold in December, I gave it a rest. I believe in perseverance but when the lake's frozen solid and the weather's diabolical, even I draw the line, especially when we're talking less than one fish per acre. I'm certainly not going to sit there and wait for the ice to thaw. I may be dedicated, but I'm not daft.

Someone did venture out and two fish were caught, one on Boxing Day and one the day after, but I came home, had a Merry Christmas and a Happy New Year, and was back at the end of February.

I had something up my sleeve when I returned, and it wasn't a present from Father Christmas. At the end of the previous season I had spoken to a bloke who'd had three runs at the far end of the Pad Lake, and when I'd had a look around I noticed that the frogs were spawning. I know from my Redmire days that carp feel about frog spawn the way kids feel about sweets - you just can't keep them apart. They were eating so much of it at one time that Chris Seager tried out tapioca and caught a couple of the famous lake's fish on it. For a while a carp that's on frog spawn won't stop for a boilie, if your bait is in there with the eggs, I believe that a fish will

'Heather' in winter

mop up the lot. Never one to pass up an opportunity, I got on the blower to London Zoo and found out that the little fellas in lakes lay the stuff about one week after their friends in garden ponds do. So I kept my eyes peeled, and when I came back in February I headed straight for the rushes at the far end. As it turned out, I wasn't there long enough for the free groundbaiting to begin.

There was no sign of frog spawn or carp, so I fished the birdfood boilies over a couple of gravel bars I had found about 25 yards out from the far bank. I'd got to know the water by plumbing it pretty extensively the previous season, and found a clear patch that I can only describe by saying that it felt like I was dragging the lead over a billiard table and then I hit the balls. Whatever it was made of, it was rough and lumpy and different from the rest, and the first time I put a bait there I caught a fish.

It was on the second session, when I had been there just three days, that it happened. At 3pm on March 5, I was having an afternoon nap when there was a single bleep. I looked out and saw the rod tip bounce down, but the line hadn't been pulled out of the clip (I use a circle of rubber tube pinned around the rod so that the trimmed ends form a 'V'). I climbed out of bed and as I did so, the line dropped back. I struck and felt a little kick a long way out, just like the tench were giving me.

The fish kited straight across the lake, and it was only when I put pressure on to bring it around a bush that I realised it wasn't a tench. It hadn't fought until then, but suddenly it surged away and got me in trouble. The line started to go through the branches of a fallen tree, and I had to release the pressure to avoid damaging it.

I called a couple of the lads around and I put on their waders and tried to get the line free, but the water was too deep. I knew it was either the big 'un or her 36 pound mate, I'll go in after it. I think I lasted about ten seconds before I had to come out. It may have been March, but it wasn't long after the thaw and that water was cold enough to turn an Eskimo's nose blue. People were saying I should throw a brick in, but that could have damaged the fish or the line, or both.

This is where I have to say a big thank you to the chap who saved my bacon, Keith Sullivan, who's been a friend for about ten years. Without a moment's hesitation he fetched his lilo (a handy piece of equipment for resting fish when photographing them, as well as for kipping on), stripped down to T-shirt and shreddies and paddled out to the end of the tree. He must have had his ReadyBrek that morning because he only said "Bloody 'ell it's cold" just the once. First he tried to free the line by breaking branches while on the lilo, but he couldn't break enough off. So, in an act worthy of a bravery medal, he plunged in up to his neck, took the rod from me and swam around the tree and back in to the bank so that I could play the fish from the other side. What can I say? A greater love hath no man than to whip off his undies and wade out into an icy lake for a friend. That's one I owe you Keith.

On the other side, the fish was still snagged in some pads, but gentle pressure got her out and then I kept in front of her, steering her left and right until she was where I wanted her to be. Then she rolled, and the big 'un was mine.

The scales were ready and waiting, and she pulled the needle down to 41lb 9oz - the fish I wanted, at the weight I'd hoped for. It didn't matter what happened after that, I'd done what I set out to do and could go home happy.

Needless to say there wasn't much fishing done for the next few hours as pictures were taken, people were informed and we wet the big 'un's head with a beer or two. People started asking what I was going to do for what was left of the season, and at first I just wanted to catch a few easy fish. But when the dust settled and I was alone with my thoughts, it seemed too good an opportunity to miss not to spend the last few days trying for *Heather*. I'd planned to be on the complex until the last day, and considering how close I'd come to catching her and how much I'd learned about good areas, it seemed a waste to go home. I had a pretty good idea of where she would be.

So, at 4am - I'd just woken up after the previous afternoon's celebration - I moved on to the point of the Car Park Lake, an area where it is shallower and warmer than the rest and there is plenty of cover, and put baits out on an area of gravel over which I'd seen her earlier in the year. Ideally, I like to anticipate the fish's movements and lay my ambush ready for their arrival. A planned surprise attack is far more effective that stumbling on your quarry and having a go. With this in mind, I put a line of baits across the channel, to draw fish to where my critically-balanced Tropicana pop-up was waiting.

Things started, as always, with tench, and then more tench, and then more tench. It got so I was dreaming about tench. It also meant that I was getting through a fair bit of bait, because when I catch a fish I like to put out some free offerings. The hookbait is likely to be the last one out there, and it's probably been in and out of several mouths without anyone knowing about it.

The weather was getting better all the time. It would rain all night but then ease off in the morning, and the sun would come out to dry the ground and warm the lake, giving everything a fresh, newly polished sparkle and lifting the water temperature by the hour. I still fish hard when the weather is bad, for someone, somewhere has caught a fish in those conditions, but there's nothing like the right weather for getting the juices flowing.

The feeling of expectancy was electric. Something just had to happen. On March 10, at 6pm it did. There was a bleep, the rod top started bouncing, and the line was pulled out of the clip. I tugged on my boots and was ready for action, like a fireman answering a call. This was it. This was the one I'd been waiting for. By the time I got to the rod, the line was peeling off the spool, I cupped the front of the reel (that method was good enough for Jack Hilton, so it's good enough for me), struck, and hooked another four pound tench. I don't mind a bit of action, but this was ridiculous.

And, still they came, getting bigger all the time. At 9pm I landed a five pound male, which gave a great fight, even on an eight pound line, and would have been a real arm-acher on tench tackle. By the end of the evening I'd had 12. The one consolation to me was the anglers around me were not getting them. I reminded myself as I slipped yet another of the little red-eyed creatures back into the lake that success with the tench can only be a good sign.

There was another tench in the early hours and by breakfast time all this tench catching had made me hungry. I got some bacon and eggs off Keith and soon had them sizzling in the pan. I don't normally cook myself a breakfast, because fried food does my face in like a dartboard, but this morning my mouth was watering at the thought. I could almost feel the grease dribbling down my chin.

A young lad called Alan, who lives locally and spends as much time on the lake as off, came around. He's going to be a great carp angler one day because he's always spotting fish and asking us questions. He'll know more about those lakes than anyone before he's much older. It was while I was talking to him and stirring my grub that the tip of the left hand rod dropped back. I struck, and straight away I knew it was a big fish, even though it was a long way away.

It didn't do a lot at first, though there was a nice bend in the rod. Suddenly it hit a weedbed. I put as much pressure on the eight pound line and six pound hooklink as I dared, and she came out of it, but instead of running away from the source of the pull, she ran towards me so that I could not apply any side-strain. I think it was when she did something as cunning as that, that I realised what I had hooked. Her movements were slow and decisive, with long, strong pulls as if she knew the situation and how to get out of it. She didn't go mad, like some people have said she does, but then I didn't play her heavily.

She tried to get among the overhanging trees to my left, and I had to get into the water to stop her reaching them. This brought her along the bank in front of me and when she rolled a little way out, I knew for certain. Here was *Heather* at last, and even after all the hard work and the near misses, I couldn't help thinking how lucky I'd been.

I gave a shout to Jock to get his video camera, and the next time she rolled she was in the net, with Alan looking on, just six days after the Pad Lake fish.

The leeches on her side and belly, which I relieved her of, showed she had been lying dormant for a while. I lowered *Heather* onto the scales and she registered 40lb 8oz. Two forty pound fish in under a week had become a reality.

As I watched her swim off, after the photos, it struck me how much narrower she was compared with when I'd seen her in July. I can only wonder how much she weighed then.

People asked me afterwards why I didn't go for the North Lake fish and try for a hat-trick of forties. But that's a fish I've already caught once before and it wasn't on my list of aims, so I didn't try for it. I will never know whether or not it would have come true in the remaining three days. To tell you the truth, I'm not really bothered, I did what I came to do and then I went home. If *Heather* hadn't succumbed, I would have been back there on June 16 to try again.

As it is, I can move on to another water, another fish, and hopefully this time next year I'll have another tale to tell.

CARP AND THE DRAW OF THE BERMUDA TRIANGLE
Tony Moore

Running like a schoolchild at holiday time, I rushed into the car park, dived into the 'carpmobile' and pointed it towards Surrey, destination Yateley. I had three weeks of fishing ahead of me but first the trip down south was necessary to collect some bait for myself and some friends.

The first few weeks of the new season had been slow for me, not a touch from my favourite Oxfordshire stillwater, Cut-Willow (which was not unusual). I spent the previous season on it's grassy banks with only Mr Tench obliging, usually at some unearthly hour of the morning.

My original plan was to collect the bait, then return home for some serious overnight rolling before driving down to Oxford for the obligatory three-week stint I endure every July/August, but things, as usual, didn't quite go to plan.

On my arrival at Yateley, and after suffering numerous horsefly bites on my way around the water, I eventually arrived at Geoff's bivvy on the Copse Lake. It was 6am and apart from Paul's endless snoring from the next swim, the lake was idyllic and peaceful. The water was low, and weed drifted aimlessly across the surface as dark torpedoes moved stealthily between Paul and Geoff's swims.

"Get the kettle on fatty."

"Put it on yourself Fat-Guts."

This was our usual jovial greeting, at which Geoff removed his hands from his underpants, picked his nose, dipped the kettle in the lake, lit the stove and scratched his rear all in one graceful movement. "*Arf* won't be here till dinnertime with your bait." This was no problem, after the initial rush to get down a few more hours wouldn't matter, and I had three weeks holiday in front of me.

We sat, drinking tea all morning. Geoff may even have caught one, but I won't mention that, his head is big enough already. Midday came and went and with my night shift taking its toll I decided on some shut-eye. I collected my bed and a bit of tackle from the car and squeezed into a swim to Geoff's right. Before I had time to tackle up I was snoring peacefully on my chair.

Geoff gave me a nudge just before dark, it looked like *Arf* wouldn't be down until the morning so I hurriedly cast a bait into the Copse Lake for the first time in five years. Myself and Paul spent the evening listening to endless banter and jokes from Geoff. We'd heard it all before but somehow the bottles of Elephant beer gave even his oldest jokes new sparkle.

After waking at first light (joke) (it always seems to stay darker longer in my swims), Geoff thrust a 'cuppa' in my hands before huddling me into the back of Paul's ex-Telecom van amidst rods and other paraphernalia for the daily pilgrimage to Angie's cafe. "Double scrambled egg on toast, two burgers well done, sausage, chips, two rolls and two teas each please."

After breakfast was gorged and a scrub with the old Izal (please wash your hands) Paul drove us back down the bumpy track to the back of the Copse Lake where I packed up my tackle and yomped back to the carpmobile in the tropical heat. It was hot, really hot.

A quick drive across the road to the other car park and I bumped into 'Arfur' who had at last arrived. After our usual mickey-take of each other and wholehearted slaps on the back with plenty of yo-ho-ho's, we transferred the bait to my car. I left him to sort out his tackle and decided to stroll around the northern side of Yateley before I went home.

It was hot and still. I risked life and limb climbing the painfully thin silver birches that adorn the car park bay, carp were clearly visible basking in the shade of the floating scum. Sliding down the tree and covering myself with that dry and musky smelling green dust I continued walking around the centre path.

Ritchie was relaxing in the shade on the Pad Lake, a quick 'wight geezer' (Ritchie-ism) and I continued on my way past the Split Lake and onto the North Lake, my favourite of all the Yateley lakes.

The heat was stifling. 'Prophet' Phil was set up on the high works bank which is simply suicidal. His bivvy reminded me of a Japanese prison camp sweatbox, nevertheless he greeted me with his usual ear-to-ear smile and we chatted for the next hour about this and that before I decided to head for home. People were waiting for bait and I was tired. I pointed the car north, pressed autopilot and arrived in sunny Coventry some two and a half hours later.

A phone call to my good mate Mark Jones confirmed that he would join me at Cut-Willow in a week, we chatted and I told him I fancied Yateley. "Get down there my son, the boats at Cut-Willow are a pain and it's just too hot." I had to agree with him, none of the Yateley biggies had been out and I really did fancy my chances.

When I had fished Yateley some years ago a chap had caught the

North Lake forty on float-fished chick pea during my annual holiday which I was now into. Maybe this fish just liked a change of scenery in late July. I decided on a change of plan... a week at Yateley, then two weeks at Cut-Willow with Mark. Makes a change I thought and off I set.

The car was once again loaded to the gunnels, and with Matt Johnson's melodic tunes playing in my ear I decided to take the scenic route and enjoy the brisk drive through winding lanes southwards.

After once again denting my fuel tank whilst entering the car park, I parked my car in the shade and stepped out to stretch my weary legs. I slipped on my sunglasses (good job the frames are indestructible). I picked myself up, dusted myself down and pulled two pints of raspberry milkshake out of the coolbox and into my waistcoat pockets then trundled off in search of carp.

Ritchie's still on the Pad Lake, his searching eyes trying to beat the surface glare. *Effort, effort, effort.* "Where ya fishin' geezer?" He asked. To be honest I was still undecided. It was absolutely scorching and Ritchie had not seen fish moving on the Pad for ages. "I'm not really sure yet me old cock sparra - perhaps the North, I don't really know."

I left Ritchie playing around in his coolbox and sauntered on past the Car Park Lake. *Heather* weather? I didn't think so. The lake was receiving a lot of pressure at the time and quite a few fish had been lost.

I had a really good look around the North Lake, I didn't see anything but felt something...

"Bloody bird-watchers' dogs" I said out loud whilst scraping the foul-smelling mess from the bottom of my boots with a dock leaf. 'Poop scoops' should be compulsory on here I thought.

One chap was fishing at the far end on the shallows where he'd seen some smaller fish earlier in the week. He'd had no action and it didn't look that good but somehow that lake was drawing me like a magnet.

There was one niggling doubt at the back of my mind. The Copse Lake had been fishing well up to now, maybe it was worth a try. Two milkshakes later I was in Paul's swim, accidentally pulling his clothes line down as I entered with all the grace of those all-dancing butter advert cows.

Paul had nothing to report and to be honest the lake looked

The North Lake Forty

awful. The water level had dropped a foot and the surface was 80 per cent weed. So the North it was. Oh well, I can blank with the rest of them.

Three consecutive journeys laden with tackle traipsing through the malaria-infested undergrowth left me lying across my tackle clutching my chest and panting. I though this fishing lark was supposed to be relaxing. "Bloody sun," I shouted, waving my fist in the air. I checked my pulse, it was back down to 72, time to search for cyprus-carpio. I made my way around the lake, peering under the odd marginal bush and climbing the odd tree. "Carp give me a sign," I said, dangling precariously 30 feet in the air trying to beat the sun's glare with some serious squinting through my carp glasses, looking like a rather tall, overweight Japanese sniper. Nothing, not a murmur, everything was still. Not to worry, there is always plan two in my never to be published book of location, the liveliest swim, fish the liveliest swim. Anything will do... the tiniest of ripples... roach splashing, or best of all hatch taking place, preferably near some shade.

At last I found a swim I was happy with, nicely positioned out of the sun. A small island was to my left and the biggest expanse of open water to my right. There was a hatch of some description taking place to the right of the island. Our little friends the mozzies or whatever they are were continually appearing from their watery birthplace and slowly making their way to my already lumpy forearms.

I returned for my tackle and eventually, as footsore as a Roman legionnaire, sat exhausted in my swim and watched the water. All was quiet, time to get the big steel mallet out. I settled in nicely, my new bivvy sitting perfectly on the flat ground. Playing around with one rod I started to discover the contours of my swim but it was hot and I was hungry. Time to get the Haunted-House spaghetti in the pot and the kettle on the go.

As usual my rigs were tied on and ready to go, I balanced some baits up and whacked 'em out. My hookbaits were something new I was playing around with and consisted of 50 per cent standard Fishmeal Base plus 50 per cent Norwegian Seaweed Meal which seems to work really well in scorching weather. Read hydrolysis, I believe.

One of the local carp chaps came around for a chat that evening, he'd started fishing before I was born... "Tried this Platil stark yet, it's only sixty thou thick?" "No I'm afraid not, modern technology and all that," best humour the man I thought. "But I still keep my bait in egg boxes." "Nice to see a traditionalist," he said. "Gosh, isn't your rod long!" This bloke was getting a little bit too friendly, time for a subtle 'goodnight'. I pulled the bivvy door down and thankfully he left me to my slumber. I heard the bloke walking away, the words 'sultanas' and 'guitar solos' ringing in my ears. I don't know who he was and I never did see him again.

It was a quiet night apart from two suicidal bream at dawn. Reeling in at midday, a trip to the shops was in order. Upon my return I found nothing had happened. I balanced up a couple of fresh hookbaits and chucked them out. I had been fishing both baits in deeper water to the right of the island in open water (this area had the biggest change of depth I could find), one in silt and one on gravel. I lay back on my bedchair and settled down to read a magazine I had just bought. I had a good view of the lake whilst lying down and was just getting into 'Luscious Lucy from Leeds' when I was caught unawares by a large crashing sound from the far bank. I immediately jumped up and sure enough a carp had leapt near the far bank, some 150 yards away.

My immediate thought was to move, but as I stood watching the water I caught a movement to my left... a tail, a carp tail, the crafty bugger had hardly left a ripple. But there in the edge down the margin a carp was moving. Best have a closer look.

Picking up a handful of 'fish sweets' I slipped on my old plimsolls and crept around as quietly as possible (which meant that every twig between me and the carp was broken). I walked out on a small overgrown peninsula and peered around the bough of a tree, the fish should be within a yard or two of my feet. Nothing, the water was coloured and I couldn't see a thing, not a dickie-bird. The fish had been moving over a small bar which was a continuation of the peninsula I was standing on and ran to the island, a distance of three to four yards. I flicked a dozen or so baits in by hand and started the walk back towards my bivvy, gathering pace as I went.

I tied on fresh rigs, leaving the old ones, still with their baits on hanging from the brolly ribs. One rod was banged out into the deeper water and the other towards the bar, but away from my free offerings which I was to add to later (another 'carp trick' that one).

The evening was very humid and as it became dark I sat on my bedchair flicking pebbles at my indicators. I stood by the water's edge as it became dark, it looked perfect, absolutely perfect...

The take would come, I knew it would. Hurry up Mr Carp! I could do with some kip, I stayed up until 4am when a couple of bleeps to the open water rod saw me standing heron-like next to the rod. Must have been a liner methinks as I decide it's time for bed, 5am and I'm just into my first perverse dream... Luscious Lucy from Leeds... beeeep... an absolute flyer to the island rod. Up in a flash I pulled in, Jesus was that one motorin' - going faster than a dolphin following a yacht. The Armalite carp-bruiser was bent double as the big old carp sought sanctuary around the other side of the island, but suddenly the line went limp. Although disappointed I'm always calm when I lose a fish, I simply reeled in. 'There will be other times', I thought as I held the rig in my hand. I was shaking like a leaf as I tied on a new bait.

I dropped the rig in the margin, the new bait sank quicker than the four ounce bomb I was using. I was trying a 'newish' rig that works best with the bait balanced just off the bottom. I didn't fancy tying a bait on again, so I leant into the bivvy and tugged an old rig off the brolly rigs. I tried it in the edge, perfick!

My first cast was a bit *too* good, I thought the line was caught on a branch so I reeled in and tried again. This time it fell short but I left it, I'm not sure why. If the fish were moving around the island towards me I was confident they would find it. My bait was good and I'm sure they'd be looking for it. Anyway one take was a miracle, two would be impossible. On the rests, in the clips, in the bed, head down to dream of what might have been (sheer poetry that last bit).

An hour later and a single bleep to the same rod. The line on the surface lay motionless, but the indicator was 'vibrating' (just like Luscious Lucy). Nothing to lose I thought as I picked up the rod and wound like fury, sure enough somewhere along the way I made contact with the fish, which didn't seem to like being impaled on my Drennan size four. As it made a big boil on the surface over the shallows to my left I carefully pumped her forward and clearly remember shouting "mirror" when she flipped her tail as she came over the shallow bar in front of me.

The fish charged off to the right and my eyes were firmly fixed on the line picking up as the fish rapidly increased the distance between her and my waiting net. At this point I honestly thought it was low twenty, its movements felt too 'sharp' to be a really big fish.

The Pad Lake Porpoise

Because of this I had no hesitation in dipping the rod and reel deep in the water to turn it away from the snags further down the bank and slightly behind me. The fish turned easily and I slowly guided her towards the waiting net. I could only see the head but managed to net her at the first attempt. I bit off my rig and then threw the rod up the bank.

After pulling the net back I grabbed the arms and lifted "Gott in Himmel" as Klink would say. This is heavy, really heavy. As I peered into the net I was greeted by the sight of the *North Lake Forty* in all her splendour. The feeling was incredible, instant butterflies, instant panic, all I can remember was running around the lake, soaked to the waist, looking for someone to take pictures (I must have walked out with the sack to make sure the fish was lying properly).

Around the corner I found Geno and Dixie, they'd heard my shout but didn't know where I was fishing, they were joined by Tony and Little Bert and we marched back in procession to weigh the fish. After an initial mistake by me which put the fish at 47 pounds-plus, we re-weighed and checked the weight several times. All were agreed at 45lb 8oz. Utopia and nirvana all rolled into one. Photos were taken and the fish was returned to it's watery home.

I let out one more shout of celebration and the lads gradually disappeared, leaving me on my own. It had all happened so quickly, from the take to returning the fish was no more than half an hour. I needed some space and sat down on my bedchair a complete quivering mess.

I eventually decided to make the long hike over to the Copse Lake to see some friends. Geoff didn't believe me at first but when my smirk hadn't stopped for an hour or so he congratulated me on my angling prowess... "It doesn't count you jammy £$*!$+D," he said (as all jealous anglers do) "why didn't you come and fetch me?" I tried to explain that everything had happened so quickly and that I wanted to get the fish back as soon as possible, but I don't think he has forgiven me, even now.

After several cups of tea and a hearty breakfast at Angie's, Geoff drove me around to the north side. I still had a few days fishing left and decided to have a 'dabble' on the Pad Lake. *The Forty* hadn't been out since my good friend Jock White had caught her at 40lb 10oz the previous winter and I was getting greedy.

The lads helped me move my tackle and after a couple of hours toil in the blazing heat I settled in a swim at the far end of the southern bank.

The occasional ripple gently blew from left to right in front of me, the swim hadn't seen much angling pressure thus far and it was nicely tucked in the corner out of the way.

After some carefree plumbing I tied on some fresh baits and folded up the rods. I chucked them in the bivvy and set off. It was celebration time 'good style' as my mate Bernard would say. A compulsory afternoon session in the White Swan was in order, the bottle of Elephant beer and brandy chasers gradually took their toll, as did my ever-lightening wallet. Eric Clapton thrashed out 'Behind the Mask' on the jukebox for the final time as we decided to leave. On the way back we stopped at a local lake for a swim, I'll never forget the sight of 'Sicky' Steve running towards the lake, stripping off Reggie Perrin-style and diving head first into six inches of water, ouch! Laugh, it was only the bolt through my neck that stopped my head falling off.

Baits chucked towards the horizon's silhouette I eventually dozed off. I awoke the next day at about two in the afternoon none the worse for my experience. The rest of the day was uneventful, seeing me recast into 'silty' areas at dusk. "If they wannit they'll have it" as Keith would say. I managed to get some shut-eye despite the once a year chap fishing on the far bank using a lamp that lit the lake up like daylight.

Dawn came and went (nice girl), the boiling heat made the morning go by very slowly until midday when I reeled in to go to the shops. The baits smelt awful, they'd been sitting in detritus all night and smelt like a baby's soiled nappy. I'd have to do better than that, but first things first - the Safeways freezer was calling. Struggling with two large carrier bags, I made my way from the car park to my swim. It was so hot I'd treated myself to a pair of shocking bright purple shorts with 'Bermuda Triangle' emblazoned on the side in kryptonite. Keith Sullivan reckoned they were lucky because he'd bought a pair but, as everybody knows, he never catches anything so I was thinking of chucking them already. However I decided against it, after all I looked like a real carp angler now!

I stopped for a quick breather, looking over the lake pretending to be stealthy with two bright yellow carrier bags under my arms. Then something strange happened, I saw carp, three carp to be precise, straight out in front of me, about 50 yards from my swim. I closed my eyes and shook my head but I couldn't make the three silhouettes disappear. I walked towards my swim to get my carp specs but the fish were obviously attracted to my new shorts and followed at a leisurely pace, eventually ending up tightly bunched up some 30 yards out in front of my swim. Sixty per cent of the lake's carp population were in my swim! Do carp really like loud shorts I thought as I hurriedly set up a floater rod. I hate floater-fishing and my halfhearted attempts saw two of the carp vanish. They don't count on biscuits anyway I said to myself as they kicked their tails and headed up the lake. The lone carp lay totally disinterested, it was one of the two big fish, at least 35-plus.

Later that afternoon the loner melted into the depths and out of sight. I ripped the floater rig off and slipped on a small marker float and two ounce bomb. The fish had stayed very close to one spot for some four hours. Whilst plumbing I think I could see why. There were two small patches of gravel lying in four to five feet of water with a dividing layer of very fine silt. The second, and nearest, patch of gravel rose slightly then dropped off straight into some weed, not the horrible smelling weed that seemed to be rife in this part of the lake but really fresh stuff, long and thin with fresh smelling leaves. I believe it's called Stalwort and the carp love it, it's a quick grower and the carp seem to get on it straight away, especially in this heat.

A few tester casts to the correct part of the surface shadow saw my Seaweed Meal pop-up lying perfectly on the second gravel patch just before the drop off into the weed, and surrounded by a dozen or so fishmeal boilies.

Ritchie (the master) set up opposite me that evening and popped in to see me on his way to the pub to meet a friend. "You're in the best swim on the lake geezer," he said. "I know, that's why I'm here," I replied. We both had an inkling that one of the big fish was going to come out. I heard Ritchie recast on returning from the pub but apart from that the night was very quiet.

The morning started very brightly and by ten o'clock the two little thermometers in my bivvy showed the temperature to be unbelievably high, so high in fact that you wouldn't believe me if I told you. No you wouldn't, honest!

The church bells started mid-morning, generally getting up everyone's nose. The morning slowly dragged on, I was chatting with Steve and Alex in my swim at 11am when the rod on the spot gave a single bleep. An enquiry, "I think I'll hit that" were my exact words. I leant forwards and pulled the rod slowly to my side, sure enough a big thud came back through the rod top, *carp on* and it felt like a bit of a beastie. The fish had me back-winding initially but the old faithful Armalite beast-tamers took on a healthy test curve as the fish leapt salmon-like a couple of times. Amazing! I knew it was the big girl after the first leap. She did nothing special and after a couple of good tugs in the edge I easily guided her into my waiting net. Ritchie was up on the far bank showing interest... "Which one? How big?" I simply held up four fingers "Forty" I shouted back.

Ritchie started to make his way around the lake. The crowd gathered and sure enough it was Jock's forty at 38lb 10oz, a gorgeous fish and nicely proportioned. One that will get bigger I'm sure.

'Sicky' Steve Rugby tackled me into the lake, I'm not sure who came off worse, me or him. The crowd left me to dry out and take it all in which was basically impossible, I was in a right state. We celebrated heavily that night and I stayed fishing the Pad Lake for another couple of nights, after the 38's slightly smaller mate, before moving onto the Car Park Lake after the infamous leather.

I decided to give Cut-Willow a miss and settled in for a ten-day stint hoping for a Yateley hat-trick. After six days my margin fished hookbait was picked up. Initially I thought it was the dreaded tufty (it was 8am and I was still half-asleep) but my delay in connecting with the fish saw it heavily weeded. A full test curve bend and the fish started to move, slowly, strongly, then the hooklink broke in half. Retackle, recast, what else can you do? Ritchie lost a fish that morning from a neighbouring swim and the next few months were to prove particularly difficult for both of us.

The last week in September saw me smiling with my first Car Park Lake fish, a common of 18lb 8oz, the smallest fish in the lake. Ritchie struggled on and had his result in March, but that's his story. For me that was my last take of the season. Yateley proving to be really difficult in the colder months.

It had been an amazing season, not only for the fishing but the friends I met, old and new. I know it's corny but a special thank-you goes out to the Steves, Jock, Tel, Peetz, P the P, Spit, The Prophet, The Master, The Nose, Hippy, Bert, Traybin, Mush, The Doc, Bucks, Geno, Arf (and anybody else who knows me). One last thing... Hello Mum!

HORTON
Dave Lane

Before I start, I realise that not an awful lot is known about Horton, being a fairly new fishery so, in brief: the fish (for right or wrong) were transferred from Longfield, Goose Pool and Road Lake in 1990. The first season was run on some farcical day ticket scheme but luckily this failed and led to the forming of a 50-man syndicate.

The lake is a 14-acre pit, basically oblong shaped with two bays at the far end being the *Barking Bay* - a featureless 13 feet deep area with overhanging trees and sporadic weed growth, and the *Church Bay* - slightly deeper at 16 feet, also featureless but always very weedy and a fairly regular visiting area for the fish. The main lake is between 16 and 23 feet, with a bar/plateau bisecting the lake at the car park end. This area is approximately four to ten feet deep and leaves a small, deep area beyond it. There are about 60 fish, from double figure commons up to the 49 pound lake record, 27 of which are mirrors. Out of these 27 there are seven, the select few, the 'A-Team' - these are the quarry. All the fish are in good condition and gratefully accepted, but the 'A-Team' members are revered above all else.

The first season was a bit of an unknown. There were a few people who had fished on the day ticket scheme but for most of us it was a complete mystery with no preconceptions of swims, fish behaviour or, as it turned out, the main surprise - depth. My first cast with a plumbing float from *The Point*, my opening night swim, revealed most of the water in front of me to be over 18 feet deep and bowl-like, sloping away at an alarming angle from the bank. After talking with some of the other anglers it turned out that this was pretty much the case everywhere.

I must admit to not being overly struck with the place at first, but after two days and a move into *The Reeds* I hooked a fish that changed that attitude for good. I'd seen a lot of fish showing in the centre of the lake after 24 hours or so of the season had elapsed. A period that had yielded *Jack,* the lake's largest resident and only known forty, to Johnny Moult at 44 pounds; plus a couple of other fish, one of which, *The Lady* another 'A-Team' member, fell as part of a brace to Noddy Stuart. He fished on full of confidence, taking his next fish a mere nine months later, on the last day of the season.

Anyway, back in the middle the fish were leaping, spooked out there by the pressure of a new season's barrage. Keith, my long time angling buddy, and I decided on a move. We knew it was at least 22 feet deep in the middle area, which had put us off at first, but regardless of this about a half an hour after casting my baits into the middle from *The Reeds* swim my alarm screamed its first Horton battle cry. I couldn't believe on hooking that fish the sheer power it showed, charging all over what had seemed a large area of open water ten minutes previously, but shrank into insignificance when I tried to keep the fish within the confines of my own swim, let alone anywhere near the net. After a while I gained some measure of control, or at least I stopped it taking any more, so it kited on a long line down into the right hand margin. For ten minutes or so it fought to gain sanctuary in the various snags along the margins and at one stage had Keith in the bushes 50 yards up the bank hurling bricks in the edge to spook it out of the overhanging branches of a particularly threatening looking tree. I held the rod tip under the water with the tip bent round and as another breeze block hit the water the fish kicked its tail and came out of the snag. I coaxed it slowly around in front of me and bit by bit it lifted higher in the water. I could feel that horrible pinging as the dorsal or tail flicked the line and the heavy thumps as it shook its angry head, it was enough to soil the most capable pair of trousers. The net was lowered as the leader knot begrudgingly left the water and then he was gone, just like that. No last-minute surge ripping the hook out, no pinging back of the rod with a broken line flapping in the breeze, just gone, I was well upset to say the least. Robbed at the net. Losing that fish had done it for me. I was hooked far deeper than he was, that's for sure! Don't get mad, get even, I told myself and I vowed to catch them all, that way I'd be sure to get him in the end. At least that was the plan.

I caught a couple of fish that week, one later that day and one the next morning, an 18 inch common and a 20 inch mirror, but that wasn't the sort of *even* I had in mind.

The summer of 1991 produced a few fish for me and Keith including a few of the biggies. A session on heavy particle baiting with maples gave me *The Lady* at 34 pounds, a beautiful near-linear mirror who, in the heat of the July sun, looked a perfect lady from where I was sitting. Keith took *Lumpy* and *Shoulders* during the summer, the latter going 38lb 1oz, an incredible fish and the one that I dearly wanted to catch myself. A phone call at 5am summoned

'Off the surface'

Two crates of stubbies and a session down the pub

me to the lake to take the photos, normally no problem but due to the fact I'd only been asleep about an hour it was a miracle the photos came out as well as they did.

My next turn at a monster, came in September when I found a few fish in the *Church Bay,* all lazing on the surface in the sun. In exchange for a few hours frustration and a few dozen mozzie bites I managed to take *Jack the Net Ripper* at 40lb 2oz, on a Chum Mixer. It was one of the most exhilarating, if not bloody frightening, battles I've ever had and left me feeling that at last I'd started to get them back for the lost beast.

The big surprise that first season though, was *The Parrot* being caught at 42 pounds. So now we had two forties to catch and another couple on the way up.

A dedicated few stayed on for the first winter, a long cold blank for every one of us, but some good friendships were forged and although we never saw a fish as much as leap for two months we managed to enjoy every minute of it. Well nearly every minute anyway. The main by-product of this weekly freezing of the anatomy were the plans. Numerous cunning plots were hatched over even more numerous cups of tea but unusually, as most bivvy talk usually amounts to nothing at all, four of us actually followed one of these wondrous 'that'll show em' plans through to fruition. After weeks of pretending we all knew what was best, a bait was chosen, a fishmeal to all extents and purposes, with bits and bobs thrown in for good measure. A deal was struck at Mainline Baits and in the close season we started prebaiting. Obviously Keith was one of the team, Phil Thompson and Chrissy made up the four, we were nearly five but Little Robbie - another winter stalwart - had to hold back for financial reasons I think. We all picked our baiting days and to a man totally ignored them and spent every spare moment we could wangle at the lake.

By the start of the 91/92 season we knew a lot more about the lake and its population and one thing we knew for definite was that they loved the bait. We had seen sights in the close season that would make your teeth curl, thirty and forty pound fish shovelling baits down them as fast as you can throw it in, well almost anyway. Enough for the old confidence sacks to be dripping at the seams.

The draw was in the lodge, a leftover from the trout fishery days, now housing a kitchen and bait freezer, armchairs and tables. A bit poncy I'll admit but wonderful in the winter. Many a winter's night has been spent scoffing roast dinners and talking crap for hours on end, all huddled around a 'nest' of Colman stoves for warmth. As it turned out this year at the start of the season a big mistake was made by many, myself included, on the draw by heading for the middle swims - hoping for a repeat of last year. The weed being the influential factor this year, totally choking the bays and a lot of the lake by later in the season. The middle was no longer their only refuge from the barrage to come and the better stamp of fish avoided capture altogether for the first week.

What with the shitty weather we had at the off it was late June before things started happening. Phil led from the front like a true team captain taking *The Lady*, down to 31 pounds after spawning and another, a double figure common, the first of many.

All last winter the name on the lips of all had been *The Parrot*, how big? It still hadn't been out so the estimates by now were stretching to the ridiculous, but when Del netted it at 36lb 4oz around the last week of June we were all a bit surprised. Personally the sheer ugliness struck me first rather than the weight. It was the first time I'd ever had the misfortune face to face as it were and what a face it was, a hefty smack with a cricket bat couldn't have made a worse job - deformed top lip, flat face, pop eyes, a slate grey colour and with a lump, and then when he opened the sack the fish looked even worse.

I drove home wondering if the other fish were down in weight as much as *The Lady* and *Parrot* and also a bit anxious about my own first fish - where was it coming from? I didn't have to wait long for the answer. The very next session, which started on a Tuesday morning, I arrived at the lake to a change of weather; hot, sunny and calm. I wandered along *The Causeway* bank stopping in *The Plateau* swim on the way. I fancied the *Gate* at the far end of this south bank on the entrance to the *Dog Bay* but pre-fancied swims don't seem to produce so well on here. Location, day to day, definitely being the answer and I was staring straight at a dorsal fin over the plateau now. I shinned up a tree and could clearly see enough to keep me happy. I rushed down and grabbed the gear from the motor and practically ran back to the swim. Sam, my faithful carp dog, was charging up and down the causeway joining in the general excitement, without having the foggiest idea why.

I'd started using long nylon hooklinks and light leads to get over the weed problems. I rigged up two of these and put them in clear

Built to a larger scale!

Four runs in one and a half hours

area between three weedbeds on the plateau, this involved about ten trips up the tree to get the area pinpointed. When I was happy with it I baited up and cracked a can of cold 'chucklehead' lager and sat back to watch. Bertie Wooster lookalike, Martin, turned up about an hour later, by which time I'd seen about 20 fish jump over the plateau. I was just sitting there blabbing I couldn't believe I hadn't had a take already when Martin set up next door, as any self respecting stroke-puller would, and I popped down to fill him in (on the day's events). I had just set foot in his swim when the wailing banshee went off in my swim. I legged it back and bent into a good fish that shot off the plateau on the surface, a big grey lump out of the water pushing up a wake. As it powered through the left hand weedbed and boiled on the back of it the line snagged in the weed. I held him on full pressure and after a few sphincter-winking moments he rolled his way up on the weed wallowing on the surface. The line pulled free of the weed and the fish dived, luckily on my side of the weedbed. The fight was a slow, heavy affair with large boils reaching the surface. Alan Taylor arrived and took the net, I knew I should have paid that last instalment, but I persuaded him to let me keep it a little longer and he used it expertly at the first swipe. I peered over his shoulders and saw *The Parrot* staring at me through bulging eyes unseen for a year and now out twice in a week. Was I upset at catching the ugliest fish this side of Darenth? Was I buggery, I was buzzing! 36lb 8oz and I even photographed it. Martin got it all on video and a few people turned up to help me celebrate. By about 9.30pm I was a little bit wobbly in the breeze to say the least and I had a swim full of degenerates in various stages of intoxication, when the other rod roared off. I should have been expecting it, the fish had shown all evening over my baits but nevertheless I still nearly fell over in surprise as I grabbed the rod, at least that's my story and I'm sticking to it.

This fish caused no end of problems, weeding me up time after time. At one stage the line was trapped under weed ten feet from the bank with the fish surging off into the lake but the line going straight down into the margins. I had to strip off and wade out to free it but eventually the fish was rolling in the darkness near the net and after a few minutes of silver boils on the surface people started congratulating me. I assumed it must have been netted so I stopped pulling and made my way through the drunken onlookers to see what I had caught, wow! Two 28 pounders, that's a result! I covered one eye and realised my mistake, only one, but a beauty at that. I sacked him up for the morning and retired for the night whilst I could still find the hole in the front of the bivvy.

No more fish came my way that session but a couple of weeks later after a brief flirtation with the *Dog Bay* and a 26 pound common to show for it, conditions once again looked good for the plateau. Although there were fewer fish present this time, the feeding spots I'd found the first time round helped me to four takes in two days, landing three fish, a 22 pound common and mirrors of 24 and 27 pounds, the last - a fish called *Black-Tail* providing the first epic boat battle.

Until that time the boat hadn't been used but the weed had grown with triffid-like enthusiasm and reached the surface even in 18 feet of water, forcing us to take to the water to free the line or pull for a break, which leaves you no guarantee that the fish is free on the other end, so to the water it was. We had decided this year to put together a purely amateur video for syndicate members to keep for posterity.

It was later in the week, sitting round Keith's house, that we eagerly wired up the camcorder to the telly and sat back with a beer to replay the all-action 20 minute boat battle culminating, so John Buckley the cameraman had us believe, in a close up of the now beaten carp sliding over the net cord and the victorious row ashore. The reality was something altogether different. What followed was a wonderful botanical study of a stinging nettle, then suddenly soaring up for a fleeting glimpse of the port engine of a passing DC-11, before settling perfectly on three sets of kneecaps and the side of a boat and then off again on a tour of land, lake and sky that left us with stomachs lurching, on the sofa, scrabbling for the remote control. So, if you ever find yourself alone on a lake with only Johnny B as videoman try quickly training a squirrel or something!

As it happened, we were to get more than enough video footage in the coming weeks. The more the weed grew the more people seemed to struggle but a few of us, Phil and myself especially, took full advantage of the reduced feeding areas by pinpointing small, clear spots and regularly moving onto the fish rather than waiting for them to come to us. It was to be an incredibly exciting method as most of it was spent up trees watching fish cruising in and out of holes in the weed and flicking a light lead or freeline into the hole while they were out. Results usually came quickly if they were

No net, no trousers!

End of a two and a half year wait

coming at all and quite often I moved off fish that were not 'having it' only to find some that were, in a different part of the lake.

Fishing mid-weeks helped a lot, with less pressure the fish moved around more and were more willing to feed. The ideal areas were new holes in the thick Canadian pondweed. One such hole appeared off *The Point* swim at the far end of the lake. It's a slight peninsula in between the two bays - the *Dog Bay* to your right and the *Church Bay* to the left. It was on the mouth of this bay, in front of an unnamed and practically unfished swim, that I noticed a hole the shape of a keyhole about ten yards out and 20 feet by ten feet in size in an area that was 16 feet thick weed the week before. I scattered a few baits in there on leaving.

The next session started on a Tuesday morning in early September, a time that has always produced good results for me. It was a hot, calm day and I found Tetley up in the *Church Bay* lazing in the sun, moaning about the lack of fish in his swim. Apparently the fish had been there a day or two before, but had not returned since he had been set up waiting for them. While he stuck the kettle on I climbed a tree that overlooked both Tetley's swim and the 'keyhole' I had baited in the next swim to the right. I could not believe what I was seeing, at first I thought Tet was pulling a flanker by trying to send me off to other pastures but he sounded genuinely surprised when I told him *Shoulders* - an upper thirty at least, *Jack* - a definite forty pounds-plus and about half a dozen other big fish were circling over his baits. OK they were 14 feet above them, but close enough. As I watched, the odd fish drifted out of the weed and moved towards the keyhole area and a couple of new fish arrived from that direction so that was good enough for me.

I put my house up, cast out and set about helping Tet finish a crate of stubbies, not that he needed much assistance. He is only three feet six inches off the ground but he can put away enough liquid life saver for at least three normal-sized people. Just before dark a big old mirror slid out of the water over my left hand bait. It just seemed to hang in the air and then slide back in without making a sound, but the ripples spreading towards me confirmed it was not just the lager playing tricks on me.

By 12.00 the next day I was getting anxious. The fish seemed to have dwindled away in the night leaving just the odd sign this morning. I strolled over to the mouth of the *Dog Bay* with Tet. We were just watching a couple of small commons cruising about when my buzzer howled. I ran back and pulled into him, there was a large swirl on the back of the hole and surprisingly the fish let me lead it across the clearing, through a small gap in the otherwise solid weed on my side. In fact, it was nearly straight in the net first go but at the last second it dived down in the clear water under our feet. We were standing on an old trout fishing platform and could see the fish ten feet below us, head buried in the weed, slowly waddling in deeper. I piled on pressure and he rolled up through the water spinning on the hook hold trying to shake it, but it held firm and the short fella slid the net under him first attempt. I don't think we had quite realised how big it was until we swung her up on the mat. Banana yellow from the belly, up to a sandy brown back with a perfectly heart-shaped tail, 35lb 1oz the scales read, and *Heart-Tail* was mine at last - my tenth fish of the season and what a fish it was! We took plenty of photos and video footage. The fish lost a bit of its yellow colour during the ten minutes it was sacked up whilst we set up the cameras, but still looked a peach in the photos. Christ, did we celebrate that fish - two crates of stubbies and a session in the pub, mind you it all ended in tears when Tet got the Napoleon syndrome and wanted to fight everyone over four foot one and a half, (everyone!).

Due to the wonderful English summers we have it wasn't all up and down trees and cruising fish though. One particular morning I battled my way down the M25 through sheets of spray from suicidal 'artic' lorry drivers and near gale force south westerly winds. As I coasted into the car park I saw the only two cars already there - Tet's van and Chrissy's new cruisemobile. The rain was pushing up the lake, driven by howling gusts of wind, and both anglers were found sodden and dripping in the club hut. A large glass front allows you to see most of the lake from there, so we sat drinking tea and looking out. Tet was set up in the north east corner with Chrissy two swims up. The fish, they said, had started to show early this morning on the wind in front of them. As we chatted a mirror carp hurled itself out of the water, half way up the north bank, about 50 yards past Chrissy's pitch - followed by another two in quick succession. The rain stopped as if on cue, but not for long by the look of the sky. I grabbed the rods and a bit of gear and raced the carp dog round to *The Reeds* swim. As I got to the swim a fish popped his head out at about ten yards, this was going to like taking candy from a baby. Only one slight problem, 'no bait'. I legged it up to Chrissy who had returned to his bivvy with renewed enthusiasm and he very generously furnished me with one single boilie, which I guardedly took back to my swim and attached to one rod. Before I could cast, however, the heavens opened again and I quickly threw the brolly and sides over the heap of tackle that I had tipped upside down all over the swim, in the frantic search for any mouldy old baits I might have forgotten about. As I sat there peering out another fish showed in front of me, this was too good to miss. I reached out and with one hand in the elements, managed a cackhanded bivvy-cast to the fish. Five minutes passed and as quickly as the rain started, it stopped. Chris turned up with a steaming cup of tea and as we stood chatting the rod lying in the mud roared into life. I hit into it and tried to gain some control whilst Chrissy bitched on incredulously about being here for days, and one of his bloody baits as well, but I was denied an instant result when the fish decided that enough was enough and tore through a weedbed, pulling the hook. In retrospect it's just as well I lost that fish as I was in serious danger of being chucked in. My request for another bait was turned down flat as well so I trudged back to the van for my own.

Over that night and the next morning Chrissy unfortunately lost two good fish in the weed but Tet managed a 24 pound mirror, a very short fish for Horton, almost round in appearance, with a perfectly square group of four scales on one flank.

Twenty four hours almost to the minute after my lost fish, I had another fast take, and after a very powerful fight in the deep margins slid the net under *The Lady* at 34 pounds. I'm not usually into recaptures but this is one nice looking fish and it was good to see her back up in weight. I was smiling anyway.

The weather soon changed again and by the next session it was sunny again and fairly calm. Decibel was in the *Waiting* swim where Chrissy had lost a couple last time. Apparently he had spodded out a whole sack of hemp and was sitting it out with just a tench so far to show for it. Later on in the week however, on a bait cast away from the hemp into open water, he hooked a whacker which, after about 15 minutes firmly ensconced in a weedbed, needed desperate measures to free it, so the boat had to be launched again. The video rolled but this time we took no chances, Phil 'doubles' Thompson in the Spielberg role and John Buckley in the oar position, man can that boy paddle. I was on the other side of the boat with a drum and

September '93 - 'Moonscale' 38lb 14oz

half a dozen manacle-clad slaves and we couldn't keep up with him. The boat was spinning all over the place, we could hear the tones of the Hawaii Five-O theme being sung over the lake as we battled against the wind and each other, slowly though we got over to Decibel's swim, and with him on board we managed to extract the fish from the weed and eventually net it out in the middle somewhere. The Gypsy's first fish and a new forty at that. The awesome *Shoulders* weighed in at 41lb 10oz and made it at least three different forties to go for, but this fish was the one I wanted more than any of them. I'd joined to catch this beast and one day I will, I hope.

This all happened around the end of August and Chrissy was the only member of our little 'team' still to catch. Even 'fat Sam' had cornered a cat in the car park, but wisely backed down at the hiss-and-claw stage, but nevertheless still a result.

September, however, saw Chris bound from despair to an almost unbearable level of confidence after banking first a 25 pound mirror followed a week later by a very special fish indeed. Not only Chrissy's first thirty but another fish on the 'up' in a big way, stocked at 21 pounds and captured in 1991 at 29 pounds, it rolled over Chrissy's net cord at 36lb 14oz of absolutely pristine mirror carp. All the waiting had paid off for him and well-deserved it was too.

October really turned up trumps for me and another big surprise fish, two personal bests in fact. First a 27lb 12oz long, lean common and then on October 14th at 9.30am, just after a recast due to bait-eating-dropback-giving-needs-a-kicking tufty attack, I had a fast take on a single bait at 80 yards out. The same spot as it happens that I hooked and lost my first Horton beast. On contact the rod was flattened and line ripped from the clutch. I was in *The Reeds* on the north bank, it is mainly deep clear water in front and the fish used every inch of it charging about with unbelievable power. All I could do was gain line where I could and shake a lot. After a few minutes of this he built up some weed over his eyes and came in comparatively easily until he hit the margins where he had another little fit or two until finally he slowly came into focus. Deep down in the clear margins, we could see he was a lump but he just kept getting bigger and bigger as he rose up through the layers. Chrissy recognised him as he slid into the net, *Lumpy* the old Road Lake mirror. Laying him on the mat he looked ridiculously big, like a normal carp but built to a different scale. Even so we were stunned when the Reubens were pulled round to 41lb 12oz.

For a lake with a known stock where you would expect very few surprises, there were certainly a few rabbits being pulled out of the hat of late. This made three definite forties and three possibles, one of which made a rare winter appearance after the usual totally dead two months. Chrissy managed to recapture his 36 pound fish, up to 37lb 4oz, in February. Four fish came out in all at the arse end of the season. I dipped out again myself but ended up with 16 fish so I was well happy. There were 63 fish in all that season, over half of which came to the four of us.

The bait idea had obviously worked and therefore, we were up for more of the same, baiting with the same amount in the close season, but this year the fish we saw looked even bigger than before.

The start of the 92/93 season saw us all at the lodge for the walk-off, the draw having been done on the previous Sunday. I had drawn 18th, pathetic, I know, but I had a trick or two left yet. Everybody was talking about bays and corners and the plateau and bar swims hot favourites. Most people had forgotten the first season when the weed was low as it was now, the fish had bolted straight out to the middle having no other sanctuary. I had drawn up a six foot by three foot map of the lake and pinned it on the lodge to make the walk-off a bit more organised. I marked every swim and they slowly got crossed off as the names were called out. I had intended originally to miss out one of the middle swims but thought it was a bit 'suss' so I settled for writing *The Blank* swim in large letters across the middle north bank swim. It seemed to work quite well as ten minutes later I was setting up my gear in there. I cannot understand why all the new members avoided it, still, never look a gift horse in the mouth. It wasn't the blinding start we all expected and 24 hours into the new season not a run had come to anybody. I had fish crashing out where my hookbaits were since about six hours into the season so that bit I had at least got right.

I'd stuck with single hookbaits just to be different but temptation got to me just after dark and I fired out 250 baits at about 65-70 yards. I popped one bait up a good eight inches off the bottom as I could not understand the total lack of action, maybe last year's bumper weed crop was laying dead and decaying all over the lakebed. First light and still no takes. I was just brewing up when the pop-up roared away. As I bent into it my mind was racing to the possibilities of two foot pop-ups and keeping it a secret until I had cleaned up etc, etc. Suddenly the other rod decided to join in , the Baitrunner was pouring out line far faster than the fish I was already playing was moving so it had to be the totally unheard of two takes at once. I knew I'd never get the chance again so I took one rod in each hand and bent into both fish at the same time 'what a feeling', like a dog with two dicks. After a lot of rod swapping and hollering for help, Keith arrived to assist. I pulled the second fish over the net first and Keith sacked it whilst I played and netted the first, second. Keith also sacked that one whilst I desperately tried to get both baits back out as quickly as possible. The fish, a 17 pound common and a 26 pound mirror, lay in the margins whilst we set up cameras. A brace shot was a real rarity at Horton and I was going to relish it. The buzzers were turned off and, as I unlooped the sack cord off the front bankstick and stood to lift the fish, the rod butt closest to me lifted up. At first I thought it was caught on my arm or something but when the spool started spinning like a catherine wheel on speed the penny dropped and I struck into yet another fish. This was obviously a better fish and pretty soon a crowd had gathered. By the time the net was lifted I had to peer over the onlookers and what a sight I saw, *C.P.'s Thirty* looking very big indeed. Keith, by now, was getting pretty good at sacking fish so I let him do the honours whilst I put a fresh bait on and whacked it back on the spot 'double quick time'. The swim was pretty hectic now, you couldn't fart without booking up in advance, so I ushered everyone to the top bank for the weighing, *C.P.'s Thirty* had been the main contender for a new forty this year and as I unzipped the sack the guesses were all either just over or just under, but before we could weigh him in, there were four or five bleeps from my alarm and then nothing. I could just see the rod butts from where I was, just enough to see one was missing, as I ran in to the swim I saw one rod jammed against the alarm by the reel. The Baitrunner was not switched on and only the alarm had saved the rod being pulled in. The line was singing tight and the back lead bouncing in the air. Just as I got a finger to the rod, there was a crack and the 11 pound Sylcast fluttered down on the surface snapped clear. 'Some you win.'

I trotted back up the bank to hear someone say 40lb 6oz, the weighing had gone on without me but the scales were held by their sides and when we hung them properly from the loop on top she went 39lb 6oz, still a long way from the mere 21 pounds she was

September '93 - 'The Linear' 24lb 12oz

three years ago - obviously never heard of the Slimfast plan, this baby.

I sat down on the bedchair long after everyone had gone, trying to take it all in, no takes all round the lake and I'd had four in about one and a half hours. I tried burning the back of my ankles on the cooker and it hurt like hell, so I was definitely not dreaming. I watched the playback on the video in case I had been hallucinating but it was still true. After a while I wound in and went for a 'float' around the lake like you do, but whilst I was gone Kevin 'Thieving Gypsy' Seymour cast a very large lead a very long way, which purely by accident landed in my swim and later in the day I sat and watched him across the lake land *The Koi* at a new all time high of 41lb 6oz, that's what I call good angling!

They say revenge is sweet, well it came candy coated the next morning when I saw a fish throw itself skywards in the Gypsy's swim whilst he was still in bed. I launched a bait three-quarters of the way across the lake into the dying ripples and was soon smiling for the camera, cradling an immaculate 32 pound common. *The Parrot* in all its ugliness also put in a rare occurrence this first week to Spencer at a staggering 45lb 4oz, (well he was staggering when I saw him later on anyway).

My second visit coincided with Alan Taylor and his mobile film crew, 'The Luvvies', on tour at Horton for the week making a video. Being a bit film shy I moved swims three times until I was right next door to him and managed to pull out a 22 pound mirror for the cameras (still waiting for my fee, luvvie).

Common carp! People wax lyrically about the symmetrical beauty of a golden flanked common carp. Me? I seem to be plagued by the bloody things. I landed five on the trot from 17 to 25 pounds in July - the largest one was half way there being a perfect, deep mirror carp shape with common scaling. It had also been on the missing list for a while, last caught on the first day of the first syndicate three years previously.

Eventually though on a session in late August, commonsense prevailed and a mirror was marked down for me, and one of the two I'd really wanted from the beginning. It was two days into the session and I had moved swims so many times I couldn't remember where I'd started off. It was almost dusk when Robbie turned up for a chat. I was sitting in *The Reeds* swim on the north bank but I wasn't really happy there so, when an offer of a hand moving swims came up, I went round to *Heart-Tail* swim like a shot. I had been talking myself into it all afternoon. The swim is on the mouth of the *Church Bay* and I had seen a few fish show there recently, early mornings, on their way in or out of the bay. I put one up the margin and one ten yards out. Nothing much showed after dark, but the margin rod screamed into action at 6am. After the ritual bivvy wrecking fiasco - trying to get out of the now cocoon-like sleeping bag - I tried to bend into it but had to wind like a madman to catch up with the fish, which had shot out from under the bush to my left, past the jetty I was on and through sub-surface reeds to my right, when I made contact. He charged about a bit and did not feel particularly large but the line was caught in the reeds so I whipped off the trousers and was just about to swim round to the next jetty, to get a better angle when I realised that the net would be on the wrong side of the two trees that separated the swims, so I put down the rod, placed the net on the other jetty and prepared myself for the plunge, but as I sat there dangling my big toe thermometer - which incidentally read bloody freezing - the line came free leaving me in direct contact with the fish, but with no net or trousers. I still thought it was a small common so I risked laying the rod down again with the Baitrunner on and regained the net by charging up the bank and back before the fish had realised I'd stopped pulling. This was rapidly turning into a farce and the fish made it worse by snagging me back up in the same spot. That was it, I'd got the piss by now, I don't mind a laugh and a joke but bugger a pantomime! I heaved the fish out of the reeds and bullied him around in front of me. Chris Haswell who had seen all these goings on from the other bank came round to see if I needed a hand, so he went to the front of the jetty with the net, whilst I struggled to get a glimpse of the fish, which was beginning to grow rapidly in my estimations. Ten feet down in the margins a grey back appeared, a very large grey back. I could see an orange lump on his side, unmistakably *The Koi*, last out at 41 pounds and one of the two remaining 'A-Team' I was after. As it rolled into the net, an action replay of all the liberties I'd just taken with it flashed across my vision. Some little common this turned out to be, all 39lb 6oz of him. He was a bit marked up from spawning but still at an amazing weight for a spawned-out fish. The year before, at this time in this condition he went 35 pounds when Richard Skidmore took him from the *Gate* swim, on the Kingsmead causeway, an area they seem to visit quite regularly in any spells of hot weather we may get.

It was becoming a bit embarrassing the way they were coming to order and the regularity with which they appeared. This was my *tenth* fish so far this season and with most of the syndicate struggling for their first fish I was starting to get some rather searching questions asked about bait, rigs, colour of anatomical parts etc and I could have beaten the Aussies as far as neighbours were concerned. I had them coming out of my ears for the next few sessions. I suppose it helped keep my food and tackle bill down though, as anybody who has fished near me will know I do like to 'borrow' the odd item or two, as my tackle box is what you might call a bit on the lean side.

By about lunch-time after *The Koi* affair the temperature was climbing steadily and so was I - up a tree overlooking the aforementioned *Gate* swim area. I'd taken the rods for a little stroll around and had soon found a few fish cruising on the back of the weedbeds along the causeway bank, but the problem was how to get them to take a bait. Floaters would have been the obvious choice, but these fish are so super-wary of surface baits that it usually just spooks them off before you have even cast out, just the freebies being enough to let them know they are being fished for. I stayed up the tree for a while watching to try to find a spot to cast to. There were five fish in all; two mirrors - one 'the long one', a 26 pound fish I'd caught the year before and the other one around the thirty mark which I couldn't identify. Of the three commons *Split-Tail*, an upper twenty, was the largest. They made a circuit of the weed coming within feet of the bank and two of them tilted up and rooted the bottom not five feet from the edge. This was the 'spot' I'd been looking for. I waited for them to drift off around the weedbed again and scrambled down the tree, placing a hookbait and ten freebies on a small sandy spot just over the margin reeds. A back-lead was slid on the line and dropped just in the edge of the reeds and the line slackened slightly so that none was visible. The rod being hidden behind the reeds and myself up the tree meant that if the fish returned there was no way whatsoever they would see anything but the bait. After about 20 minutes the fish came back on another tour of the weed, this time led by the 'thirty'. They moved over the weed heading straight for the baits but as they came to the clearing they froze with fins erect and then bolted out of the area. I went and checked everything but the only thing different for

September '93 - 'The Parrot' 43lb 12oz

the fish could be that someone had thrown boilies all over their feeding area, obviously they were smarter than I thought. I was back up the tree looking for the fish, thinking they probably hadn't gone far when I glanced down and realised they had gone into hiding under the tree I was standing in. In fact, if I had let go of the branches I would have landed on top of them, but there was one more fish now, far bigger than the others. He came slowly into view as *Lumpy* the 41lb 12oz which I had taken last season. This time I decided a single bait was probably the best move so I quietly flicked a half ounce lead and bait tight under the tree and lay in the long grass a little way back from the edge, in the sun. I must have drifted off and I awoke covered in spiders and various other creepy crawlies. As I stood up to brush them off a large swirl erupted under the tree.

I thought I had spooked a fish and then the line shot out after him, and after a fairly uneventful fight the 'thirty mirror' was laying in the net. I could recognise it now as a 29 pounder which Chrissy had caught two years previously that had been on the missing list ever since. At 30lb 8oz it hadn't grown as much, in comparison to some of the other beasts, but was a fish I'd always wanted. A leathery fish with a pronounced lump and grey back, almost two tone with a creamy belly. I enlisted Pete Springate and Big Foot to do the honours with the cameras and then called it a day and headed back down the M25 a very happy man indeed. Little Robbie had just arrived as I was packing up the van, full of confidence as ever. We had a little chat in the car park and he was harping on about some new wonder anti-eject rig he was trying with a 35mm bottom bait and 23 pound mono hooklinks. I think the theory was that if they got it all in their mouths they would need a shoe horn to get it out again. But when the phone rang on Sunday evening it turned out shoe horns had been in short supply in the carp world that week, and Robbie had ended a two and a half year wait for a big Horton mirror with *C.P.'s Thirty* at 39lb 7oz and worth, he assured me, every minute of the wait. I was just sorry I had not been there to see it. It's funny how things turn out, I had wanted more than anything when I joined to catch *Shoulders* a fish I had now seen four times on the bank in three years, once as part of an amazing brace taken with *Jack* at an all time high of 49 pounds by Alan 'Wiggy' South, who is, I think, still on an all time high of his own. But it remained the last of the biggies left for me to catch, or at least so I thought.

I had been getting a lot of stick from the weekend anglers who assured me that from Friday night to Monday morning the fish became super difficult to catch so when I fluked out a brace on my first Saturday session of the season in September I considered it open season on pisstaking. Putting 'weekends are easy' in the log book started the ball rolling and when six days later on a Friday I had another brace session I was in a position to really give some stick but I put my personal safety first and kept my mouth firmly shut, well almost!

The ides of September have always been kind to me, providing me with numerous personal bests over the years but this year was to be something special. That first Saturday evening, about 5.30pm, Robbie and I were struggling to put up the 'barbel tunnel' as it became known - a long Nissen hut type bivvy - to house my good woman who was due to arrive at any minute. We were surrounded by bits of pole and canvas on all sides when I had a run on my left hand rod to a single bottom bait on a light nylon link in the margins down to my left, in the mouth of the *Church Bay*.

I had moved in to the *Heart-Tail* swim at midnight the night before after seeing monsters leaping all over the bay and I was firmly attached to one of these now. The weed had grown to such an extent here that it was not long before I was in the lake trying to free the line. This involved swimming up the edge to an old overgrown jetty in the brambles where Phil had battled his way in with the net. From here the fish was only about 20 feet out in front. Due to the bushes there was only one position I could hold the rod and as the fish and weedbed came slowly to the surface I tried to give it some side-strain to free the weed, but only succeeded in cracking Phil round the nut with the rod butt. So, I settled for pumping the entire mess straight to the net, how Phil managed to figure out which bit to net I will never know, but we were soon roaring "*Moonscale*" across the lake, another fish off the missing list. Last out two years previously to Bertie Wooster at 29lb 8oz, it looked now like it might make forty pounds, but it settled just shy at 38lb 14oz.

Yet another whacker for Horton, this place was beginning to look awesome for the future.

Later that night, all tucked up in the barbel tunnel with the woman, a screaming take had me frantically searching for the exit.

A fly on the wall would have been a fly on his back in fits of laughter as I charged around in the dark ripping at bits of canvas and zips etc, while the alarm screamed on. Eventually though, I found the rods and netted a 26 pound linear after a battle royal whic'ı wiped out both lines and lasted the best part of half an hour. Both the carp were fish I had not had the week before. My first double-up came the second weekend when I found some fish at the other lodge end of the lake taking a 26 pound common and recapturing *C.P.'s Thirty* at 38lb 8oz. The fish had changed totally to night feeding, even showing at night and not at all in the day. Obviously this made location a bit tricky as you could hear large crashes in the early hours but with a bit of wind could not see where they were. It sounded, however, like a large amount of fish were present all over this top end.

Conditions changed drastically by the next trip with a gale-force westerly pushing down the lake away from the area. The car park was packed, but from the lodge steps I could not see a single bivvy. The rain thrashed down relentlessly and everybody was obviously 'domed up' in the bays at the far end. I donned an old gas cape affair and trudged up there to get the latest news. I must admit it looked perfect up there with the waves slapping the bank and the reeds bent double in the wind, but it was well busy and nothing of note had been seen, so I set up at the lodge end in a swim known as *The Salt Circle*.

A short while later Richie trudged past and, having pulled his back or something, he enlisted Tetley's help in carrying the gear and was away down the road. In all there had been 14 new members that year but by now any preconceptions of easy fishing had been blown into the wind, as Richie's 17 pound common on the first week was the only fish to fall to a new rod up until now, (mid-September that was) and even some of the more experienced regulars were struggling. I think the green colouring of the water had made it particularly tricky this year with the fish harder to find.

Phil had suffered a bit of bad luck this season as well, when on a two week holiday he first lost a forty pound fish - when the hook pulled near the net - and the same afternoon some sleazeball pinched his motor complete with video and camera. And, as if to prove the theory that shit 'happens in threes', he awoke 'the Kraken' one evening when he hooked a monster of some description in the *Dog Bay*. He fought it solidly for 13 hours, five of which were spent

Admiration all round!

on the boat and at no time did it snag or weed him up but just kept moving, taking him up to 250 yards up the lake and back, round and round the two bays. Eventually, the line, now frayed to buggery, just gave up the ghost and the unseen leviathan slid back to the depths. Quite what occurred that night nobody is sure but a large catfish seems the most popular theory. I personally have my own ideas. I firmly believe that the forty pounder Phil lost three days previously, which incidentally was *Shoulders*, swam across the dam end of the lake after shedding Phil's hook, flopped up the steps, climbed into Phil's Sierra and reversed it down the ramp into the lake. It was then a simple matter of attaching Phil's hook to the back bumper and driving around the lakebed all night while his mates, having seen their fair share of camera equipment over the years, videoed the whole saga to be shown at carp reunions for years to come.

Anyway, back in *The Salt Circle* I chose an area just a bit closer to the middle but not a million miles from last week's spot. A small clear patch at about 65 yards, slightly shallower than the surrounding area being 16 feet in 18 feet of water. The weather was still atrocious so I cast out just hookbaits and zipped the door down for the evening. There are certain nights for staring out at the lake and nights for being zipped up in the sleeping bag with the fat carp dog as a hot water bottle, and this was definitely the latter. I had the portable telly on with headphones as the noise of the rain on the bivvy roof was deafening. By 11pm that evening I was totally 'monged' out, having suffered four hours of mindless crap being fed directly into my protesting brain. I switched off the box and put the kettle on for a last cuppa when a typical bream bite occurred on the left hand rod.

I started to put a jacket on, not wanting to get soaked for a 'snotty', when it roared away. I burst out of the door, jacket dragging in the mud and bent the rod into a good fish, in fact if it *was* a bream it was about 200 pounds and fighting fit. The rain was still lashing down and before I had it half way in I was soaked through to my pants, water was running down my back and legs inside my clothes as fast as it was on the outside. I had not got around to boots either in the rush, so I was left standing in a muddy puddle in socks. It was pitch black and I wasn't really in the mood for this type of self-abuse, so I hauled for all I was worth, (which isn't much) and soon had the fish within 25 yards of the bank. To the right of the swim 20 yards out is a snag, an old piece of frayed wire cable embedded in the bottom. If a fish reaches this it is lost. The only way out of it is to slacken off as soon as you feel it and get the boat out, any tightening of the line and it cuts like cotton. Well, I was buggered if I was getting the boat out in the middle of the night, on my own, in the pissing rain, so as the line kited toward the snag I clamped my hand over the reel and walked up the bank in the other direction, putting far more pressure on the fish than I would usually dare but if it made it to the wire it was lost anyway. The rod bucked and lurched as the fish used everything he had to gain the last few feet and then, with a horrible jolt backwards on the rod tip, he rolled over, deep in the margins, an admission of defeat.

The next hardest thing was getting him in the net. It was unusually dark for Horton due to the storm clouds, and a bucketful of salty water in each eyeball didn't help matters either. The net was at full stretch as I steered a grey shape between the arms. I kept on the pressure trying to get it up to the spreader block and safely over the net. I was on my knees by now and when the grey shape eventually touched the spreader block I couldn't lift the handle. I was too stretched out with no leverage so I threw the rod down and unceremoniously scooped my prize into the edge. I left the fish in the margins, safe in the net, while I found a torch which I fumbled and dropped in the mud, breaking the bulb, 'great start Laney' I thought. I tried lifting the net out into the bivvy where my bivvy light would make things easier but the net seemed to be snagged on the bottom. It was only when I followed the line down to the carp's mouth I realised what I had caught. Where there should have been lips there was a hard lump of bone and as I stared hard into the dark net, bulbous poppy eyes stared back - *The Parrot*, and the net was not snagged. I just hadn't lifted hard enough. I put the mat in the bivvy door and swung the beast up on to it. It was still ugly but now it was fat and ugly. I sacked him up and got Tetley to help weigh him in, 43lb 12oz, a new personal best and September strikes again.

The next morning over on the other side of the lake, in the *Church Bay*, Big Tony had a result, taking his first fish from Horton in three years so a double pub celebration was called for.

Somehow that afternoon I caught a small common of about 19 pounds, but I am not sure how, all I know is that by the time I went to bed that night I did not feel exactly 'kosher'. What I really needed was a 24 hour lay-in, but all plans of that went out the window when a rod that I can't remember casting roared off at 6am. I was bent into the fish long before I was even awake. For some reason I had no trousers on and I was bloody freezing, so playing the fish with my right hand, I tried getting dressed with my left. What with this *and* the need to answer the call of nature, the first half of the fight was a strange old affair, but I soon got it all under control - until the fish decided to charge away from the snag and straight into solid weed, totally and completely solid ten feet thick, 'not budging for anyone' type weed. I tried everything I could think of for about an hour, and then Del and Chris Haswell came round with the boat. Another hour on the boat, using every trick in the book but still no joy. I could feel the fish kicking but it obviously couldn't take any line. Thumping the bottom of the boat with the oar seemed to make it move every time but only two or three feet and then nothing. Plus the oar was getting a bit irate but what the hell, we had paid her good money. Two hours had elapsed and we were no nearer a conclusion so we stopped for tea and toast, leaving the rod on the rests. Three hours after hooking it, he was still stuck firm, then Del remembered a rake in the shed at the lodge attached to 20 feet of metal conduit tubing. So all tooled up we went back out in the boat, the fish was only about 30 feet from the bank in the weedy bay.

I started 15 feet away from the line pulling large lumps of weed in, slowly working to the middle where the fish was snagged. On about the third pull through, still ten feet away from the line the rake came to life. I had snagged the line and the pole was running through my fingers. Luckily I managed to disentangle it with only inches of pole left. I grabbed the rod and wound down but nothing had changed. I must have picked up the line beyond the actual snag which meant there was no guarantee the fish was anywhere near us, maybe the lead was just snagged here and the fish could be off in any direction. I turned the rake up the other way and pushed the pole deep into the silt beside the weed, then slid the pole under the bed, by levering against the boat I lifted the entire weedbed up to the surface. The lead was nestled neatly on top and I tore at the weed freeing the line. As I thought might happen, the line pinged free and was leading away further into the weedy bay. I took the rod and wound the now very frayed Sylcast onto the spool and gingerly bent the rod into the fish. What happened next will remain etched in my usually dubious memory forever, *Shoulders* - the fish of my dreams - my own personal quest, rose slowly to the top. His

September '93 - 'Shoulders' 40lb 12oz

whole back, and his namesake, an enormous set of shoulders, lifted out of the water and we just stayed stock still for a moment staring at each other.

Luckily I woke up first, and leading him slowly towards me started screaming to Del to net it quickly and as it slipped in the folds of my battered but trusty net I went absolutely mental. I'm surprised I didn't capsize the boat, I was hollering and shouting, Tony was clapping me on the back and I could smell the Guinness wafting across the field from the pub. I'd done it, the whole 'A-Team' and a brace of forties to finish with. Phil turned up with a bottle of Champagne and Chrissy and Keith and God knows how many other cameramen did the deed for me. I just smiled a lot, speechless for once.

HAREFIELD
Stuart Gillham

Season 1
My first visit to Harefield Lake was in June 1989, and my first impression of the water was it's one of the ugliest pits I have ever seen. Reputed to be 60 acres, it doesn't seem that big. To make up for its ugliness it holds a fantastic stock of big carp and at the time I fished it some of the friendliest and most helpful anglers I had ever met were there.

The first day I went to the lake I called on my mate Bob Baker of Richworth Bait on the way. He asked me to take some bait with me and to drop it off in the Horse and Barge at lunch-time to a chap called Dougal. "How will I know who he is?" I asked. Bob's reply was "he's a big ugly bastard with a hooter bigger than yours!". I arrived at the lake, walked round and met some of the lads. I asked if they knew a bloke called Dougal, silence fell... then questions, what did I want with him, on answering that I had his bait it turned out that they were friends of his who thought I was looking for other reasons (after meeting him God knows why they would think that). We went to the pub and this man-mountain walked over, "you must be Stuart," he said. "How did you know who I am?" I said. "Well, Bob said to look for an ugly bastard with a big nose." "Snap" I said, and from that day a friendship was forged with one of the best mates I've ever had.

The first season I struggled, due to three things. The first two being too much beer in the Horse and Barge, 'Christ these boys can drink'. I was rapidly becoming an alcoholic, also the pub held some of the best specimens of the opposite sex you could see anywhere, wall to wall women. Good mates and unlimited supply of lager - my fate had been sealed. On the occasions when the pub was closed and we weren't up the cafe I started to learn about the water; the third problem was soon discovered, horrendously sharp bars everywhere. I ended that season with two fish over twenty, one double, a personal best tench, seven cut-offs and two stones heavier wishing I was 18 again.

Later that season Dougal took the job as Head Bailiff, a decision he was later to regret. By the time he took up his new appointment a firm friendship had been formed between us and his first question on arriving at the job was, would I be one of his bailiffs? My reaction

'Little Pecs' 34lb 4oz 7/9/90

'Black Spot' 33lb 2oz 19/6/92

was to say no, as it is a thankless job and only leads to trouble, but if you ever meet Dougal he is not the kind of man you say no to. He insisted, and me being the brave bloke I am became a bailiff. By now I had a nickname for Dougal. He became the 'Monster' and in no time at all the name stuck, everyone calling him by it. As the season passed I made many friends and being a bailiff didn't seem bad, it had an added bonus that you could fish an area called *The Workings*, which is out of bounds to the other anglers, (only bailiffs can fish at this end of the pit as it is still being worked). I mainly ignored the swim the first season as nothing much was caught from there. By the end of the season I was slowly learning a bit about the water, the main thing being if you stayed out of the pub you caught more, easier said than done, when you are weak-willed like me. Two lads, Frogger and Care Bear did exceptionally well that season as they had in previous seasons. On watching them they were obviously extremely good anglers but also stayed clear of the pub when they thought they were in with a chance. Obvious really, but in my case I visited the pub thinking I was in with a chance, them hoping for thirty-plus results, me hoping for upper doubles in the pub. They did a damned sight better than me on their chosen quarry so by the end of the season I'd decided I needed to work harder at my fishing. I spent the close season out in my boat most weeks with a fish-finder, sussing out the lakebed. I intended to make a map of the lake, but this was an impossible task. It was like an egg box, craters, bars, gullies and plateaux everywhere, one second 15 feet deep, next the boat was running aground. Through the close season I slowly built up a picture of the lake. As the weather warmed up the carp showed themselves, it was amazing how close you could get to them. Life was looking good, I started to know where to expect to see fish and soon had several promising areas sussed. I decided to concentrate on certain swims the next season, so learnt all I could about certain areas, not bothering with any long range areas as I prefer to fish only as far out as I can bait up accurately, not being a very good caster and loving to fish over big beds of bait. It made sense to me, also it's easier to cast when pissed!

Two areas started to fascinate me more than others, one was called *The Stick Bar*, the other *The Workings*. Both have very pronounced bars where most weeks, if I sat quietly and watched, I would see fish travelling up and down. Being at either end of the lake it soon became clear that certain fish preferred different ends of the lake, splitting them into two separate groups. When I joined the lake I didn't know whether to join Boyer's other water Rodney Meadow or Harefield. I chose Harefield mainly on the strength of seeing a picture of a fish called *The Orange One*. My mate Ritchie McDonald had previously caught this fish at around 32 pounds. To me it was the ultimate carp and this alone persuaded me to join Harefield. Later that season luck played a part as Boyer's, for reasons known only to themselves, shut Rodney down as a fishery and moved the bulk of the big fish to Harefield including the ever-popular, most-caught big carp in Britain, *Nelson*. Although caught many times, it is still a fine-looking carp which must enjoy eating boilies and being photographed.

Getting back to my close season observations, most trips to *The Stick Bar* saw me meeting *The Orange One* and *Nelson*, at the other end a beautiful linear kept appearing off *The Workings*, a very long fish which if carrying any gut I felt would be well over 30 pounds. He was later to prove the weight wrong but not appearance. Also down this end I regularly saw a fish of tremendous proportions which hadn't been out for a couple of seasons called *The Italian*, this was one big mother. More experienced anglers than me who saw her guessed her to be over 40 pounds, the only forty I had ever seen was Walker's fish in the zoo, probably not forty when I saw it, but having seen numerous 30 pound carp I certainly believed this fish was over forty. So a good selection of swims were sussed, *plus* a new bait flavour to try for Bob, things certainly looked good.

Due to trouble over swims the Monster had decided this season that everyone was to draw their swims two weeks before the start of the season. They would belong to you for the first day and as long as you stayed in them after that. The day before the draw I helped peg the swims, noting all my favourites as I went. My first choice swim would be *Someone's Coming*, it gained it's name I understand not for its view of courting couples but because when the wind blows, the bushes sound like someone is coming through them (fascinating stuff eh!). I chose this swim because 90 per cent of fish I saw moving around the lake passed this swim. Second choice was *The Stick Bar*, second only because anglers would be either side of you, so cutting down the chances of finding my bait first. Third, if I couldn't get a swim I would double up with Tony Cheadle, one of the other bailiffs, who had already stated he wanted *The Workings*. So I had two chances in the draw as I could

'The orange one' 33lb 8oz 22/6/92

The fish I joined to catch - Ritchie'the orange one' 33lb

use Tony's draw if he was out before me. The day of the draw arrived, most of the lads asked me what swim carried which number, I suddenly realised what a prat I was (anyone who knows me realised this years ago, I always have been slow) I could have pulled a master stroke and mixed the numbers up. My first choice went early, Tony drew out before me so it was to be *The Stick Bar.* I know I had two weeks to bait up my swim, a few pints of Fosters later the Monster gave me permission to bait up with my boat as long as I did it late in the evening or early morning when the pit workers were at home. The first week I baited every three days, the second every other day and the last three days every day, 20,000 boilies, half a hundred weight of maize and one hundred weight of hemp later, I was buzzing every time I baited up. I saw fish on two occasions, *The Orange One* and *Nelson* were clearly seen. The day before the off the swim was heaving with fish.

I surely couldn't fail? That night the wind changed, blowing hard to the opposite end of the lake. No problem, I thought all that food would hold them. Wrong! On the 15th not a fish was seen over my bait. I had decided to leave the pub out this season, the first three days I managed to keep out of it and away from the cafe. This was made easier due to decent blokes either side of me and a massive supply of food and drink. One fish had been out to the chap next to me, an upper double. Most fish were coming out from the opposite bank to where the wind was still blowing. A decision had to be made, I had four days left and I was the brunt of many jokes, all that bait and no fish, 'teach you to use crap bait' was the main joke. The next morning the bream moved in so I went to the cafe for a decent breakfast, fish were still coming off the other side and the person in my first choice swim was leaving. After bribes of much lager I found some skint mates willing to help move my gear to the other side of the lake. Once moved, I had to break the promise made to myself to stay out of the pub, purely to pay my debt to the lads for moving my gear you understand! That night I made up for lost time and drank three nights' lager in one, had a mega-nosh up the Indian and had an undisturbed sleep apart from the bushes vibrating. They call the swim *Someone's Coming*, but after the Indian and the vibrations I was making it would be a brave man who came anywhere near.

The next morning around the unearthly hour of 10.30 I appeared, bleary-eyed to be greeted with the wonderful news that Care Bear

and Knacker had moved onto my baited area and had a right result
- *Nelson* at 36lb 8oz to Care Bear and Knacker with fish to 27
pounds, magic - that's all I needed, another excuse to take me up
the pub to drown my sorrows. I blanked for the rest of the week but
what should I have done? Whatever I'd chosen could have been
wrong. As usual I chose wrongly. The next few weeks you couldn't
get on *The Stick Bar*, it produced many fish but was never vacant.
I fished a few different swims with no results, things were now not
looking good. Around the end of July Big Rob, one of the other
bailiffs, moved off *The Workings* leaving Tony Cheadle on his own.
Knowing Tony neither has any money or food, it wasn't hard to
persuade him I should move on with him. The good thing about this
swim is that as it's reserved for bailiffs, you can leave your gear in
the swim as you're not depriving anyone, not that many people
would be interested anyway, as it hadn't produced a fish all season.

I moved in, remembering the big golden-scaled linear and Italian
beast I had seen in the close season. Tony was fishing away from
where they always showed so I was well chuffed. Over the next two
weeks I baited heavily with boilies and hemp, Tony was panicking
about all the bait going in, so I assured him it would draw the fish
in plus make them bigger. The first two weeks I kept up the baiting,
fishing four nights a week leaving my bivvy up the other three. Life
was easy, no lugging gear or setting up house, just turn up and cast
out. The hardest part was feeding Tony and treating him (most
nights) to lager. Very quickly Tony cottoned on to a good thing
rapidly becoming an alcoholic like the rest of us. On the third week
I suffered two cut-offs and two missed takes. Things were starting
to happen, fish were rolling over the baits most nights, the only
problem being the bar in front of me was horrendous, pulling back
the leads to the gravel resulted in cut-offs, something had to be
done. The season before one of the members had given me some
leader material called Bowstring, claiming it eliminated cut-offs. All
I had to do now was track down where to get the stuff, 10,000
phone calls later I located a supply, only trouble was it had to be
ordered in bulk from America. I bought a box full and conned the
lads on the lake to buy it, since then Harefield Tackle buy it and sell
it in convenient spools, so the problem was solved. The next
problem was hooking the fish. A quick trip over to Savay saw me
grovelling to (the legendary) Albert Romp.

Albert was brilliant, coming over to the lake and showing me rigs

'Nelson' 35lb 8oz 7/7/92

'Round-Tail' 33lb 2oz 7/7/92

and other tricks. Along with advice from the Monster, I now felt confident, all they had to do was pick up my baits, simple when you have good friends. Returning the following week on Thursday, fish were rolling when I arrived. I had brought my son Sean - a good excuse to keep out of the pub. At this time he had no interest in fishing, but liked coming to annoy the other anglers and play with the Monster and another mate, Essex Jon. That night I felt confident, around one o'clock in the morning one of my Delkims burst into life, out like a shot I struck and yes, plunged over the bar - no problem. Leader on the reel, all over bar the netting. Next problem the fish powers off, no stretch in the Bowstring, twang! The hook pulled, my son Sean has now learnt some brilliant new words. As I am baiting up the monkey on the other rod suddenly drops back, pick up rod, strike, thump, thump, sod it a bream. Being an unselfish sort of bloke I offer the rod to Sean, "want to catch a bream son?" "No thanks Dad." Pumping the bream in: "Sure you don't want a bream son?" "Get stuffed Dad." Even he didn't want one. As the bream is under the tip it suddenly turns into a bleeding great carp. Suddenly Sean wants it and tries to grab the rod. A quick cuff round the earhole sorts that out, "sod off ," Sean replied with his new found words questioning my parenthood. Playing the fish gently now I persuaded Sean to net it (threatening to throw his Teenage Turtles in the lake if he messes up the netting). Fearing for the safety of *Donatello* he nets if first time. On the scales 29lb 8oz of big, plump lovely mirror. Great stuff, my season has eventually started.

Next morning it's mushrooms. Albert is up the cafe, I thank him for his advice. Life is sweet! Next day is so hot we spend the day in the pub, purely to keep cool - that's my excuse. Stay on the lake Friday night, more fish rolling, confidence high (the first Friday I haven't been in the pub). Around 11pm off we go again 24lb 2oz; 11.30pm away again 19lb 8oz, fully-scaled - what a lovely fish; 12 midnight another take, must be a dream this, any minute now I will wake up, not a dream 17lb 12oz mirror this time. As I'm unhooking it the other rod screams at me - leaving Tony and Sean to sack it up. Strike as the fish nears the net I give it too much stick in the excitement and the bloody hook pulls. Cast the rods back out and fall into bed a happy man. At 2am life really looks good, another take... 21lb 12oz this one. Up early next morning, the heat is coming on already. It's only 7am, four fish in sacks and it's not a dream.

Monster arrives, gives me a friendly slap and knocks me flying. Picking myself up, Sean is killing himself laughing, threatening next time I belt him he will set Uncle Monster on me. As we get the first sack out for the photos my mate Rob appeared with his video camera, brilliant - now I can be a film star. As I posed for the filming one of the lads on the other bank shouts out something like golden rollocks. Bleep, bleep, a drop-back on the nearest rod, shove the fish to Sean and tell him to sack it back up while I land the bream, him convinced it's a bream is well happy being filmed sacking a fish, he can bullshit his mum into thinking he caught it. In the meantime the bream turns into another carp, sorry son - I didn't know. This time he makes up stories to Monster hoping I will get another slap and he can grab the rod. His plan backfires, Monster doesn't believe him and he gets it. Life can be tough sometimes. This fish fights like mad, some ten minutes later one mental 27lb 8oz is in the net. Aragh! The peacock call goes out, (this is a ritual started by Essex Jon). The noise resembling a peacock being grabbed by the cobblers. All summer I had listened with envy as Essex had built up a great tally of fish. Now it was my day and what a day, photos done and up the cafe, double mushrooms please and sit and smirk as everyone notices them on my plate.

That day I had to get some shopping, Sean went off with Essex to the pub, I was to meet them later. Glad of the peace I took my time shopping. On arriving at the pub to the sound of laughter, I walked in and Sean was performing in great style, blowing up balloons supplied by his new mate Essex from a machine in the toilets and learning new sayings from his hero on what to say to any unattached women. On seeing all this Dougal decided to pull him up and he immediately threw a glass of orange at him, Dougal ducked and it hit Frogger full-on. What had Jon put in his orange? It turned out to be Malibu so it was back to the bivvy with one-not-so-well and not-so-tough eight-year-old menace. That night he slept like a log, not for me though - I landed another two - 18lb 8oz and 27 exactly, plus three fish lost. Home the next morning, Sean relates the full story to mum and immediately gets himself a month's ban from playing out or going fishing. Me, I get the biggest rollicking ever and escape back to the lake licking my wounds. That night I lost two more, some curse the missus has put on me. I go home, no dinner, no nookie, no chance of getting round her. I sort out the work and sod off back to the lake. Essex has done me a right favour, normally I would have to grovel for extra fishing, but she is glad to see the back of me and run my business on her own. Arriving back at the lake it is pouring rain with thunder and lightning, I cast out as quickly as possible and dive in the bivvy, put the kettle on and have a well deserved cup of tea. My mate, Chris Perkins the famous 41 year old teenager, appeared round the bivvy, "want some fish and chips, I'm off up the chippy golden balls?" He asks. Excellent - this is better than being at home. As he disappears over the gravel pile one of my rods screams off, playing the fish in the pouring rain, it feels like another good one. Just as it comes to the net the rain stopped and the sun appeared from behind the clouds. At the same time Dougal and Chris appeared, much insults were thrown at me, only in fun though. This is what fishing is all about: good mates, good fishing, life is great, 21lb 12oz this one, a big long battle-scarred fish. "Well old son it's time you left the fish alone and bought your mates some lager," said Dougal. I didn't need any persuading - one happy carp angler staggered out of the pub that night to the sound of Dougal saying: "See you in the morning for photos golden balls."

Some time that night my dreams (of Kim Basinger) were interrupted by another fish. Wanting to get back to my dreams, I was just about to get on board after Kim had put a bag on my head. Why? I don't know, I think I am very good looking, the fish quickly weighed, at 19lb 4oz a nice common sacked up, ready for Dougal. A quick peacock call just to piss the lads off. I went back to my dreams. Around 6.30am suddenly shoved off my bedchair, one day I will belt him for this when he gets older and I get bigger, Dougal questions me: "What's in the sack old son?" "A 19lb 4oz common," I replied as I opened the sack, Dougal says: "You daft prat it's a fully-scaled," me looking back at the fish arguing back that it's a common. On looking at the side facing Dougal I saw it's fully-scaled one side and a common the other: "Two freaks together," says Dougal. I agree because he's too big to argue with.

Back home later that morning I had promised to take a break from fishing until Sunday when I had to take 12 kids for a day's pike fishing, this had been arranged with my good friend Mark Simmonds, who runs Broadlands Lake. He had promised me the lake for a day during the week before he normally allows pike fishing. I had fished this week in the past and you normally get some very good sport. We were to go down on Friday night with

'Big Robbie' 30lb 6oz 8/7/92

some friends, meet Dougal and Christine for Saturday night and the kids on Sunday. I persuaded the missus we would have a better night up the Horse and Barge staying at the bivvy. To my surprise she agreed. Arriving at the lake Big Rob had moved in for the weekend, the swim looked like a refugee camp with mine and Tony's bivvy and Rob's tent. Rob had brought his big tent as he had his wife and her sister with him. That night after the pub we had a bit of a party at the swim, sometime in the middle of it I caught a 23lb 12oz which was the 24lb 2oz I'd had ten days previously.

Saturday arrived and the conditions looked ideal, the worst thing was that I had to pack up and wouldn't be back until the next weekend, as I had a full week of appointments and paperwork to do. The Sunday was a success for the boys, landing 24 fish, 12 of which were doubles. This made missing the fishing worthwhile just to see their faces.

The following Friday I returned to the lake, it was hot and calm and when a breeze did get up it blew to the other end of the lake, not ideal conditions for fishing so we had a few beers and a romantic night out for 30 up the Indian. On waking the next morning I looked out at the rods and saw the tip pull over on my rod, leapt out and hit it - 25lb 4oz, that'll do for me. The rest of the weekend was quiet, too hot and calm. In the weedbed to my left there were several fish lazing in the sun, one was the big Italian who dwarfed the other fish, and the linear was there too. I put mixers over them all day but they showed no interest at all. Home Monday morning, it stayed hot all week so I caught up on work. Come Friday the wind was getting up nicely, getting stronger by the hour. Grabbing a fresh supply of bait and food, I replenished my wallet. I was off knowing that with a wind blowing hard into *the works* that conditions were right., I was in a hurry to get back, three hours later I had moved about five miles in a massive traffic jam on the M25. Eventually, after leaving the motorway and driving through the back roads I arrived and cast out, then started sorting out my bivvy. Tony had been rummaging through everything, he had left it in a right mess. After I sorted it all out, I'd just got the kettle on and the rod on the weedbed rattled off with the fastest take I have ever seen, line was going off so fast I was worried about turning the Baitrunner off, the fish fought like crazy. After some 20 minutes the big linear rolled about ten yards out, my legs turned to jelly, this was one fish I really wanted. Playing it extra gently, it was another ten minutes before it was in the net. Aragh! The call went out. She weighed 29lb 4oz, a big long fish not carrying any gut, she was under the weight I estimated her at but who cares, what a beautiful carp, definitely the best looking fish I have ever caught. Sacked up, cast back out and on to the phone to the Monster, (he would be down in half an hour). Sitting drinking tea with the wind blowing nicely into my face, I thought tonight I will stay on the water. Dougal had other plans, "after a fish like that you must come and celebrate," said the Monster. I told him I had planned to stay on the lake as conditions were ideal. You greedy bastard was Dougal's reply, the fish will always be here but your mates won't. Thinking about what he said, the weather forecast had said wind all weekend so over the pub to celebrate. Leaving the pub, apart from my legs not working and my eyes not focusing properly something was wrong, being quick witted and observant it took me ten minutes to realise the bloody wind had dropped, it was absolutely flat calm and stayed like it all weekend. The lying git on the weather forecast had set me up, no more fish that weekend. Still it didn't matter, I had caught the linear.

Back home that week the weather reports were for more wind by Thursday, so, after bribing the missus, I was back for Thursday morning. I had been baiting up with a lot of hemp every other week and using some 1,000 boilies per night. I had struck up a friendship with the manager of the gravel works and in return for helping him run the barges to and from the workings he always let me use the tug on the last trip to get my hemp out. They weren't using it today but tomorrow morning I could use it. The next day I was sitting in my bivvy when Keith, the manager, suddenly started shouting. Looking out I could see the tug had come untied with the engine in gear, and had pulled off over the lake on its own leaving Keith stranded on a barge. It was merrily chugging up the lake towards the islands. Suddenly after hitting a bar it veered off to the right and was dead on course for an occupied swim on the bank. Much shouting across the lake, no one appeared, the tug slammed into the other bank straight into someone's swim. I ran round expecting to see all the rods smashed, this was one lucky bloke - the tug was between his rods, still in gear, flat out. I jumped on the tug, slowed the engines and the other angler appeared. "Some place to park," he said, thinking I had put it there. Taking the tug back across the lake I made a detour, picked up Tony, 6,000 boilies and half a hundredweight of hemp, out to the swim and baited up, picked Keith up and back to our bivvies.

We cast out and sat back in the sun. Usually when we baited up it took a few days for the fish to get going, usually rolling over it before getting their heads down, so it was a surprise some ten minutes later when Tony had a 22lb 8oz. Thirty minutes after this and I was away, the fish went round to my left very slowly but feeling like a good lump it was heading for Keith's barge which I knew had two anchors out on wire cables, it was now... shit or bust. Putting my hand over the spool and holding on, the rod bent double and started groaning, the line was singing. Suddenly a dirty great mirror, definitely over thirty, crashed over on the surface, Tony turned to me, "30-plus," I would rather he hadn't confirmed it, the legs were now shaking. Suddenly Tony's Optonics burst into life he had another take, so dropping the net he ran to his rod, leaving me on my own with one angry thirty on the other end of my line. As I netted it Tony's fish went behind a bar and jammed up solid, so putting his on the rests with the bail-arm open he helped me sort out my fish. To say I was chuffed would be an understatement - 34lb 4oz, what a season this was turning into!

Tony returned to his rod only to find the fish gone but two hours later he was to get his reward. He had another take, hit it and the fish isn't doing much, zig-zagging about then swimming towards him "feels like a pisser" said Tony, I jokingly said it was probably *Nelson*, they reckon he doesn't scrap. Suddenly up came *Nelson* ready for the net. I don't know who was most surprised *Nelson* or me. Last time out he was down to 33 pounds. This was his tenth visit to the bank that season so we reckoned about 32 pounds, *Nelson* however had other ideas as he had been on the bait around three hours and being one greedy bastard he had probably scoffed all our bait. His weight was 36lb 12oz, still 1,000 baits is around four and a half pounds, so in reality he could have gone 50 pounds. All this commotion was old hat to this old warhorse of a fish, he just wanted to have his photos taken and get back on the bait, we just wanted to go to the pub or stay on the lake. Dougal holding his throat convinced us along with the saying about your friends and the fish.

At one o'clock that morning two very drunk idiots staggered out of the Indian and back to the lake, Tony didn't know whether he could cast out or not so I reminded him of one of Roger's sayings, "if you're too drunk to cast, drop 'em in the edge." It's worth a

'The Linear' 30lb 12oz 23/7/92

couple of fish a year, obviously tonight wasn't the night because Tony blanked. Me, I just cast out, heard two splashes and fell in a heap on the bedchair. Sometime later I woke up, (what's that bloody racket, Tony must have a take) put a pillow over my head and tried to ignore it, still it went on. Suddenly Tony is at the bivvy: "Don't you want this one, shall I hit it?" He asked, knowing he would hit the run, I was out and on the rods in a flash, only to fall over them flat on my face, much to Tony's amusement. On striking I fell over again so decided it would be better to play it sitting down. The fish was swimming towards me quite fast, after a couple of minutes winding I remarked to Tony that I must be able to cast further after a couple of gallons of lager. Thinking that with this brand of lager you can reach the spots other lagers can't reach, the daft prat said: "Stu you're back-winding, the fish must be half way round the pit." Sometime later after pulling myself together, 26lb 9oz of common was safely tucked up in his sack for the night. Another magic weekend was over.

For some weeks there had been a lot of aggravation on the lake caused mainly by one man. I don't want to put it in the book, as it isn't the time or the place, but Dougal lost his job, redundancy was the excuse used, so enough said about that. The following two weeks were sad times, the magic atmosphere which had surrounded the lake for the last two seasons had disappeared. I didn't feel like fishing much but Dougal persuaded me to carry on, so every night I spent with him drinking and remembering better times. About this time Sean's ban ended, so he was back on the lake and for the first time in his life was mad keen to fish. Not wanting to put him straight onto carp I sorted out my old match rod and set him up for the roach and bream. Every ten minutes saw me or Tony sorting out tangles but Sean was really enjoying himself catching plenty of roach and bream. To tell the truth so were we, we had set up spare rods and fished with him in a small bay to our right. It was on one of these days three weeks later, when we were sitting there bashing out roach, that Tony remarked quite casually: "Isn't your Optonic making a racket?" With the wind blowing away from me and not having very good hearing I hadn't heard it. After dashing to the rod and a lively scrap I landed yet another good fish, a short fat one at 27lb 12oz.

After the last few weeks' aggro this fish cheered me up no end and the old enthusiasm was creeping back, funny what one fish will do for you. The following day Sean was out at first light, he was really getting into his fishing and I was pleased, just wish he wouldn't wake me at the crack of dawn each morning. Ten minutes later I am just nodding off when Sean shouts for me. "If you think I'm getting up to sort out a tangle for you have another think, use mine or Tony's rod or better still get Tony up." I answered. "But, Dad I have hooked a monster." With this I can hear his clutch screaming, dashing out I am just in time to see a massive bow-wave going up the lake and Sean hanging on for dear life to what is obviously a big carp. The next second his two pound line has parted, to be honest with all these bars and the light tackle I don't think anyone would have stood a chance but it was still worth cuffing his earhole for fishing for carp when I told him he couldn't.

The following week we were back, Sean, now fishing for pike, had several up to seven pounds. I had three fish, 22lb 12oz, 19lb 4oz and 19lb 12oz, two commons and a mirror. The fish were obviously getting their heads down. We were sure there would be more to come through the winter and were really looking forward to it. We decided to keep the bait going in, cutting down slightly but a nice steady supply through the winter.

The next weekend Tony had a 27lb 8oz, so it was looking good. Sean was catching plenty of pike and roach and everything looked rosy. On the Sunday the forecast gave a hurricane warning, the direction would be straight in our faces so we decided to pack all our gear away just in case. The wind never arrived on the Monday. This was a bad enough blow as, being a scaffolding contractor, bad weather like that forecast is a licence to print money. However, a far worse blow was in store. I got a phone call at 2.45 that afternoon, Keith had got the sack and I was banned from the water for using his office phone even though he had given me permission, three days later Tony was banned for the same reason as me. So the rest of the winter was spent messing about as I hadn't made plans for anything else. I caught a few fish here and there but my heart wasn't in it, I could only wonder what would have been. Towards the end of the season I was told I could come back for the last week as a guest but wouldn't be allowed on *The Workings*. I wasn't sure whether to go, as there had only been the odd fish out all winter, but decided it would be better than fishing elsewhere, also I wanted to see if I could still catch them on what was obviously a good bait from swims other than *The Workings*. Arriving on the Friday and

'Goldfish' 31lb 4oz 26/7/92

'Little Pecs' 37lb 8oz 20/8/92

setting up home, I was here for the week. On phoning home that evening, *not* from Keith's old office I hasten to add, my wife informed me that my old mate Ritchie had caught the fish he was after from Yateley at 41lb 9oz from the Pad Lake. Knowing the stick Ritchie had been getting from a lot of people because he had been having hard times I was over the moon for him. Up yours to the knockers, which this sport is full of.

On the Monday after a couple of bleeps around 7am a full-blooded run occurred on my long-range rod. A few bumps and pulls later, I was convinced I had a tench on when under the tip appeared the big linear, again straight into the net. Will it go thirty this time I wondered? Not to be, but at 29lb 12oz still a cracking fish. Somehow though it didn't seem the same, yes the fish were still there but my friends weren't.

Suddenly I realised what a true saying it was - I decided then that I would meet Dougal and Tony, as arranged, in the pub that night and pack up the next day. On getting to the pub a good carp party was under way. Ritchie and a mob of the Yateley lads were there. "Guess what?" Said Ritchie "I had a forty." "Yes I know, you phoned me." "Not that one," says Ritchie, "another one, *Heather* at 40lb 8oz from the Car Park Lake." Magic. After a brilliant night in the pub I packed up feeling happy yet sad, a mixed season and one which will be hard to repeat.

Season 2

Since writing the first part of my story for the book I have had another amazing season and as Rob hadn't finished his book he asked me to write about my 1992/1993 season back at Harefield.

As I wrote earlier the reasons for the end of my fishing at Harefield were political, so I won't bore you with the pathetic details. I felt I had unjustly been denied the chance to show just what the capabilities of the lake were and it hurt not to be able to finish what I was doing. However things were about to change in a big way. Dougal and another good friend of mine, Ben Tucker, had been asked to run Boyer Leisure and had asked if I wanted to come back as their Head Bailiff at Harefield. Did I? Is the pope a catholic? This was like a late Christmas present. I had to meet the head man of Boyer's. It was actually the first time I had the pleasure of meeting Miles Boyer as in the past everyone was kept away from the 'man'. I nervously went for the meeting, as without his say-so I couldn't return. After an interesting meeting and clearing up all the bullshit and controversy I was welcomed back to what was to be a new era for Boyer's and in my opinion the best set-up they ever had. I was to take up my new position for the beginning of the 1992/1993 season. I was buzzing with anticipation for the coming season. The lake was to be run differently this season, for the first time rotas were to be introduced, fishing one week on, one week off, Monday to Monday. I was given a golden opportunity in so far as I didn't have to fish on rota and could go when I wanted. To some this set up may seem unfair, and normally I would agree, but I felt I was owed this chance, having been denied finishing my last season on the water as I wanted. Apart from that, when someone offers you the chance of a lifetime you don't say no.

At the beginning of the season Rob was making a video for the first two weeks and I was asked by the management to fish with him. This was agreed with pleasure as Rob is a good friend and an angler I respect. I was really looking forward to the occasion. We chose a swim known as *The Point* as it offered the best place for filming where we could both be in view of the cameras. Rob was to fish the left side of the swim on what is normally an island but as the water levels were down it was joined to the main bank by a small pathway. The cameraman, Len Gurd, would be in the middle, myself to the right casting to a different area of the lake to Rob. We knew three weeks prior to the draw for swims that we would have this area so we had plenty of time to plumb around and find areas to fish and also introduce our bait. My swim was opposite the area I mentioned before known as *The Stick Bar*. To cast to an area where I had seen fish feeding involved casting over two steep bars to the right of two small islands, which in normal conditions would be underwater. As the bars are covered in mussels and sharp stones I planned to fish Bowstring leaders of approximately 25 yards to eliminate cut-offs, and at the end of these approximately three feet of lead-core fly line to sink the business end of the tackle and save spooking fish. To this was attached a four ounce attractor lead fished helicopter style, a brilliant new product was on the market - the CV safety rig, which meant in the event of a break-off the whole lot comes free so as not to tether fish. With all my plans made I cagerly awaited the off, my only worry was if Rob totally out-fished me, I would look a prat on video. Knowing Rob as the capable angler he is I thought I would settle for a third of what he caught.

Come the 16th Rob started in fine form taking three twenty-plus fish the first day, my worst fears were coming true. Rob had the fish stacked up in front of him and was doing a very efficient job of baiting up and holding them there. Still it didn't matter as I was in great company, back on the lake with a full season ahead of me, and Rob deserved to catch as he had put his head on the chopping block laying out hard-earned wonga to make a video on this usually hard water. If we blanked he would do his money, so for Rob the pressure was on. My only chance the first day was early in the morning which I fluffed by my own fault, forgetting the sharp bars, I left my hooklink at approximately one foot and had it cut off on the take. I had forgotten previous lessons learned when fishing other waters that it is best to fish short hooklinks of a maximum nine inches. Cursing my luck I changed rigs but no more action was to come that day, putting pressure on me to catch. The first fish of the season is always the hardest and with the added pressure of doing it in front of the cameras I really felt up against it.

The next day Rob started as before, catching from first light, around 11am my chance came in the shape of a nice common of 22 pounds, it felt like a ton weight had been lifted off my shoulders. Rob finished the day with three more fish, two over 20 pounds. The following day the fish were still stacked up in front of Rob, he landed four to 30lb 2oz, I had one hook pull and a nice mirror of 26lb 8oz. the only other excitement that day was that all Len's notes for the filming blew into the lake and I had to swim out and collect them. We were staying on the lake, not bothering to go to the pub, but it was great fun just to be back. That evening we had a big barbecue at the lake with a few friends and plenty of beer. By now the weather was warming up and the fish were cruising in the surface layers so by fishing pop-ups straight up from the leads we continued to pick odd fish up - Rob another 29, myself two twenties - one common and one mirror. So by the end of the first week we had caught a good few fish, Rob with the lion's share.

That evening we decided to take a break and let our hair down, so it was over to the Horse and Barge then up the Indian, by the time we got to the Indian we were in a sorry state. Some friends of mine who were fishing another lake for bream were just getting their meal as we walked in. One of them had ordered a Phal for a bet and couldn't eat it, so we bet them I could and we had a little earner as I love hot curry. After eating that one my meal came. I

'Fully-Scaled' 36lb 12oz 29/9/92

devoured my meal, and Len couldn't manage his as it was too hot (and he was too drunk), so, being the gentleman I am, to save his face I scoffed his as well. After staggering back to the lake I waited for Rob to fall asleep so I could put my next plan into action. Rob had kept the fish in front of him for the last week and I needed to tempt some my way. When he had passed out I put my spodding aids together, ie my life jacket, flippers and two buckets of hemp. On my second visit out to the second bar Rob woke up and caught me, he said he thought proper carp angling had died till he saw my antics, I gained his admiration. Belly full of beer, three curries and a midnight excursion - my trap was set. The next day Rob caught my old friend the linear, still looking as good as ever and up in weight at 30lb 12oz. What a result Rob was having.

By the afternoon things were looking good for me, there were certainly a lot of fish showing over my carefully spodded area. For this season I had got myself a puppy to keep me company, a little black terrier I called Jack. In the last week he had got into a habit of peeing under Rob's rods, and at first I thought it was funny, but it seemed to be bringing him luck, so this day I squeezed his head over my rods to see if it would bring me luck as well. As normal it was another well thought out plan that seemed doomed to failure as the only take I had was when I was having an afternoon kip. I woke up to a strange noise which consisted of a series of bleeps. On dashing out of the bivvy I found Jack making a meal of eating my rod handle, after beating him up I returned to bed for another blank day. As it got dark that night a lot of fish were showing over the bait and it looked good for a change of fortune. The rotas were due to change the next morning and the evening was spent having a few cans of beer with two of my old mates, the Dodgy Northerner, Eric Hattersley and my other good friend who I planned to fish the rest of the season with - No Legs Tubby Terry Thompson. At around 1am it started to happen - first a 22lb 8oz mirror, followed half an hour later by one of the original stocking of Harefield, a lovely old common of 26lb 8oz. Just as I landed it the other rod rattled off and, after a short scrap, the fish I had originally joined Harefield to catch rolled into the net, *The Orange* fish at 33lb 8oz. What a result, I was over the moon. The fish wasn't in the best condition as he'd been unfortunate enough to have been dropped by somebody during the previous season, his tail was broken and his pec was twisted, he was also carrying a bit of fungus. So on his return we trusted he would avoid further capture this year and hopefully recover. When we photographed the fish I was on cloud nine and wasn't thinking too straight. For the video I wore Rob's hat with the *Big Carp* logo on it but I meant to take it off for the photo session. However I forgot and as Rob's head is like his belly, the only thing that stopped it falling over my head completely were my big lug holes. So the only photos I have are wearing a hat which is too big. I still have the memory however, and I hoped to catch it another year, hopefully in a better condition.

At around 6am, after sorting everything out, I had just got the kettle on when off roared my left hand rod. On hitting the take it felt like a right lump, the power of this fish was incredible. It took off straight behind the island to my left, the line catching on the mass of stinging nettles on top of the island. Holding the rod high above my head I ran over to where Rob was fishing to the other side of the island. The Bowstring cut through the nettles and with a sudden twang I was back in contact, finally, as the fish approached the net, I had a great pile of silkweed up the line and jammed in the top ring. I was crapping myself. Rob got out as far as he could in his wellies but the only thing I could do was walk backwards. As the fish rolled into the net, we could see it was one known as *Black Spot* at 33lb 2oz. I was over the moon, what a brilliant few hours... it was great to be back and having them. The rest of the week carried on in brilliant style with me catching a further five fish and losing three others, one felt a good lump but such is life. These things happen but you still feel gutted, even when you're hauling it's still annoying to lose fish. The video finished on the Sunday, I planned to fish on till Monday morning. As I was packing up I had my final take of the session, as it came to the net I could see it was a fish known as *Humpy* which I had taken before at 29. It had been out the year previously at 34 pounds so the old legs were shaking. When its head was inches from the net the hooklink caught the lead and cut off on a sharp chunk in the lead which had been damaged on a bar. I was devastated but what a session we'd had with a final tally of 24 to Rob and 12 fish to me, all on video. Rob finally had to make two videos of the trip, giving us a lasting memory of a fantastic trip in great company, just to give Rob a plug, get the videos *Harefield Haulin' 1 and 2.*

Well after that little lot it was home for a week to recover, throw the milkman out and get to know the family again. I planned to return the following Monday for another week's fishing with my old mate Tubby Thompson, planning to fish the same swims, with Terry in Rob's swim and me back in my previous swim. On arrival back at the lake the fish had been getting their fins over and only a few had been landed, with two doubles from our intended swim. The Monday was spent without seeing any fish, but we baited heavily with the same bait as the last season, (Richworth Condensed Milk). I knew the fish really get on these so my confidence was high. Tuesday morning at 5am my sleep was interrupted by a nice 22lb 8oz mirror, as Terry was still a-kip I sacked it up and recast. Not feeling tired any more on went the kettle. As is usual, just as the kettle boils, off roars the same rod, on striking the fish I felt a good lump. The water levels had dropped even further in the last week, and to get the fish in past the first bar involved hanging on till they swam past a gap in the bar of approximately 12 feet wide, then pulling like hell to get them through the gap. Sounds easy until you try it with a big angry carp on the other end. As the fish ploughed past the gap I heaved it towards me and missed the gap, the fish stuck on top of the bar in about two feet of water, wallowing about over the bar rocking this way and that. I could see its big shoulders and guessed it at over thirty. Luck went my way and it rolled over my side of the bar and chugged around in open water. Calling Terry, there was no response from the little-legged git so I had to net it myself. On the scales he went 35lb 8oz, I recognised the fish but couldn't place it straight away until I turned it over and spotted its blind eye, *Nelson*. What a start to the week. I sacked it up, woke Terry, then shot round the lake to my old friend John Bevan, woke him up and asked him to bring his video to do the honours as it was my personal best. John wound in and, as he had a bad leg, limped round the lake whingeing about people catching fish too early in the morning. After the photo session John limped back to his swim. Just as he cast out off went my same rod again. As it came to the gap I said to Terry "if it gets stuck on the bar it's over thirty" and with that it did the same thing as the last one and stuck on the bar. With a bit of pressure over he came and into the net - 33lb 2oz - a fish known as *Round-Tail*. What a brace, and still only 7.30am. Poor old John wound in and limped back again. After the photos the other rod shot off, this time the culprit was a small tench. John said it wasn't worth going back to his own swim as the fish were obviously stacked up in front of me and Terry. He proceeded to demolish all

Terry with 'Round-Tail' 36lb 6oz 30/9/92

my lager, his excuse was then "to celebrate!" God knows how anyone can get on the drink at eight in the morning, but then Old Bevo is the master at drinking. An hour later, in again at 20lb 12oz, the fish is one of the first I ever caught at Harefield, a really ugly, old, wrinkled fish with a smashed up face named the *Little Turd*, we renamed it *Bevo* as it's a dead ringer for him. Around midday Bevo staggered out of my swim having demolished all my beer and disappeared to the pub calling us wimps for not joining him. I had decided this season to stay out of the pub and concentrate on the fishing. It seems on this lake that things have a habit of not lasting long, and politics can change the face of things rapidly, so I wanted what I felt I was owed after the last fiasco. Plenty of time for drinking when the season changes and things get hard, also as we were in the middle of the worst recession for years my finances were low. No work gave me plenty of time to fish, but not a lot of money. Unfortunately you can't have it all unless you're a rich tackle dealer like Old Bevo.

The next day Harry Haskell, a good friend of mine over the years, was coming up as Ben and Dougal's guest to fish with me. Over the years I have known Harry, he has helped me with rigs and I have tested lots of inventions Harry has come up with. Harry is a very 'thinking angler' and has a great deal of knowledge. He had heard all the stories about Harefield and wanted to see for himself what went on there. He arrived at first light, we told him of yesterday's captures and another fish of 22lb 12oz I had caught during the night, he was certainly going to see Harefield on top form. Luckily he has been around long enough to know it was exceptional fishing. They weren't the best of weather conditions for his first sight of the lake, raining heavily off and on all day. My first take of the day at around 9.30am resulted in a hook pull. When fishing over large beds of hemp I have come to accept hook pulls, as I have observed carp at close quarters over big beds of hemp. They swoop down on a long run, sucking up the hemp. My personal theory is, if they pick up the bait on the first part of their approach, you hook them well back and get a screaming take. However, if they get the hookbait towards the end, you only prick them and get a short take. My belief is this is when a hook pull will most likely occur. Certainly I was getting some belting takes, with fish hooked at the back of the throat very rarely resulting in hook pulls, and the short takes always hooked just in the bottom of the mouth.

However, going back to the day in question. At ten o'clock Terry had two small doubles in quick succession then at 11.30 off went my right hand rod. After a lively scrap we took a fish which didn't feel that big as it was coming to the net, all we saw was a short fish with a small head as normal. We were guessing its weight on the way to the net and all reckoned it might go twenty. As the fish rolled over the net it seemed to grow, being short but very deep, we reckoned it may just ring the bell. On the scales at 30lb 6oz, it was an absolutely immaculate mirror in pristine condition without a mark in it's mouth, we certainly didn't recognise it as one of the known thirties. Showing the photos to the other lads on the syndicate, no one recognised the fish. Everyone said I should name it, personally I don't like fish with names so replied, can't you just call it a ****ing carp so the poor sod ended up being called ****ing *Carp*, what an unfortunate name for such a lovely fish. In the next five hours I had two more hook pulls and three doubles. Harry had certainly seen some action, and as he was staying till the next afternoon, we were hopeful of more to come. That night as we sat around drinking tea, Terry got a take which went straight through a small gap between two large islands, every time he got it back to the island it got stuck. Terry reckoned it felt like a good fish so I volunteered to swim out and free it, on with the lifejacket and flippers into the dark. It was very creepy swimming out in the middle of a pitch black night. Reaching a shallow bar between the islands I found Terry's line and slowly worked my way to the fish. Once located, I slipped my hands down till I found the head, put my other hand under and lifted. It was only a small one so I carried it over the bar. Terry, not knowing what was going on thought the fish was coming back through the gap, I could feel him pulling the line and the fish moving, so as I released the fish back on his side I gave a big tug on his line. I could hear him telling Harry that it felt big and chuckled to myself. Quickly swimming back I arrived while Terry was still playing it. To keep him at it, I said it was big which made him even more nervous. By the time it reached the net Terry was convinced he had his first thirty. Upon netting, he realised he had been conned as it only just went double. Harry just shook his head at our antics and went to bed.

The following day the action didn't start till around midday when I had a good fish go left and get stuck behind the second small island in front of me. Whichever way I pulled the fish wouldn't come free. We tried our full repertoire of tricks to free it, first firing stones with a catapult to try and spook it. We then tried our favourite scheme, where I sit on Terry's shoulders and fire the catapult. This had worked well on previous attempts, but not this time. Next we found a short ladder which Terry held while I went up it. Still no joy. So it was down to the last option, strip off and swim out with the rod to free it. When I reached the island I crept over to the other side, behind a sheer ledge of gravel was the fish, a mid-twenty, rubbing his face into the gravel to try and rid himself of the hook. Suddenly, being confronted with me, he bolted off into open water with me swimming in leading him to the bank. Once there I played him in, shivering. At 27lb 8oz I was well chuffed, after photos Terry put the kettle on while I put on dry clothes. Just then Bevo appeared back from the pub pissed as a cricket, whilst hurling insults at me, he fell through my Hutchy Dome smashing the poles amidst hoots of laughter from Terry. Harry, who by now had seen enough to know you have to be mad to fish here, announced he didn't think he could cope. So, after final farewells, Harry left for home leaving me and Terry to dwell over the last 36 hours. Thinking about what Harry had seen it must have seemed a strange place to him. That evening we rounded off another day with a 22lb 4oz mirror to me and yet another double for Terry, and finished the trip with one more twenty for me.

Back again for another full week, and No Legs Terry at last had his first twenty of the season, a mirror of 24. "This will be my week," announced Terry, "now I will get all the monsters and you will get the pasties." He followed this prediction with a nice 16 pound linear within the next hour. An hour after that I started with a fish of 20lb 4oz. The next day I made acquaintance with an old friend. The common one side, fully-scaled the other, up in weight at 21lb 8oz, and followed it up with a personal best common at 27 pounds. I had no more fish that week but Terry continued to catch, not the monsters he predicted, but three fish, two low doubles and a single. I was now calling him my pest control officer. Terry was asking what the hell he was doing to get all the small fish and myself the bigger ones. I decided to get him at it by telling him it was all down to the boilies you use. As he was on the same bait as me he said it couldn't be. "Well" I said, "have you ever noticed I search through the bag for my hookbait, and with the two coloured baits we are using I always pick the one that appears to have a big smiling face on?" "Rollocks,"

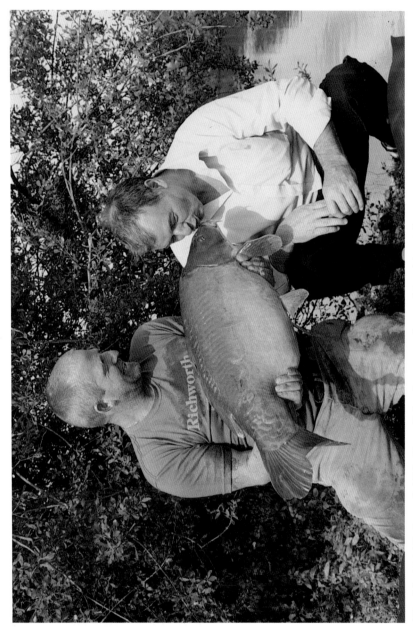

'Bite Mark' 30lb 8oz 1/10/92. Fatty Baker kissing it for making him rich

said Terry, but the seed of doubt had been sown, so the next few trips I made a point of searching out baits to wind him up. Home again for the week, rushing through work to get back up for the next rota. As usual towards the end of the week I phoned Dougal to see what was coming out. "Not a lot," he replied "but a lot of fish are showing off *The Workings*," which was the opposite end of the pit to where we had been concentrating. I phoned Terry to give him the news and we decided to have one last week on *The Point* and then move down onto the *Road Bank* casting over to *The Workings*. What a shame *The Workings* was out of bounds to everyone as it would have been a little 20 yard cast to the fish instead of one hell of a cast from the *Road Bank,* some 130 yards-plus. This would suit Terry as he can cast as far as anyone I have seen, but I knew I would struggle with my two and three-quarter Armalites. It was a case of raiding my piggy bank to purchase two long-range rods and two Daiwa SS3000 reels. The next week we were down for 'the off' and at night we sneaked out to *The Workings* and started baiting up the swims ready for two weeks time. Dougal agreed, after bribery with wicked amounts of Fosters, to bait up the week we wouldn't be there so that the area would have seen baits for two weeks prior to us fishing. That Monday in the car park Bamber (of Premier Baits fame) was doing his usual whingeing of how unfair the world was. Looking at him you would tend to agree. He was unfortunately blessed with the looks of the Milky Bar Kid (hard to live with when you're 30-plus) and a fine head of bright ginger hair, making him look like a Duracell battery. All the same he is a really nice bloke (sometimes), and, up until he reads this, someone I would regard as a friend, but God can the bloke whinge! He had renamed the lake Unfairfield, as Terry and I always had *The Point* swim. Like true gents we didn't tell him this was our last trip there, but told his mate Paul Selman of our plans so he could get there early on the next rota and stitch him up. The next day we decided to go and wind Bamber up some more, so we went to the other end of the lake and proceeded to take the mick. I convinced Bamber to give me one of his T-shirts with the dreaded Premier logo on it, and promised that if I caught a fish I would wear it for the photos. Getting back to *The Point,* wearing my newly-acquired shirt I cast out the rods and put the kettle on. Bamber had come back for tea and as we were drinking it off went one of the rods. After a short scrap I landed a nice 20lb 12oz common, turning to Bamber I couldn't resist another little dig, "the shirts are OK but your bait's crap," I joked. Duracell was raging now, his dear little face the same colour as his hair. Just after returning the fish the other rod was away. After a hair raising scrap, with the fish going all over my swim just under the surface like a Polaris missile, eventually over the net came my old friend the linear at the same weight as when Rob had it at 30lb 12oz. I was over the moon, off came the Premier lucky shirt, "I can't be seen with a proper carp in this shirt," I said. With that it all became too much for poor old Duracell so he stomped off still muttering on about Unfairfield. Never mind Bamber, the Milky Bars are on me!

The next couple of days went by quickly with no action to either of us. On Friday night it had been planned for a good drink and curry with Dougal and Bob Baker the famous boilie maker. I was forced, screaming, to the pub, protesting that the 'new me' no longer went in for these type of antics. After at least two seconds I changed my mind and was ready for the off - Terry being skint and not liking curry had decided to stay on the lake. He reckoned that whilst I was gone he was going to clean up. I reckoned that he fancied my dog so I wished him luck and was over the pub waiting patiently for opening time. The night was spent in good company with the other lads of the rota, plus some of the Savay syndicate, Bob and Dougal. Out of the pub at closing time and up the Indian, arriving back at the lake around 2am. I was in one hell of a state. Leaving Bob at Dougal's swim, I bade my farewell and stumbled and staggered back to my swim in the pitch darkness. After some effort I arrived back at *The Point*, checked Jack the carp dog to see if he was intact after his night with Terry, woke Terry up and took the piss because he had blanked. I cast both rods out somewhere, heard two splashes, and collapsed on my bed. Sometime later I remember waking up to the sound of a buzzer screaming, and after a few minutes I realised it belonged to me. Terry filled me in with the details the next morning, so the following is as he told it to me. I don't believe any of it. Apparently he heard the buzzer and the next thing he knew I was knocking hell out of the top of his bivvy saying: "Lawrence I have got a big bream on." (Lawrence being another of Terry's aliases started on a trip in the past to Holland, the name having somehow stuck). Terry stuck his head out of the bivvy, looked up and saw my rod bent double with me saying "it's a monster bream Lawrence." Terry kept saying "OK, take it easy, you don't want to lose it" and me replying "it's only a bream." In a short

'Stripes' 31lb 2/10/92

space of time the fish was within netting range and 'boiled' under the rod top. Terry decided to net it as quickly as possible before I lost it. As it went in the net he could see it was a dirty great common, I looked over his shoulder and said "it's the biggest bream I've ever seen Lawrence, it must be a record." Terry told me to 'go away' and he would take control of the situation. He weighed it and carefully placed it in a sack, then as he was putting it in the water it smacked him straight in the kisser with its tail, at which I burst out laughing and said "don't suffer that off a 'snotty' Lawrence, give it a slap back." By now poor old Lawrence had had enough so he tucked me up in bed and went back to his own bed to dwell on the injustice in the world. He had stayed on the lake and blanked, then I reappeared, and get another big fish. By now he was starting to believe that perhaps there was something in the 'smiling boilies' story. In the morning I woke up with a dreadful hangover. Terry appeared with a cup of coffee for me and called me a flukey bastard, "why call me that" I asked. "Don't you remember?" He said. "Well," I replied, "I dreamt I caught a big common," then spotting the sack in the margins and looking at Terry's face I began to recall some of the events. "How big is it?" I asked, "31lb 4oz and I hate you!" was Terry's reply.

The following week Dougal baited the *Road Bank* swims for us. Mysteriously, two new markers appeared right on the edge of the weedbed where the sand bar runs behind the weed from the gravel workings. Albert Romp, who was on the opposite rota to us, reckoned the lake was haunted as markers appear in the middle of the night. If it was a ghost that put them out, you certainly wouldn't want to bump into it.

Our first rota in the new swims was the beginning of August. The wind was blowing strongly towards the gravel workings, making the long cast very difficult. Terry was reaching the area, but my attempts were dropping short. Terry took two more doubles and was now getting ratty about being dubbed my pest control officer. By Thursday the wind dropped and I could cast to the sand bar. Within an hour my luck continued to shine through, taking a twenty-plus mirror and, later in the evening, a somewhat ugly fish called *The Turd* at 28lb 12oz. My confidence was now running at a high, the bait was working for me and all my mates were on it, the fish certainly had a taste for it. The next day Terry was thinking of going home, but I persuaded him that night would be his night. "If you think so pick out a lucky bait for me" he replied. "The luck doesn't work if someone else touches your bait," I told him. By now he was paranoid about the smiling baits. After carefully sifting through his bag of 1,000-plus boilies he produced his choice, a nice white bait with a great big red smile on it. "That's the one Lawrence," I told him. As is often the case with these stupid games, that bait was picked up around midnight. After a long fight No Legs was over the moon with a nice 27-plus - a personal best for Terry and a well deserved fish. Poor old Terry had so far netted most of my big fish only to catch all the beaneys himself. Terry wanted the photos just right, so myself and another mate, Ian Gotty McEnzie, arranged flowers in the greenery behind Terry. When Terry was satisfied we had all the reds and yellows in the right places out came the fish for its snapshots. The final twist for poor old Tel came a week later. I sent his pictures up to the fishing comics for him and put his profession down as a ladies hairdresser. Now Terry is rather proud of being a 'macho' tipper-truck driver, so this antic of mine really pissed him off. Still that's the penalty for fishing with a horrible git like me!

Another week at home then back again for another full week. The first three days were spent confined to the bivvy as it legged down with rain for three continuous days. God how I hate fishing in these conditions. No fish showed over this period in front of us but they were showing well opposite so they weren't far away. Meanwhile on *The Point* on the Monday another bloke, Gary, had a right result. Calling over to us to bring some large scales as he had a fish of 38-plus. On the way round the lake we were discussing which fish it could be and on arrival another mate, Nick the Tree Feller said it's *Little Pec's.* It can't be, we thought, as the fish had been out a few weeks previously at 33 pounds. When Gary lifted the fish from the water we could confirm that it was, and definitely up in weight, looking absolutely gorgeous at 38lb 12oz. We wondered if we had made the right choice moving swims. Mind you, poor old Paul Selman had fished *The Point* the week before taking several fish, only to see fish moving this week at the other end of the lake. Deciding to fish there instead of *The Point,* which he had come early to make sure of getting, he blanked. Still, such is life, and Gary deserved his prize. As is the custom on Harefield the captor of a big fish has to stand the rest of the lads a drink or three. It was just as well Gary had it and not Selman as he is so tight someone would have had to give him a permanent loan to buy the beers. By Wednesday night the rain had stopped and the weather was turning better. Thursday morning dawned sunny with a nice ripple towards the works. At 11.30 I'm in again with a nice 21lb 8oz common. That night Terry, Ian, Bevo and myself sat around till late, guzzling cans of beer. At 3am I was woken by an absolute belter of a take. On the strike the rod hooped over and I was forced to back-wind straight away at 130 yards-plus - this was obviously one big mother. In the dark it was hard to tell how far the fish had gone but I was worried it might reach an island. Putting my hand over the spool I hung on for all I was worth hoping to turn the unseen monster. The fish kited left and up the lake only to jam solid behind a bar. There was a really fierce bar which I knew was somewhere in the direction the fish had gone, and having only 20 foot leaders on to get the range required and only eight pound main line, I was somewhat worried. The fish wouldn't budge, so the only thing to do was put the rod back in the rest and wait for it to move off. After a cup of tea and chain smoking a few fags, line started to trickle back off the spool. Picking up the rod and leaning into the fish, it was kiting left and straight for Terry's lines. A big fish on a long line is a devil's own job to control, or at least that was my excuse, as it ploughed through all three of Terry's lines (three should have been two but it was still dark) cutting all three straight off. No Legs was well chuffed. After 15 minutes of ploughing up and down the deep margins, eventually she rolled on the surface ready for netting. In the net it was obviously a right chunk, and under the torchlight we realised it was *Little Pecs*, the same fish as Gary's on the Monday. She went 37lb 8oz. Yes! A personal best. Into the sack and run up to John Bevan two swims up to inform him of the good news, shaking the old git awake. "John, John, I have a personal best!" His reply was charming I thought, as I wandered back to Terry who had the tea brewed to celebrate. "Bevo is in a good mood" I informed him, "miserable old bar steward."

At 8am Dougal wandered up from his swim, "what you had then?" When I told him he slapped me on the back "nice one son." After getting my breath back from his friendly pat we decided to go and wake up the old git. John woke up still humpy. On asking him what was up, he informed us that when I woke him with the news, he also had a personal best of a different kind, his first hard-on for three years. Sorry John, I didn't know, it must be sad when you get old and senile! Photos done, fish back and all up the cafe, mushrooms for me and a big silly grin on my mush for the rest of the day. After the cafe a quick trip to Harefield Tackle to replace Terry's line and stop him moaning, plus more expense for the ale to cheer John up. I bought all his drink and had to arrange a bank loan to pay for it. On our return to the lake I helped Terry renew all his line, then retired to bed in a drunken stupor to sleep off the effects of a good lunch-time session. An hour or so later I heard the warning blast of a hooter fitted to the gravel workings tug, a signal they give to warn they are towing a barge to dump rubbish up the other end of the pit. If you hold your rods high they go under the line and all is OK. Shouting at Terry - no response, he was dead to the world. He only woke when he got two screaming takes caused by tons of tug and barge. By the time he got to his rods both new lines were cut at the rods. I didn't laugh much at his continued misfortune. Terry didn't bother to retackle, going back to bed to sleep it off and be fit for an early off in the morning for a day of raw sex. Saves my poor little dog the pain - so he was happy.

Terry and John went home on the Sunday morning. As conditions were ideal and fish were showing in front of me, I decided to fish on till Monday. Around midday another friend, Nigel, moved into Terry's swim and we sat around drinking tea watching fish after fish lump out over the baits. Surely it was only a matter of time? Around 4pm a take occurred on my left rod. Just single blips and the spool clicking slowly away. On striking it felt like another lump. A very heavy fish, it just kited left, the fish in total control, as I followed it up, gaining line, it came towards the bank past Nigel's rods. Holding the rod high over a small tree it came in between two swims under a steep bank, under stinging nettles and brambles of about chest height, and laid on the surface about ten feet from the bank. A great beast of a common well over 35 pounds, it certainly looked bigger than *Little Pecs* - what a situation to be in. Did poor old Nigel risk ploughing through brambles and nettles and jumping into some 20 feet of water to take a chance of netting the beast. If anything went wrong he would either spook it or get caught up in the line. "What do you want me to do?" he asked. "It must be well hooked," I replied "I will lead it to the next swim and you can net it comfortably with no risks." What a bad decision on my part. As I started to apply pressure to lead it to the swim, the sodding hook pulled. We were left with the awesome sight of one big mother of

a common giving a final wave of his big tail and sinking back to the
depths out of view. Poor old Nigel, he didn't know what to say and
just shook his head. Me, I threw the rod up a tree and said "oh dear
me" or something along those lines, packed up all my gear and went
home to recover.

On reflection you put things in perspective, I had certainly caught
a big common earlier which I hadn't deserved so you win some and
lose some. I only wish I had won *this* one, I would have swapped
that one fish for all the others. There had always been rumours of
a massive uncaught common in Harefield, but I had always
dispelled the rumours as every lake holds a big uncaught common.
If Nigel hadn't been there I wouldn't have told anyone. One day,
hopefully someone will land this beast and I will be the first to
congratulate them, it will certainly open some people's eyes.

I was to miss the next rota, taking the family for a week's holiday
in Holland to coincide with my good Dutch friend and fellow carp
angler Marco Spiering's wedding. I promised under threat of
castration from *'er indoors* not to take my fishing rods or talk about
fishing for a week. Not easy when you're at a wedding with Dutch
carp anglers, whose secret waters you could discover while they
were under the influence of Dutch lager. The rota I missed
apparently blew a hurricane and even Terry couldn't reach the area,
I would have stood no chance, so I missed nothing.

The following week's weather forecast was for high winds with
no signs of letting up. We planned, if it was the same on Monday,
to move back to *The Point,* where the wind would be behind us
instead of in our faces, plus a nice easy 70 yard cast. I was going to
stay for three weeks which meant a week in the middle of rota to
gain my missing week back. I was also being put under pressure to
keep catching as I was now on eight thirties, and with September
being a good month, everyone was willing me to beat Andy Little's
record of 12 thirties in a season. I must admit the idea sounded
good, but four more thirties was a lot to ask. I had already had a
lifetime's fish squeezed into the one season. Still my confidence was
sky-high, and all the lads on the rota I was fishing were behind me
willing me to do it and give their lake the record. What a smashing
load of lads they were.

Back at the lake and onto *The Point* for the next session, it felt
I had been away for ages, not just three weeks. No fish showed all
week, the only excitement being on the Saturday when we had a

monster barbecue for about ten of us, good company, good food and untold Dutch Grolsch supplied from my trip to Holland. We started early afternoon and by early evening, with us all full up and on the way to another hangover, Terry suddenly got a take. Stumbling to his rods and striking he announced to his audience '*monster on*'. With this statement the fish proceeded to chug off behind the small island between his and my swim. Without any hesitation off came all Terry's kit, and handing the rod to Nick 'the Tree Feller' Roberts he proceeded to swim out and free the unseen monster. Arriving at the island he freed the fish, too pissed to notice it's size (still I suppose when you have 18 inch legs, the alcohol gets to you quicker). Nick started to wind the monster back, "it didn't feel like a carp," announced Nick, getting the fish back before No Legs to reveal a tench of at least three pounds. Poor little Tel took some stick off the lads, and we got some good photos of Terry naked for my slide shows. Not a pretty sight as he has an upper body resembling a Sumo wrestler and legs the length of normal blokes' ankles. After the food and drink had run out we decided to carry on over the pub where Nick Roberts put on an absolutely awesome display of self indulgence. Having to be held up by two of us (one each side) while Skinhead Lee poured more Fosters down his throat. What a player! Poor old Nick woke up the next morning, after coming out the back of his bivvy in the middle of the night, in the brambles behind his swim. That was the first blank week of the season and things were looking grim.

On Monday the rotas changed and I had *The Point* to myself. Steve Allcott was fishing farther down the lake in *Someone's Coming* and called me down in the morning to show me loads of fish coming through a gap in the island towards me. There were incredible numbers of fish passing through so I hastily returned to my rods. All that day fish were crashing and rolling over my baits but still no action. The following morning was the same. I had plenty of fish, but with no action. I wound in and went to the other end of the lake where my old friend Pete 'the Burglar' Jones was fishing. We discussed the problem of plenty of fish showing with no action, and Pete showed me a new rig he was trying which had resulted in him having a couple of good fish the previous trip. I was amazed it worked as it consisted of approximately six inches of 30 pound Amnesia hooklink connected to the swivel by a small loop to give it movement. Apparently when a fish picks it up they can't reject the hookbait. I couldn't see why it worked as it went against all my beliefs of fish behaviour towards rigs. Still, if it worked for Pete, it was worth a try. So after poncing a spool of the Amnesia off him I trotted back to my swim to give it a bash. Within half an hour of casting out I had a 19lb 8oz mirror, so with confidence in this 'stiff' rig I put it on the other rod as well. An hour later I lost another fish due to a hook pull. Still, at least things were happening after ten days without a fish. The next day I went on to take a double and two twenties, one being the fully-scaled one side/common the other, up in weight at 22lb 4oz. The next day no fish showed and I had no action. The following morning produced another fish at twenty-plus, so the rig was certainly working. No more fish came that week.

Terry arrived on the Monday for another week so I showed him Pete's new rig to try. That day no fish showed in front of us but we baited heavily that night in the hope of them moving in. The following day, coming from our left, big fish started showing past the baited area, and they continued to show down to the bottom corner of the lake and worked their way up the bottom bank end back up towards us, showing all the time like porpoises until they were over the bait. A lot of the big fish in Harefield swim around together and are called the A-Team. Well the A-Team were certainly here and in numbers.

Dougal had just turned up for his morning tea and chat before doing his day's work. On seeing all the fish he said "you're going to have them today." As he said it Terry saw a big fish roll over my left hand rod and said "it looks like the fully-scaled." Just as the kettle boiled a single bleep occurred on my left rod. Looking at the rod top, I noticed it pull over slightly and as I struck Dougal said: "Bream." Some bream this one, the water exploded over the bar and a lump swam off to my right. After some ten minutes the fish had come into the bay on my right about 30 yards out and over rolled this big scaly fish. "The fully-scaled," I said, and the old legs went to jelly. Dougal said that it wasn't and to pull myself together and get it in. Thinking it wasn't I calmed down, the fully-scaled was last out at 34 pounds and was a fish I really wanted to catch. Then I heard Terry say to Dougal "it *is* the fully-scaled isn't it?" "Yes," said Dougal "but don't tell him, he will only panic and muck it up." Hearing this, I got into my usual state of mind which consists of slagging off whoever has the landing net. Poor old Terry had suffered this abuse all season and was in stitches to hear someone else on the receiving end. It normally goes something like this. As the fish shows some ten yards out in deep water, which would be over anybody's head I start. "Go on. Get in. Get out there. Don't 'muck' about. Net it. Get in." Terry was used to this but Dougal wasn't: "Shut your gob before I knock you out," came his reply. Terry by now lapping it up and winding me up saying that Dougal should have guessed that I was in my normal panic-mode as the fish approached the net. We could see it was the big fully-scaled in all his autumn colours, looking really grand. We could then see the half-straightened hook just hanging on a bit of rubbery flesh, just nicked in his bottom lip. As he came over the net Dougal paid me back for all the abuse. He lowered the net. Just as the fish was swimming back out Dougal scooped it back up, turned round and said "had you worried there!"

Most of the lads of the rota came round to see the fish and congratulate me. At 36lb 12oz he was at his biggest ever weight, what a fish... I was over the moon. Just to add pressure they were all saying that there were only three more to go (for the record). As the fish were there in numbers and Harefield goes from hard to near impossible after the first heavy frosts, we decided to skip the celebrations and fish on. I readily agreed to this as buying the lads drinks after each result was becoming an expensive pastime. Because of the amount of time I was fishing, neglecting my business, my resources were at an all time low. Later that afternoon I lost another lump near the net which looked like *Black Spot*, which I had in the video at 33. The hook pulled and I launched my rod after it, much to Terry's amusement, as I had to go in for it after I had calmed down. The next day I had to go to work to keep my workforce in jobs. Leaving at 7am was extremely hard as the A-Team were still in residence and leaping out waving their pecs at me. I couldn't get out of my appointments that day so with regret wound in ready to go. Just before I left, my mate Matt 'the Male Model' Skinner arrived. He had only joined the lake that season and had done very well for his first season, landing several twenty-plus fish. He asked me if he could borrow my long-range rods to fish from the bottom bank to cast up towards the fish showing in front of my swim. So, lending him the rods and telling Terry to get a bait into my swim, I bid my farewells and rushed off to work knowing I couldn't get back till late that evening.

Dougal and Ben were doing a survey on a lake near my house that day and arranged to meet me at home for lunch at 1pm. When I arrived home at lunch-time Dougal said: "Guess what, Terry's had a lump, *Round-Tail* at 36lb 6oz." I was really chuffed, if anyone deserved a big fish he did. He had fished his little legs off and finally got his reward. I rushed round for the rest of the day knowing Terry would be in the pub that night and wanting to celebrate with him. I finally got back to Harefield at ten that night, straight into the pub, all the lads were there and well pissed. On congratulating Terry it turned out to be a double celebration as Matt had caught *Maurice the Mirror*, his first thirty at 30lb 6oz. At closing time I was the only sober one to look after a gaggle of carp idiots. Normally I am one of them. It is only when you are sober you notice what prats you look and sound. Covered in fish slime, unwashed and unshaven, it's amazing you can't pull the lovely young crumpet in the pub when you think you look and sound so good. I ran a drunk Dougal home with an even drunker Terry sitting in the car with us. After hearing Terry relate his capture to Dougal's poor wife, plus some other crude comments which luckily for Terry, Dougal took the right way. I dragged Terry away (much to the long suffering Christine's relief). Imagine poor Christine's life. Every time they go out in the Colne Valley all she ever hears are carp idiots and tales of monsters caught and lost.

Back at the lake Terry was too pissed to fish, so I made him loads of coffee. All I really wanted was to go to bed but I had to hear him relate the tale of how the fish took off, it's exact route around the swim, in the bay, out the bay, seven times under the rod tip. I was well pleased for him but on the tenth repeat I pretended to be asleep. For the next two hours Terry kept waking me up, he had one of those miner-type lamps on his head and kept turning it on and shining it in my face to relate the story again. What a star! He eventually passed out at around 3am, leaving me to get some well earned-kip. The following day the A-Team were still there. Around lunch-time Bob Baker the boilie maker turned up with a fresh supply of bait for me. We were just sitting down with a cup of tea when off went the right hand rod. After a short scrap, into the net came a fish I had caught two years ago at 27, *Bite Mark*. This time going 30lb 8oz, me informing Bob I caught it especially for him so he could see his bait work.

Things were going extremely well - only two to go. That night we had the first hard frost, hard times were just around the corner. The next day Terry was going home so he packed up and another mate, Hampshire Chris, moved into his swim. Chris is my hero, having been around for many years. One of the unknown men of big carp fishing and one of the few people I know to have caught a twenty-plus fish on spuds. I was looking forward to a couple of days of good company swapping yarns. Half an hour later the right rod fished in deeper water on a pop-up rattled off, and after a mental scrap, over the net came another fish from two years ago, *Stripes* which I caught at 27lb 12oz. Rob had it earlier in the video at 29-plus so with fingers crossed it went onto the scales. It certainly looked thirty, but being an exceptionally long old warrior of the original stock fish you couldn't really tell. No worries, he did me proud at bang on 31 pounds. All the lads came round for photos and Terry reappeared, he had been gossiping at the other end when news reached him. His tale sounded better. He was driving home on the M25 when the screen over the road lit up 'Gillham has another one', so he turned round and came back. After returning the grand old fish the lads decided to throw me in for being greedy. Regaining the bank, I was just down to my skids getting changed when off went the other rod. Whilst playing the fish I had to put up with all the lads mucking about and trying to remove my kacks. Christ I was freezing, so I tried to rush the fish in, at 16lb 8oz it was to be the last fish for me for a while.

That night we had really hard frosts and in the morning I watched the A-Team leave the way they had arrived. As they reached the bottom corner another mate of mine, Brian Ingram, picked one off at 30-plus, his first thirty. He was so chuffed he came round and kissed me. All these foreigners are tarts, he returned to Birmingham a happy chappie. Why they don't eat Tunes is beyond me, it cured Malcolm's blocked nose so it should work on them. After the last week's action I went home for Sunday night, risked divorce, and returned for another three-week trip. Not a fish came out from anywhere on the lake. Hard times had arrived and I still had one fish to go to equal Andy's record. After three more weeks with no signs of fish anywhere I was turning into a robot. The most exciting part of the day was changing the bait. Boy was I glad to pack up at the end of that trip. By then it was November, and as there are no rotas on Harefield after November, I planned to fish four nights a week until the last three weeks of the season. Then I would do a final three week trip as the lake normally fishes well at the end of the season.

On the next four day trip I lost a fish from the other end of the lake due to a hook-pull. This was the only take on the lake for four weeks, so while it wasn't fishing I decided to decorate the front room (to get some much needed brownie points from 'er indoors). Normally in my house I pay a decorator to do this chore, but as money was at an all time low this was out of the question. After a few days working up the enthusiasm, just up to my knees in crap, Rob phoned up. Clarkie's just had *Little Pec's* at 39 plus another thirty and lost a couple. Just my luck - the fish decided to go on a munch. As I was rushing through the poxy job, Dougal phoned the next day to say that Clarkie's had another upper twenty and Gaylord's had a thirty and a 28. This was too much for me, down the pub that night I found a skint painter and talked him into finishing my front room for a pittance and the promise of a cheap scaffold next time he wanted one.

Back to the lake Clarkie's swim is empty, but I don't know where he had them coming from. Knowing he is a mega-caster didn't help, so I set up in the next swim knowing he was turning up later that day. I thought I could watch where he casts and suss it for my next trip. Later that morning up rolled Martin 'superstar' Clarke, a legend in his own lunch-time. Martin is a very capable angler, and he proceeded to cast into the horizon. Christ I thought if that's where they are I'd better get a helicopter to reach them. Within an hour Clarkie was away and I netted *Maurice the Mirror* for him, at just over thirty. The next few weeks were spent in this area to no avail, the fish had gone off as quickly as they came on. With Christmas approaching I was to be out of the game for three weeks. We always take our family holiday over Christmas, being the only time we can shut the business down and get away. To be honest I was looking forward to the break. Having done over a thousand hours fishing for one lost fish, I needed to recharge my batteries.

Returning home in the New Year Dougal phoned with two lots of bad news. The lake was frozen over but worse *The Orange* fish was found ill just before Christmas swimming aimlessly around on the surface. Dougal netted it out but nothing could be done for the poor old fish so they released him to take his chance. Shortly afterwards the lake froze over again so we could only hope. The second week of January Dougal phoned again to say that the lake was thawing, so next day I went back up there. That morning *The Orange* fish washed up dead, it was like losing a friend. The fish I had joined to catch and which meant so many things to me. The making of many good friends and the capture of all my fine fish were down to the pursuit of this fine old fish. So long old friend, may you swim forever in that big carp world in the sky.

At the end of the summer Miles Boyer died after a very brief, unexpected illness, leaving the power base at Boyer Leisure in turmoil. Ben had carried on till the end of the year but the knives were out for him and he went. Dougal stayed on but a new team were at the top. Here we go again I thought. Sure enough I was back on the lake for the last three weeks of the season, one week into my final trip of the year with a 22lb 8oz mirror under my belt, and looking good for that desperately needed last fish, when down comes Dougal looking glum. "Do you want the good news or the bad news?" He asked. "Give me the bad news first," I said. "The management don't want you here any more," he said. "Christ, what's the good news," I asked. "Well," he said "you can stay until the end of the season as they want you to achieve the record for their advertising." "They can stuff it" I told Dougal, "it doesn't mean that much to me," so I packed away all my gear and left. The end of an era for me. Still at least this time I nearly got a full season out of it and caught all the fish I wanted. At least this time I could leave satisfied without a bitter taste in my mouth. Plus I could have a close season to myself instead of working for free on their lakes and supplying and fitting scaffolds for them at a loss to my own pocket.

Len Gurd had asked me to be a bailiff on the excellent Linear Fisheries for next season, so I phoned him and accepted, he was well chuffed and asked me to bailiff his Elstow syndicate. This fishery has around 18 thirty-plus fish so it was a good move for me. I finished the last week on Linear's new lake at Stanton Harcourt in Oxfordshire, catching a few good doubles which wasn't bad considering they hadn't been fished for all winter. The last two days I was to fish Savay on my days-only season ticket. I wanted to buy all the lads a drink and say farewell.

So the season ended and what a season! Eleven thirties, all different fish; 24 twenties and 13 doubles. That weekend Boyer's offered me a syndicate place so I paid my deposit, but my heart wasn't in it and when in the close season I was offered a place on the Leisure Sport Horton Lake I asked for my deposit back and

decided that my love affair with Harefield was finally over.

This season has brought me back to reality, struggling to learn about new waters. Business is booming so I've had only 15 nights fishing up to now (October) but new places and new faces - I can't wait for next season. Hopefully I will sneak a few out and as my business gets back on its feet I will get more time off next season. The Horton syndicate is magic, great crowd of blokes and extremely well run. I am slowly falling in love with the place. There are also some lovely fish to catch in Elstow so roll on the good times.

I would like to end with a big thank you to all the lads who were on Harefield last season especially Rota Two for all their support and encouragement and putting up with me living there. Cheers lads. Also thanks to Dougal and Ben, Richworth Baits and Kent Particles. Harry Haskell and Lee Jackson for help with rigs. Mark Dean at A1 Photos for handling all my pictures, and last of all Tubby Thompson for being an *Ace Ghillie.*

Chapter 5

ADVANCED TERMINAL RIGS III

I have seen no major breakthroughs in rig design, with only a couple of exceptions, over the last few years. The bent hook rig as described in *Fox Pool* came under much criticism when its use became widespread on the carp waters around England.

What people didn't seem to realise was that this rig was designed for a specific purpose, it was designed to fish a water with very few fish in it, most of them very large, fish that were well clued up with around 40 years of experience on all of the terminal rigs that were current at the time. The problem came when people began to use it on small-fish waters, where fish of 10 to 15 pounds were caught easily because it was a very effective rig. The trouble was that it tended to double-hook or tear the fish's mouths. These smaller fish would rush along the margins opening and closing the bent hook, making it more like a can opener and tearing the fishes' mouths. There were of course many alternatives which appeared after this problem was noted. People used lead wire pushed into silicon tube and over the shanks of ordinary hooks, bending the lead wire into the shape of a bent hook. As soon as the fish was hooked, the lead wire would straighten out giving you a normal hook hold. I personally have not used the bent hook rig since I fished Fox Pool. I have never found it necessary to use it on any other of the waters that I have been fishing, even waters such as Yateley. I have tended, over the last couple of years, to keep my rigs as simple as possible and I must admit to being horrified at some of the rigs and combinations of tackle that I've seen published in magazines, books and in videos.

Only recently, somebody sent me a rig through the post which comprised of four Berkeley swivels, three beads, a hook and various other rings and bits and pieces. I should imagine that the total cost of this rig was in the region of four pounds. God knows where this fellow was fishing because the waters that I'm fishing at the moment, where you have to cast very close to snags and fish in thick weedbeds, means that of course you do lose rigs from time to time and if you are losing them at four pounds a go it wouldn't be long before you couldn't afford to go fishing at all.

We seem to have strayed a little bit from where rig design originated. The simplest rig of all is of course, a freelined bait with just a hook tied onto the line, but we know that we need a lead to enable us to cast this out into the lake. So where do we go from here? A hook at one end of the rig and a swivel at the other and then perhaps something which either makes the fish pick up the bait and bolt, or prevents the hook from being ejected. I'm certain that we don't need these complicated set-ups that some people are advocating at the moment.

Rigs have always been of great interest to me and I spend many hours on the bank and during the close season playing about, tying up different rigs. I must admit to getting a few strange looks from my wife sometimes as I'm trying to suck these rigs up off the bottom of the bath using a plastic tube with my head under the water. This must seem very strange to anyone that doesn't go carp fishing.

So what has happened in rig design since *Fox Pool* was written? Well, the next most popular rig to appear on the scene was the barbaric, if not very effective, big hook rig. I never found it necessary to use these, but I knew many people that did and had good results on them. The thought of a two or three 'O' hook impaled through the bottom jaw of a carp meant that my conscience would never allow me to use such a thing. In the right hands of course and with a suitable pair of tin snips so that the hook can be cut, this rig can be used safely. In the wrong hands it could be a very dangerous weapon indeed.

When designing rigs, two important factors must be considered: 1) that it will hook a fish should the fish pick the bait up, this of course is obvious; and 2) that it won't tangle in casting or pulling back. I think this is often ignored by some people who sit down with pen and paper and draw lots of different rigs that look very nice but always end up in a ball when you try and reel them in.

The two types of rigs that I have seen experimented with on various lakes around the country by other people are the stiff link rigs, which I will go into in more detail later on in this piece, and rigs which involve small Drennan rings with the bait sliding either on the line, on the shank of the hook, or on some other extraneous piece of tackle. This anti-ejection principle by using the Drennan ring was first used by me over ten years ago, with the rotating hair rig and of course the excellent 'D' rig.

The two rigs that I use for 75 per cent of my fishing have both been widely publicised. I will mention them again briefly for those of you who are perhaps a bit new to carp fishing. The swimmer rig is the one I normally use for pop-up fishing and for bottom bait fishing, which is something I seem to be practising more and more these days. I just use a size four Drennan Boilie hook, taken back

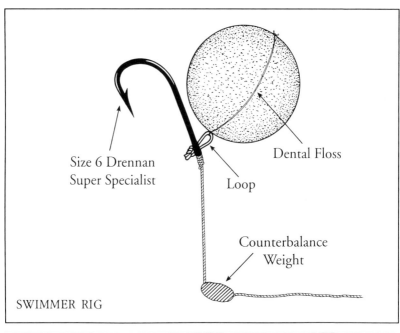

Size 6 Drennan
Super Specialist

Dental Floss

Loop

Counterbalance
Weight

SWIMMER RIG

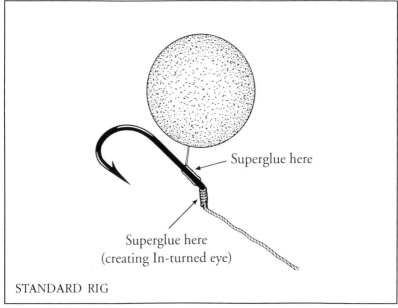

Superglue here

Superglue here
(creating In-turned eye)

STANDARD RIG

through the eye with a dab of superglue on the knot so that you can angle the knot, making it an in-turned eye, and another dab just on the hair as it comes through the eye, attaching it to the shank, thus creating a tangle-free set-up. These are both very simple rigs and ones that I have found effective on almost every water I've fished.

In particular the swimmer rig has caught literally on every lake I've fished over the last eight years. You can find a diagram of both of these rigs within this chapter for those of you who have not used these rigs before, but I shan't go into any more detail on their use because, as I've said, they've already been widely publicised and I've written about both before.

The Weighted Drop Hook

So let's look at what's new... One rig that I feel has great potential, although I haven't finished perfecting it yet, is a rig that I developed on the Yateley Pad Lake: the weighted drop hook. This rig is different from most conventional set-ups in that the hair, instead of pointing towards the bait, points back up the main line and the counterbalance weight for the pop-up instead of being on the main line is on the hook. Therefore, this means that the bait and weight

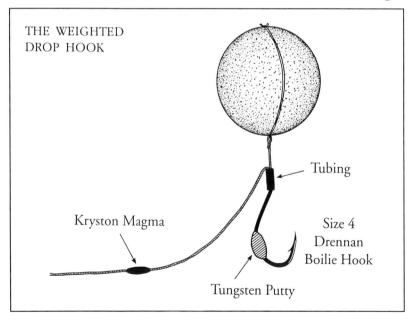

THE WEIGHTED
DROP HOOK

Tubing

Kryston Magma

Size 4
Drennan
Boilie Hook

Tungsten Putty

have changed places. The theory behind this rig is that the bend of the hook sits nicely on the lakebed and the pop-up of course rises above this.

Should the fish suck the large light boilie into its mouth, the hook could then swirl around inside the mouth cavity, but because the hook is weighted it tends to drop onto the floor of the mouth and should the fish try to eject the bait, the hook acts as a claw, clawing its way along the bottom of the mouth as the fish tries to blow the hook out. The point usually goes in somewhere along the floor of the mouth or in the bottom lip.

The first weekend that Steve Newman and I tried this rig on the Yateley Pad Lake, we had caught nothing for the previous three days, and the first day that we used it we caught 17 tench, a pike and a roach. This left us in no doubt that something about this rig was right. I must admit that after using it that winter and the following close season on Farlows, taking quite a few carp on it, I haven't really used it since. But I was talking to some of the lads from Summit Tackle down in Kent and they'd used it on the Railway Lake and on the Road Lake at Johnson's and had caught quite a few of the big fish using this rig. I think something like five or six fish over twenty in a couple of days.

Whether they've actually developed this rig any further than my original concept I'm not sure, I did show it in the *Harefield Haulin'* video and for those of you that have seen it, you must admit that it looks very effective as it sits on the bottom. There is obviously much room for improvement in this rig and it does have a tendency to tangle, probably one cast in 50, but that may be the one cast when the big fish in your water comes along and I just cannot live with that.

Stiff Hooklinks
Now let's have a look at the stiff hooklink rigs. Much has been written about them, especially in the *Big Carp* Rotary Letter, with the various contributors putting their opinions as to the effectiveness of this rig. Rod Hutchinson said in his piece that it was no different to that which he'd always used, since he always uses 11 pound Sylcast, the hooklink material is stiff in itself. But there is more to the stiff hooklink rig than just a stiff piece of nylon. The method of attaching the hook and the swivel by means of a small loop means that the hook and swivel have totally free movements from the hooklink. It

creates a hinge effect, allowing the stiff hooklink material to be lifted freely should the fish suck the bait from the bottom. This means that the normal stiff hooklink does not have to bend up from the swivel as the fish sucks, which of course would give the bait an unnatural movement, a restrictive movement due to the bending of the line. There are many different opinions about this type of rig. I was talking to Lee Jackson the other day and he'd used it on some waters that he was fishing and said that it was the best fish deterrent that he'd ever used. He had watched fish mouthing and sucking at baits in the shallow water and said that they were put off every time by this hooklink. So maybe it's not the stiffness which is the effective thing. The original thought behind the rig was that the fish could suck the bait into the mouth but because the hooklink was now rigid, the hooklink being made out of 25 pound line or thick Amnesia, it created the effect that the bait was attached to a stick of stiff material and instead of your normal flexible link, which can be swirled round inside the mouth and blown out easily, this stiff link could not bend back and double up on itself and be blown out of the mouth quite so easily. If the hook is then hinged, using this small loop, it can then catch on the mouth as they try to rid

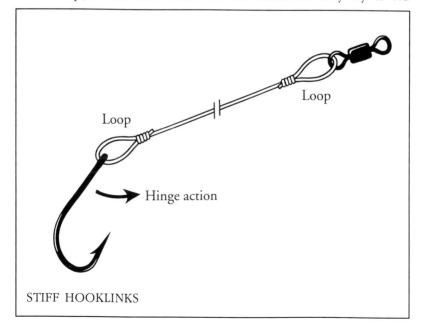

Loop

Loop

Hinge action

STIFF HOOKLINKS

themselves of this stiff line pushing in towards the throat area.

If Lee is right in what he says about the ineffectiveness of this rig, perhaps there's another reason why this rig was so productive. One other train of thought is the fact that the stiff hooklink keeps the bait away from the lead completely whereas with a normal flexible hooklink, the tackle could be in a heap around the lead, thus enabling the fish to suck the bait up on a very slack line, swirl it round sucking and blowing and blow the whole lot out easily without ever feeling the lead. With a stiff link, the bait is always at its maximum distance away from the lead or fairly near to that anyway, which means that when the fish picks the bait up it has only got to move the bait a small distance for the hook to become an effective pricking tool. You are effectively fishing the equivalent of a very, very short flexible hooklink, which we know has been very effective in the past.

I did try this rig when I became aware of it, I believe that it was 'invented', for want of a better word, in the north of England somewhere and the people that used it up on their lakes had outstanding results, though I personally have come to no positive conclusion about the effectiveness of this rig. Fishing one flexible and one stiff, side by side, I did not seem to have any different results although I know that Steve Briggs has used the rig over the last few years and done exceptionally well on it.

The rig that Steve has been using, and I'm sure he won't mind me mentioning this is actually a combination of stiff and flexible. The top eight inches at the swivel end of the hooklink is made of stiff 20 pound Amnesia. The bottom two or three inches is made of ordinary Kryston flexible link, the two being joined together with a small Drennan ring. This Drennan ring can then be used to mould the tungsten putty around for your pop-up weight, this also has the added advantage of holding the putty in a positive position. The thought behind this rig is that the stiff section of the hooklink keeps the bait away from the lead and also will act as an anti-eject section whereas the flexible two or three inches which is the distance that the pop-up is fished off the bottom can then swirl around and catch inside the fish's mouth. This seems to be one of the best combinations of flexible hooklink rig design that I have seen in use and I know that Steve uses it for 90 per cent of his fishing.

One further development that Ginger Steve brought into effect down at Farlows a couple of close seasons ago was a three-part rig

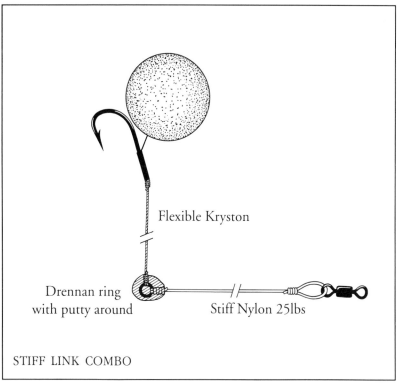

Flexible Kryston

Drennan ring
with putty around   Stiff Nylon 25lbs

STIFF LINK COMBO

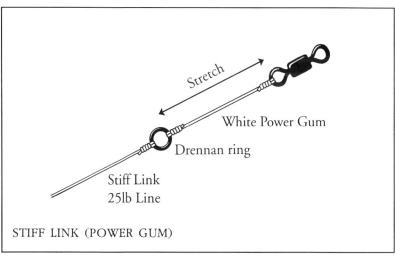

Stretch

White Power Gum

Drennan ring

Stiff Link
25lb Line

STIFF LINK (POWER GUM)

comprising stiff hooklink material as the middle section, flexible hooklink material for the last couple of inches and a two inch section of strong powergum, the clear not the red. This clear powergum breaks at about 20 pounds and is used in combination with a very heavy lead. The thought behind this method of fishing is that when the fish picks the bait up, should it prick itself it pulls against the elastic part of the hooklink. It pulls against the lead, stretching the powergum and this in turn has the effect of pushing the hook in at a much stronger rate.

You have only got to try this rig out on the kitchen table and you will see that, if you use an ordinary stiff hooklink, put the hook point onto your finger and drag the lead along, there is no give at all in the hooklink and the lead is at its maximum weight but the point of the hook never seems to actually penetrate the skin, instead of that the lead just slides along the table. When you incorporate this elasticity at the swivel end of the hooklink, the elastic stretches until it reaches the point that the lead begins to move but this spring effect has the action of pushing the point of the hook in.

I have personally only used this rig on a couple of occasions so cannot really comment on its effectiveness but I can see the thought behind it and I am sure that there is much room for improvement in this type of rig design. Of course this has to be the next step in rig design. We've had freelining, then we had bolt rigs and now of course, the fish speed off with the bait once they've felt the heavy weight or the large hook. The obvious next step is a rig which actually drives the hook in, out in the lake. This way the fish could never pick the bait up and get away with it. This is slightly unethical and I think I'd be very careful about what type of rig could be designed for this.

I remember many years ago hearing Kevin Maddocks talk about a rig that he and Lenny Middleton had used up at Waveney Valley in the late seventies, which comprised of a small brass tube containing a spring or elastic which was held in a trigger. When the bait was picked up and the hook point pressed against the skin, the trigger was released thus taking the tension out of the spring which was held inside the brass tube and pushed the hook point into the fish. They too felt that this rig was unethical and gave up with it after a short period of time, but is it really any more unethical than fishing a four or five ounce lump of lead attached to three inches of hooklink? A few years ago the fish had no chance of getting away with this type of rig. Of course, these days as we know, they are a little bit more clued up and do seem to be getting away with it, or not picking it up at all.

I personally am not convinced that this stiff hooklink method is any better than a flexible one although I do see possibilities and of course, I am leaving myself wide open to criticism saying that I don't find it any more effective, because in the next six months something could come along which proves me entirely wrong. But I always speak as I find at the time and, at the moment, the rigs that I have seen do not seem to be any more effective than the straightforward rigs I've been using.

Many of the little edges that top carp anglers had to themselves five or six years ago are now widely known by fishermen country-wide and there seems very little difference between many of the anglers fishing on the lakes today in terms of rigs, baits and tackle. Of course the only thing which is different is the anglers' fishing ability and there will always be those who have excellent water craft, casting capabilities and fish-finding methods who will out-score the anglers fishing with identical baits, rigs and tackle. Those are the things which can't be bought in shops.

Carp fishing is generally a lot more equal for anglers these days, there are far more people with a lot of time to go fishing and there are far more anglers on waters which were kept secret or exclusive ten years ago. Carp fishing is out in the open and most anglers can get on the majority of big fish waters in the country, either by joining a waiting list for a syndicate or just by buying a club ticket for waters such as Yateley, Wraysbury etc.

False Stringer

So where does that leave us now? It seems as though no one has an advantage over anyone else but of course there will always be thinking anglers who are trying to fool the fish by various methods. It was Albert Romp who, a few years ago, found a method which accounted for several large fish for him from Savay Lake - it was a false stringer rig. A stringer as you all know has quite a few baits attached to the hook by PVA string, this enables you to have a few free offerings close to the hookbait and also if you are fishing at very long range, enables you to have some bait around the hook itself. Stringers have been used at Savay for many years and of course when you think about it the 20 anglers fishing stringers on the lake and casting five, six or ten times a day, each time they reeled in they left a small line of bait lying on the bottom with three or four boilies lying in a line. Perhaps we are giving the fish too much credit for their intelligence but Albert's theory was that fish began to find these small strings of baits lying on the bottom and ate them in total confidence because there was never a hook attached to them.

After the anglers had gone home, dotted around the swim were 20 or 30 of these small strings of bait just lying there in a line. When you think about it, if the carp has any intelligence at all, it must be able to tell the difference between just one bait and a line of baits lying on the bottom. So Albert's idea was to imitate this string of bait lying on the bottom but instead of it being attached to PVA, it was attached to his hair.

Albert fished a long hair and by hair, I don't necessarily mean a piece of hair or fine line, that's just the name that we give to a tied on section for putting on the baits. It can be the main hooklink material just pulled through the eye or a separate piece of material such as dental floss or nylon attached to the shank by means of a piece of tubing. So instead of Albert using one 18 or 20 millimetre

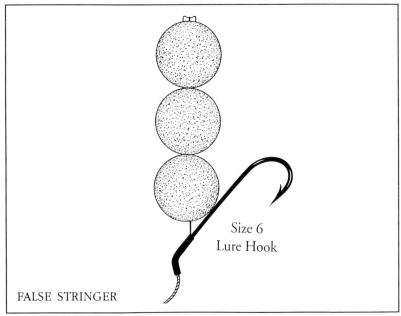

Size 6
Lure Hook

FALSE STRINGER

boilie, he left this section of hair longer and put three, four or five baits with a bait stop at the end, this was then cast out in the conventional manner. Now if the fish did feel confident picking up these long strings of bait, this is where they were going to come unstuck and Albert caught some very big fish using this method and it wasn't long before many anglers in the area were using it on waters such as Savay, Harefield and Harrow.

Whether it was actually the stringer principle that was catching the fish, I don't suppose we'll ever know. I remember years ago seeing the Greedy Pig rig publicised, which was basically a long string or group of baits. Carp being naturally greedy animals would always go for the larger group of baits anyway. I've noticed that when mixer fishing, if you get a few mixers which tend to congregate together, the fish always tend to home in on these, ignoring the single ones and sucking in with one great gulp the five or six mixers floating close to each other. So it may just be this idea which has been the carp's downfall at Savay. Albert got great mileage out of this type of rig. I used this rig at Harefield quite a few times and I've caught several fish on it but again I wouldn't rate it over just a normal stringer rig with a single pop-up.

Whisker Rigs

Now I did say at the start of this piece that there had been very few major developments in the last few years, that was with a couple of exceptions. The first being a weighted drop hook and secondly, the whisker rigs. Whisker rigs are a relatively new idea and became fashionable about two years ago when anglers such as Martin Locke and Steve Allcott caught some big fish using them. I know that Martin caught his two forties in the winter from an undisclosed gravel pit in south England, using the two whisker rig.

This rig is a little bit tricky to tie so I will go through step-by-step so that you can try it out.

First of all of course, you need a hook, the excellent new Owner Cutting Point Thick Wire Hooks are ideal for this, or Drennan Boilie Hooks used in size four or larger. You need a five millimetre length of 1.5 Kevin Nash rig tubing, semi-stiff and a three inch length of either 20 or 25 pound line or Amnesia. Taking your five millimetre length of Nash rig tubing, make a hole through the side of the tubing two-thirds of the way down and push your three inch length of nylon through the hole and out the other side, leaving an equal

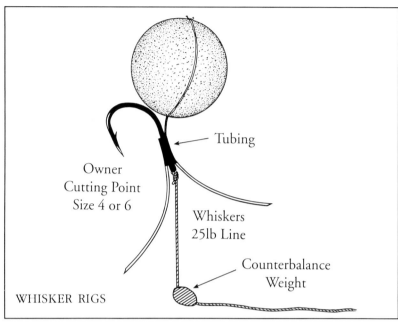

Tubing

Owner
Cutting Point
Size 4 or 6

Whiskers
25lb Line

Counterbalance
Weight

WHISKER RIGS

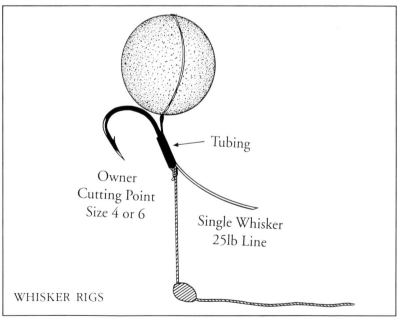

Tubing

Owner
Cutting Point
Size 4 or 6

Single Whisker
25lb Line

WHISKER RIGS

ROB MAYLIN'S TIP FOR THE TOP
"THE SLIDING WHISKER RIG"

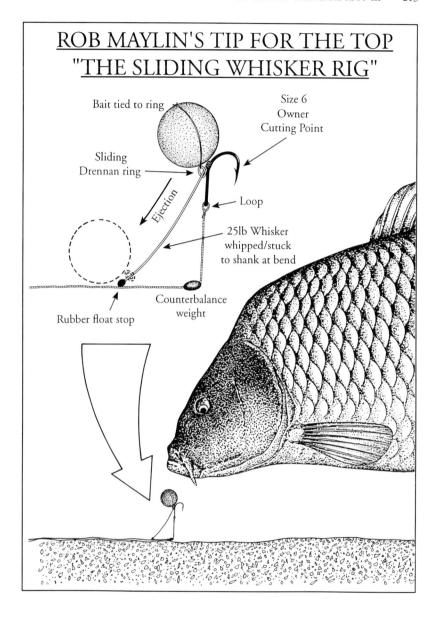

Bait tied to ring

Size 6
Owner
Cutting Point

Sliding
Drennan ring

Ejection

Loop

25lb Whisker
whipped/stuck
to shank at bend

Counterbalance
weight

Rubber float stop

portion of line each side of the tubing. Now slide this piece of Nash tubing over the point of the hook and down the shank, ensuring that the longer piece of tubing, the two-thirds, are at the eye end. This tubing is then forced over the eye protecting the knot, you now have a hook and on the shank of the hook is a piece of tubing which has a piece of 25 pound line running at right angles through the wall of the tubing and out the other side. Now take a small baiting needle or crochet hook and push this down the tubing, hook up the three inch length of thick nylon using the needle and pull it up in a loop through the tubing up the shank of the hook. This has the effect of angling the two ends of the line downwards, pointing down the hooklink and gives you a loop above the Kevin Nash rig tubing for you to tie your bait on to. This thick line can now be curved into a whisker. The counterbalance weight should be positioned on the main line at the same level as the end of the whiskers, then when the weight sits on the bottom of the lake, the two whiskers are like legs, either side of the weight touching the lakebed beside it.

This is not 100 per cent necessary but I have found it the best way to do it. Therefore if you started with a three inch length of thick line, you will be fishing your baits about one and a half inches off the bottom. Should you wish to fish your baits higher than this, you will need a slightly longer length of thick line. The pop-up then holds the hook above the whiskers, because the whiskers are angled, when the fish sucks the bait in, the whiskers are sucked into the mouth easily but once inside, they tend to open and make it very difficult for the hook to be ejected.

I realise that this all sounds very complicated but I would advise you to try this rig because it is probably the most effective rig since the bent hook rig was invented and I personally have used this rig to great effect and caught many fish, including quite small fish from Farlows, using the bait three inches off the bottom.

The only way that I can see this rig can be improved upon is a method of allowing the hook to tilt over once inside the mouth and I must admit that I haven't used this rig this season because I'm trying to keep my rigs simple where I'm fishing, and I haven't experimented fully with the rig to try and allow this tilting action to happen. The only way that I have used it with a tilting action is by using the stiff link method with a small loop attaching it to the eye of the hook. This, of course, allows the hook to tip over but I am

Hemp on
Kryston Bogey

Pop-up version
using cork ball insert

'BOGEY' RIG

still sure there is room for improvement, the single whisker version of this rig is also very effective and a lot less fiddly to tie. All you have to do with this rig is attach one piece of thick nylon to the shank of the hook, pointing back up the hooklink and curl that like a whisker. That too sits very nicely on the bottom although I have not found this method to be as effective with anti-ejection.

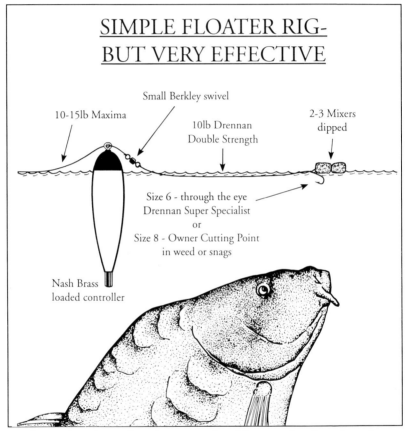

SIMPLE FLOATER RIG- BUT VERY EFFECTIVE

Small Berkley swivel

10-15lb Maxima

10lb Drennan Double Strength

2-3 Mixers dipped

Size 6 - through the eye Drennan Super Specialist
or
Size 8 - Owner Cutting Point in weed or snags

Nash Brass loaded controller

I hope that these rigs give you a few ideas to develop rigs of your own. The concept behind chapters like this in the books that I write is not that you should just go out and use exactly as I say, but to look at what I do and then sit down for yourselves and think 'how can I improve on that' and I am sure that sooner or later somebody looking at one of these rigs will come up with something which was as devastating as the hair rig when that first came into carp fishing.

Chapter 6

NELSON THE ONE-EYED CARP

This was to be my first summer on Harefield Lake. The lessons that I had learned the previous autumn and winter would serve me well and I intended to fish the whole year, although if the action slowed down towards winter, I intended to pull off and select another venue on which to spend the rest of the winter.

The previous winter on Harefield had been hard and I only took one fish after Christmas. I really didn't want to fish another winter like that. John Stent was still in charge of Boyer fishing and the system they had at that time was, one week before the start of the season all the anglers that were in the syndicate at the time would draw a swim, in the car park at Harefield, they then had one week to carry out plumbing, baiting and learning about their swim before the start of the season. The system of drawing a swim before the start of the season has advantages and disadvantages. The main advantage is, of course, that you know what swim you're going to be in, you don't have to be down there a week before the start of the season bivvying up. The main disadvantage is that you don't have the chance to choose a swim depending on weather conditions. When you draw the swim a week before, the wind may be hacking down to your end of the lake and conditions looking perfect. At the start of the season, all that could have changed, the weather might have gone colder and pushed the fish out of the shallows down into the deeper water, so it's a bit hit-and-miss.

Anyway, I turned up for the draw a week before the start of the season. Several mates were going to fish it at the start with me, including Dave Whibley. Steve Allcott was thinking about it although he'd just started getting into Wraysbury at the time and couldn't make his mind up whether to have opening week on Wraysbury or to come down to Harefield and have a laugh with the boys, Phil Harper, Paul Brooks, Peter Jones, Travolta and the infamous Knacker.

There were 100 anglers in the syndicate plus bailiffs, making a total number nearer to 120. After the lake was pegged out for the draw there were only 40 swims, which meant that if everyone turned up for the draw over half the people there were going to be disappointed. This of course was prior to the rota system which is now employed at Harefield - a much better idea I think.

Come the day of the draw, about 60 anglers had turned up. Dave Whibley and I decided that if one of us drew a decent swim we would double up, of course if the other angler didn't draw a peg at all then he would double up anyway. Dave Whibley was first out of the hat and chose *The Point* swim, a very, very good choice indeed. The swims went slowly, everyone seemed to be getting the best swims and then finally it was my turn. I think I was about fifteenth out of the hat and I chose *Loftus Road* - a swim that I'd never even fished before. I didn't know a thing about it but it seemed as though it would be a good bet on the day because a long chuck would put you out in front of the workings.

The workings is an area of the lake which is out of bounds to anglers. It is the east bank and only your favoured bailiffs were allowed to fish this, but a cast of 150 yards from *Loftus Road* could put the bait in the same position as the anglers fishing from that bank. This, I thought, would be a very good spot to start. The water in this area, I knew, was about eight feet deep, there were lots of gravel bars, in particular a gravel bar almost centrally in the lake with about three feet of water on top of it. I'd been out in the boat in the close season, something that you were allowed to do at the time, prodded around with a long pole all around that area and found some likely looking spots. There were obviously several anglers that didn't get swims and Essex Jon was one of them, so I asked him if he'd like to double up with me at *Loftus Road*, it seemed as though we'd have a good social, a good laugh and more than likely a good drink, and he decided that he'd come in with me. I didn't prebait this close season, with only a week to go and everybody else chucking God knows what in the lake, there didn't seem a lot of point. There was going to be plenty of food all over the place so after a quick look round in the boat one last time about four days before the start of the season, that was it. Home, get the tackle sorted out, all long-range gear. I knew what was required of me, I knew the tackle I needed to get out there, just a matter of getting down there and doing the business.

I arrived at Harefield on the 15th at about two o'clock in the afternoon and had a walk all the way round the pit. Several of the anglers had already set up, rods pointing skywards, big reels. Most of the anglers that were on there were kitted up for long-range fishing, although to be fair many of them didn't have the technique of getting those extra few yards that you needed when the fish were showing in the middle. At that time, the only anglers on there that could cast that distance (that I saw) were Zenon Bojko, Martin Clarke, Simon Day, Gary Bearman, Steve Allcott and myself, which

Tim Spencer and his opening morning brace of commons

Lake record at 38lb 4oz

meant that there were only a handful of anglers that were able to fish one of the best areas of the lake. I forgot Essex Jon, and that is something I shouldn't do. He had two absolute beasts of rods, about four pound test curve and 13 feet six inches, that could hurl nine ounces of lead to the horizon. I'm not suggesting that any one should try and use nine ounces of lead but I did see Essex do it a couple of times and it was, to quote his famous words: "Absolutely awesome!"

Jon arrived late that afternoon and we had a few cans of beer, sat down and looked at the lake like you do before the start of the season. It was sunny, not very much wind - perfect conditions - and we could see fish cruising about out in the middle. We made our minds up that if we went to the pub we would definitely be back by ten o'clock, we wouldn't get too drunk and be ready to cast in at 12 o'clock with a chance of catching a fish at first light. The best laid plans of mice and men they say and it certainly didn't go according to plan. I'm afraid we had rather too much to drink and a rather large Indian afterwards and ended up in the car park having more cans of beer till about two o'clock in the morning. Neither of us were in any state to do any long-range casting when we got back, we decided to put Plan B into operation - we would just go to bed and get up at midday and cast out, we thought we'd be alright by then!

As it happened, at 9am we both decided to get up and fish - keen as anything. We'd already heard several indicators going off on the lake and somebody had just popped down and told us that a lad called Tim Spencer had a 30 pound common and a 20 pound common out of *Someone's Coming* and they were about to do the photographs and would we like to come up and see it. We'd also heard that on the road bank, Simon Day and Gary Bearman had a couple of fish each. It was obvious that the long-range fishing was paying off. We went down to see Tim Spencer and the fish were absolutely beautiful, a really long 30 pound common and a nice twenty to go with it. What a superb brace shot these two fish made, it certainly whetted our appetites for what was ahead. We scurried back to our swims and got everything ready to start fishing, and it was 9.45am when we cast in unison. The formalities over with, it was on with the kettle, a cup of tea and some breakfast. About ten minutes later, as we sat there eating our breakfast, Jon suggested that we have a little bet... we had a pound on who would catch the first fish of the season and we'd also have a pound on who caught the biggest fish of the session, we shook on it and sat down behind our rods.

Two minutes later my left hand rod, which I had cast as far as I possibly could out in front of the workings, gave a quiver and then ripped from the clip and took off across the lake at an alarming rate. Because of the height of the swim above the water, the line was dropping down and flying out up and down, up and down, streaking out across the flat calm water into the sun. I picked up the rod and immediately knew I was into a very, very big fish. It tore off along the far side of the bar, snagging the line from where it had picked up the bait and then moved out more centrally into the middle of the lake. I pulled the fish back, using very heavy pressure, this was only possible because I was fishing ten pound main line with a 15 pound leader, any stronger breaking strain then I wouldn't have got the distance, any lighter and I'm sure that the line would have already cut. Begrudgingly the fish came back towards me and eventually you could see it wallowing behind the bar where I'd had the pick-up, but no way could I pull it over the top. I put the rod down in the rest and it took line again, picked it up, tightened it up, pulled it back towards me. I repeated this exercise two or three times but the fish was getting nowhere, neither was I. Putting the rod down on the rest for the last time, I just didn't know what to do. Jon suggested that he could swim out there and perhaps get the fish to an area of the bar where it was able to come through and I could carry on playing it with rod and line. I thought this was a very good idea as I'm not a very good swimmer anyway, but of course Jon's physique enabled him to do this sort of thing in seconds. He quickly went off back to the car to get his swimming trunks when along the path came the Veg.

Now I haven't mentioned the Veg up until now, but there is a funny story that goes with this fellow. I fished with him down at Longfield and he is deaf in the extreme. He never hears any of his takes, never hears anything you're saying (especially when you ask him to get the drinks in), but when he wants to hear he can. Now we call him the Veg - a little bit unkind. When I first went onto Harefield the year before, I was talking with Simon and he told me that one of my mates was fishing down there. I said "Oh who's that then?" He said "Oh he fished with you at Longfield, you used to call him The Edge." I said "The Edge, I don't know who that is, why did

Two lake records to the 'Famous Five' in the opening week!

Tate Gallery upper twenty

they call him that?" He said "They called him The Edge because he had the edge over everyone." I said "What does he look like?" "He's a little fellow with a pointed nose and great big ears." He was so deaf that for all those years at Longfield he thought we were calling him The Edge.

Still never mind, along he came. "Have you got one on?" he says, stating the obvious. "Yeah" I said "it's snagged up behind the bar." I picked the rod up to show him and lo and behold the fish came straight over the top, not only did it come over the top but it swam straight towards me as fast as it could. It looked as though it was going to go for The Edge, sorry the Veg. Anyway the Veg went down with the net, slipped it underneath and wallop in it went and it looked big. Having never seen *Nelson* before, I didn't really know what I'd got but when we turned the fish over in the net, there was his blind eye. I let out a cry across the lake and shouted across to Simon down on the other side "*Nelson*".

Just then Jon came round the corner in his swimming trunks. "No need for it this time mate!" I said "it's in the bag and I think you owe me two quid." I weighed it straight away as you do so it didn't lose a dram and it went 38lb 4oz. A new lake record for Harefield, I was absolutely elated. I ran down the bank as fast as I could to get my old mate Steve Allcott because he is without doubt the top photographer. Steve was thinking of packing up and going to Wraysbury, he just couldn't get the place out of his mind but nevertheless he was very pleased for me. Steve wound in and brought his camera up. Then along came Dave Whibley, Martin Clarke and the whole gang. I really did feel like I was on centre stage, *Nelson* the big boy, 38lb 4oz, a new lake record, what a result!

Jon handed over the two pounds, I let out a cry like a banshee across the lake and the fish was returned. It wasn't long before *The Anglers Mail* was on the phone to the Horse and Barge, they'd heard that I'd caught a 40 pounder but I think Dougal put them right, telling them that it was indeed a new lake record of 38lb 4oz and also promising to tell me to send them some photos, (they appeared in the paper a couple of weeks later).

So I was off to a flying start. The rig, the bait, the technique had worked yet again, it did seem a very, very good method and I didn't think I could better it. At this time though, I didn't realise the potential of close fishing with a lot of bait placed accurately and I was to learn a hard lesson later that season, taught to me by probably the two best anglers that had been on there for many years, Care Bear and Frogger. Their technique of fishing the first bar enabled them to fish accurately with lots of bait and of course not to lose many fish. Having only to pull them over one bar is a great advantage, but you've got to be spot on with your fish location. There's always fish out in the middle, you can always chuck it and chance it right out into the horizon but if you can find the fish close in and feed heavily, that's the way to catch the big bags of fish from Harefield. They really do love a bit of bait.

Someone brought us a few cans of beer back from the off licence and Jon and I sat there and had a beer, laughing and joking and prodding each other, saying what a fantastic start it was to the season. A little after two o'clock that day I had another pick-up from the same place and it did the same thing again, backwards and forwards to this high point on the bar. If you can find these high points when a bar suddenly rises to within a couple of feet of the surface, this is a brilliant spot to put it when the sun is out. They definitely home in on these areas, swimming round them, cruising over the top and will pick up a single bait positioned there 90 per cent of the time. This time Jon *was* needed to swim out, he had his swimming trunks with him of course. In a few minutes he was out there, standing on the bar and I could see the water just up to his knees, in his hand however was a sad sight... my rig - the fish had gone. Again it felt like a very good fish.

We didn't move that night but neither of us had any action for the next couple of days. All over the lake however, there were other fish coming out and at the end of the first week Dave Whibley had a new lake record common at 31lb 8oz from *The Point* swim, a very distinctive fish because of its punctured swim bladder which had left a lump on one of its flanks. We heard the take from where we were fishing and ran down the bank to see the action. The fish had taken in front of the second bar, run along the side of it and through a gap and disappeared into the gully behind, it had then swum strongly behind an island, Dave's line had picked up and the fish could be seen wallowing in the shallow water on the other side of the island. This time it was Knacker's turn to go in for a swim, he stripped off down to his pants, his fantastic physique showing up Essex Jon completely. His huge belly hanging over the top, we all fell about laughing. A powerful swimmer though, he was soon out there, standing on the island trying to find the line. When he went

Steve Nine/One and Paul Hodgson with over 60 pounds of Harefield carp

A long 29 for Steve Allcott from the Tate High Spot

Nelson at 37lb 8oz for Peter Jones

down the line with his fingers, he found the fish just under a piece of weed below the surface. Grabbing it in his hands he then lifted it up onto the island and called over to Dave, who was some 40 yards away on the bank "it's a common - over 30 pounds, what shall I do with it?" A shout came from the other side of the lake: "stick it down your pants Knacker," and everybody fell about laughing again.

Dave, being the great sport that he is, told Knacker to put it back on the nearside of the island as he wanted to play it in by the rod. I don't really know what I'd have done in those circumstances, probably got the net out to him somehow to make sure that I didn't lose it, a 30 pound common is a big prize to lose. Anyway, it paid off for Dave. A few trips up and down the margins and this lovely common was in the net, took some pictures and away it went. What a great start to the season! The Famous Five had caught lake records of both mirrors and commons. We certainly celebrated that week!

The wind was now blowing hard down towards *The Point* which is the other end of the lake to where we were fishing and a move was certainly in order. Essex decided that he would go home and do a few days work and then come back down again. After all, you could fish all season and as there were no rotas, there was no hurry to do a few days when the swims were packed. I decided to move into the *Tate Gallery* after Martin Clarke had moved out. Martin had caught a 17 pound common on opening night (well actually half an hour before the start of the season - sorry Martin). That had been all that had been caught out of there that week, this was now empty but I knew the *Tate* quite well, having fished it a few times in the winter and had caught *Maurice*, at 27 pounds in the March of the same year and I knew that particular area was one of the high points on the bar. It meant a cast slightly to my left, well it looked 'slightly' from where I was standing but when I actually looked, I was casting right across the swim to my left and almost in the next swim down. Both these swims were taken, Steve Nine/One was next to me and he didn't seem to mind as I was a lot further out than him. He was only fishing the first bar and I was out the other side of the third, so using the same technique again, a single bait, small pop-up a couple of inches off the bottom, I set up in the *Tate* for the rest of my holiday.

Everything started off sweetly, the first day I was there I had a take on the left hand rod, I landed a 27lb 12oz mirror, an absolutely cracking fish as you can see in the photograph. I was well pleased, that was now two to me. I felt confident, cocksure and certain that I was going to take the place apart, this was a big mistake because from then on things started to go drastically wrong.

Over a short space of time I lost 11 fish, the next 11 fish I hooked. Three more that week due to various reasons, one cut on the bar, one because the line came off the spool and tangled round the needle holder, and another time a fish came off in the edge. There was nothing I could do, no one loss was the same as another, every time I was losing a fish it was for a different reason.

I popped next door for a cup of tea one morning, only to find someone with my rod in their hands when I returned to my swim. "I was just walking past," he said "and I saw the rod tip nod so I decided to strike it, I didn't want it going in behind the bars." I said: "Well you could have shouted for me." With that the line went slack and he turned to me and said "I've had it close in once, it was a 30 pound common." "Great" I said "just what I needed."

When I eventually landed one a few weeks later, it was hooked up on a load of trailing tackle. A six pound common without any fins, this really was the last kick in the guts, 11 fish lost and when I did land one it was an Ethiopian common hooked up on someone else's tackle. Things certainly weren't going my way now.

It was about this time that I learned of the potential of floater-fishing on the water. I'd done a little bit the autumn before but it was a little bit late in the year, the fish weren't really interested, a lot of the fish had been caught by then and were very wary. But of course only a month or so into the season many of the fish still hadn't been caught and were suckers for floaters. It was Frogger and Care Bear that again showed me the potential of this lake for floater-fishing.

Over a two-week period these two very capable anglers took 11 fish off the top, seven of them over 25 pounds. Now this sort of floater-fishing for this stamp of fish was something that I couldn't miss out on. Floater-fishing has always been my favourite form of fishing, very exciting, very visual, looking for the fish all the time, walking around with just a pocketful of tackle and a bag of mixers, something that I enjoyed doing. A lot of people say that fish off the top don't count, well I reckon that's rubbish - it's horses for courses. There's only a few days of the season on these big fish waters where you can catch fish on the surface and an angler that floater fishes

Care Bear taught me a hard lesson

The Top Bays

At last I've landed one

all year will end up with a lot fewer fish than an angler who fishes on the bottom as well. So, it's when conditions are right - if they're cruising about on the top and look as though they're going to have a floater, have a go for them. They count just as much as the ones on the bottom and I, for one, prefer that sort of fishing, having done so since I caught the big fish down at Longfield a few seasons before.

I use standard floater-fishing tactics, a three to four foot trace made of Double Strength, usually ten pound breaking strain, a size six Super Specialist which is very sharp and very light and doesn't seem to change the shape of the mixers as they sit on the water. The controllers I normally use are either Kevin Nash or Midi, heavily weighted with brass. The large Nash ones can be cast upwards of a hundred yards with ten pound breaking strain line so they're ideal for this type of fishing. I don't actually stop my float, I have it free-running on the line, I find that I can see when the fish takes the bait the lines snake across the surface through the ring on the top of the float. This enables me to make an instant strike on those occasions when they haven't hooked themselves and exploded on the surface nearly pulling your rod in. Most of the takes that you get when you're fishing exposed hooks like this tend to be very violent.

The next two sessions that I fished down at Harefield were mainly on the surface behind the barge on the causeway between Broadwater and Harefield. There was a strong easterly blowing, pushing the fish up to the top again but this bay was sheltered from the wind compared to the rest of the lake. However, it was blowing in behind the *Someone's Coming* island. Frogger and Care Bear had already set up in the best spot directly behind the barge and had been feeding mixers consistently throughout the morning. I believe they'd taken two 20 pound fish when I turned up. I decided to go two swims to their left and try putting a lot of mixers out to draw some of the fish up out in front of me. I still hadn't recovered from the bad patch that I'd been going through and knew that things were still going to go wrong.

The swim I was fishing was where I'd caught my first ever Harefield carp, a 17 pound common. I knew from catching that fish that you had to apply a lot of heavy side-strain to keep it away from the bushes which went into the water on both sides of the swim. I made my mind up to feed the fish in close, not to give them too much line and not to give them a chance to get into the bushes at all. Two large sacks of mixers later, I eventually got two or three fish up in front of me and decided that I would make my first cast. I cast amongst the three backs as they were coming out of the water and within seconds that my float had disappeared and I was into a hard-fighting fish. The fish swam immediately left and I pulled heavily to the right to make sure that it didn't get into the bushes, this however was exactly what it did do, as soon as I pulled, it kited into the bank and a heavy fish could be seen beneath the overhanging branches. I pulled backwards and forwards two or three times and the double strength went. A double strength link is an excellent line for floater fishing, but it has hardly any abrasive resistance because of its low diameter. It is not recommended unless you use it in a heavy breaking strain for fishing in snags. I was gutted, another fish lost. Anyway, not to be put off as there were still two fish out there and one of them was still taking, I kept feeding the mixers. Gradually more and more fish came to my half of the lake. There were now no fish out in front of Frogger and Care Bear and both of them kept popping down to my swim to see how I was getting on. "Any minute lads," I kept saying "I'll have one." I made two or three casts towards fish that I could see which looked bigger than the one or two small doubles cruising close in. A huge back came out of the water, a mouth was just about to engulf my mixers when something exploded three feet closer towards me and my rod was almost wrenched out of my hands. 'Yes, I'm in' I thought, but hold on a minute, I didn't see the mixers go, what the hell was going on? The fish charged up and down the bank, it felt like an absolute monster, streaking up and down with me holding the line at breakpoint, keeping it away from the bushes several times. Suddenly this huge length appeared out of the water in front of me, it was an 18lb 8oz pike foulhooked in the top of the head. I couldn't believe it, however I actually landed this one. I popped down to show Care Bear and Frogger and they laughed their socks off. Maylin was struggling, loads of lost fish and the only thing he was catching was pike, hooked in the top of the head! When would my luck change? Five minutes later, that's when!

Colin Martin just popped down for a look around - he hadn't been down to Harefield before but had heard a lot about it. When he saw the fish taking floaters he knew that he fancied getting a ticket on there. Colin's another angler who likes to take advantage of floater fishing when it's possible.

A deep 28-plus taken from the Top Bays

Whilst waiting for the 'Point' I caught this 26lb 8oz mirror from the 'Tate'.

A 32lb 'Goldfish' for Stevie Brillo

As I say, five minutes later the floater was gone and I was into another good fish. I knew immediately it must be around about 25 pounds. This time I decided not to give it an inch of line and cranked the handle round half a turn at a time until I got the fish on a short line. No way was *this* fish going to get in the snags. Within seconds, I'd got it in the net, I pulled it up onto the bank, I lay next to it and looked at it. Got one at last! On the scales, 25 pounds exactly. Result!

The next session down there was again in hot weather and I found the fish up in the top bays. I was the only angler floater-fishing at the time, the other two, Frogger and Care Bear, had pulled off and gone down to Frampton. I located three big fish in a small bay at the top, fed a small amount of mixers getting the largest fish with a humpback coming up taking them at my feet. I literally just dropped the mixers into its mouth. It charged around under the rod tip, didn't really seem to know where it was going, I had it cornered in the small bay and to get out it had to come straight towards me.

Again it only took a few seconds to net the fish, an absolutely immaculate one, just a fraction over 28 pounds. Two anglers then appeared round the corner, one I recognised as Zen, the other a big guy with a silver grey beard was soon introduced to me as Steve Morgan from Mainline Baits. This was the first time I had met Steve. I'd heard a lot about him and from what Zen had told me, he was a really nice guy. Steve and I were going to turn out to be quite good friends. Anyway he introduced himself and asked me how the fishing was going. Just as he said that, I saw two fish in the corner of the bay, and I flicked out a mixer towards one, "there Steve, over there." Now his eyesight's not too good and I don't think he actually saw it until two lips came up and the rod buckled over. Whack, I'm in! "Got one Steve." "Christ," he said, "I thought it was going to be hard over here." "I had a 28 a few minutes ago," I said. "Blimey." With that the line came back, the hook had slipped out. "Oh no," he said "what a gutter, I bet you're absolutely devastated ain't ya?" Just then I looked across and the other fish was still there. I cast out towards that one and within two seconds that one turned round and took the floater and I landed it. A nice fully scaled, round about 19 pounds. I didn't weigh it because my scales were up in the other swim but 18 or 19 would have been about right. Steve was well pleased to see a Harefield carp on the bank, however, that was to be my last Harefield carp from the surface that year.

I decided that September would be my last month on Harefield for the rest of the season. I'd arranged a ten-day session with my good friends Steve Allcott and Phil Harper to coincide with this the last month on the lake. I arrived a couple of days before them to find the lake quite busy for the time of year. Normally after the early season rush was over the lake became a lot quieter and there were plenty of choices of swims, however this was not to be the case. I fancied going in *The Point* area or *Someone's Coming,* both of these swims were taken but only for a few more days so I decided to go into my old friend the *Tate Gallery* to see if I could take one from there and then move onto *The Point* when that became free in a few days time. That was when Phil and Steve were turning up anyway and that's when the holiday would begin.

I'd also made my mind up to fish a different method when I got on *The Point.* I'd started using Kevin Nash Liver Palatants and I'd had a large quantity of boilies made up ready for this session. However, fishing the *Tate Gallery* which was all long-range fishing, there was little point in putting any free offerings out as you could get them nowhere near where you were fishing. I fished the high point on the left hand side of the swim, where I'd taken the 27 at the start, and was rewarded on the second day of the session with a nice fish of around 26lb 8oz. This was a fish that I'd seen caught previously by Steve Briggs at about the same weight, I also lost another fish which felt about the same size.

Three days went by, the anglers fishing *The Point* left and I moved onto the hump - a small island surrounded by a couple of feet of water which puts you out more or less in the middle of the lake. The advantage of fishing this swim is you can get your free offerings out almost centrally in the lake just with a catapult, an obvious advantage on this very difficult water. Phil soon turned up and moved onto *The Point* swim proper to my right and Steve Allcott went into the *Someone's Coming* swim. He quite fancied this area, although I knew from my last few days that the fish were further down the lake and that if anyone was going to have the fish it would be Phil and I. What a marvellous last session this turned out to be for me. Absolutely fantastic fishing, everything went right and it certainly stood me in good stead for a future session that I was going to do on Harefield at the start of the following season. More of that in the next chapter!

I put out quite a lot of bait in two areas, one to the left of my

First twenty of a mega-session

Liver Palatant 25 pounder

Two at 29lb 8oz, lucky or what?

swim which was a gap between two islands and one straight out in front where a series of bars ran parallel to the bank a few feet below the surface. As the water temperature was already beginning to fall being late September, I decided to fish the gullies and filled in the gully with bait between bars two and three at approximately 60 yards range. When I say I put a lot of bait out, probably about 20 pounds of dry mix each day over the ten-day session (which is a lot of bait for me).

I started the session with mirrors of 15, 21 and 25 within the first couple of days but carried on with the heavy baiting. Then on about the fourth day of the session the most amazing thing happened... we got back from the pub that night about 11 o'clock, and I was able cast the baits out quite accurately because it was a very moonlit night. However, there was a strong wind blowing that night, incredibly strong and because of my precarious position on top of this hump I was hanging onto the bivvy like grim death. In the end I had to get up and hammer an extra set of pegs into the eyelets. Once I was secure and I knew the bivvy wouldn't blow away, I could get my head down and relax. I remember laying there on the bed, looking up at the sky lit up by the moon and the clouds racing along with this most powerful wind. All of a sudden a huge gust of wind blew my rods from the rod rests and I looked at them lying there on the floor and noticed that the line was still going through the rollers, back through the indicator on to the Baitrunner. I thought this was probably the best place for them because if I put them back on the buzzers, they were going to blow off again, so I lay there looking at them laughing to myself thinking 'what a night this is, I must be mad'.

Suddenly the left hand rod, which was laying on the floor screamed off, the tip bent round, cutting through the water. As I leapt out and picked the rod up, I hadn't realised the strength of the wind and I was almost blown off my feet. I could feel no sensations from the fish at all due to the powerful wind blowing against the rod. I just kept hanging on and winching in, every now and again the fish would take a few feet of line and then come towards me again. I looked up at the moon and the clouds and I laughed to myself 'what a night to be out playing a fish'. All of a sudden a golden flank flashed at my feet and I noticed that it was an enormous common. I've got to admit that even my bottle went at this stage as I'd never had a 30 pound common and I was certain

that this fish was going to do it. Luckily it went into the net at the
first attempt and I sacked it up in the margins. I wish now that I'd
weighed it first but I didn't, I just put it in the sack and climbed back
in the bed (after recasting my rod). In the morning I woke up about
seven o'clock, put on my boots and walked across the shallow
water to the point where Phil was bivvied up, this was my normal
routine to wake him up as early as I could and get him to make tea
for me. As I got halfway across to his swim, Phil's head popped out
of the bivvy and he gave a big smile, I thought for a moment he
might have had one. All of a sudden there was a scream of the
buzzer behind me and I legged it back across the water, picking up
the right hand rod. This fish absolutely tore off up the lake and I
thought I'd really got a monster on the end. Five or six powerful
runs of around 20 yards at a time. Phil came across, and got the
landing net ready. Suddenly we saw it was a huge common, very,
very long, but very thin. Into the net it went. "Christ" said Phil "that's
got to be 28 to 30 pounds." I looked down at it and said "I've got
one bigger than that in the sack." He turned round to me in
disbelief, "honest?" "Yes mate, one bigger than that." We sacked that
one up as well and got the cameras ready. Steve Allcott came down
to do the pictures.

There on the bank were the two fish, two immaculate commons,
both had previously gone over 30 pounds but now were both 29lb
8oz. If I'd weighed the bigger of the two fish, the fatter one may
well have been over thirty several hours before. Who knows?

The photos over, I put the fish back and went back to my swim
and cast out in the same positions and carried on my routine of
heavy baiting, accurately, to the hookbaits. Fifteen minutes later the
right hand rod was away again. Surely this couldn't be another
common? It was tearing around again. Phil came over with the net,
we looked down and couldn't believe our eyes, was it one of the
same two? No, in the net another 29 pound common. In the space
of a few hours, three 29-plus commons. This one was 29lb 4oz, a
fish they called *The Chinese Common* because of its sloping eye and
sloping head, a beautiful fish I am sure you will agree and a
marvellous trio of commons. A record I believe - three big commons
in less than 24 hours. The jewels of Harefield. Fantastic fishing!

Now Steve Allcott couldn't resist it any longer, he had to move
down where Phil and I were fishing. There were loads of fish
moving around down there although they'd certainly moved more

29lb 4oz 'Chinese Common', that's three 29's in six hours!

Judgment day

At last Phil strikes gold

to my right out in front of Phil. I am not a greedy angler, I certainly like my share of fish but I was *willing* these lads to catch some fish. There was only one thing for it - it was onto the Nash Liver Palatant for both of them. I gave them a bucketful each, which they gratefully accepted. Both of them put both rods out on the new bait, double bottom baits, Drennan Boilie hooks size four, 25 pound Kryston, nine to ten inch hooklink, four ounce fixed lead; exactly the same rig that I had on.

It all went quiet for me but the next morning Steve Allcott was to take one of the best fish from the lake. It was shortly after ten o'clock when we heard his buzzer go, by the time we got to his swim he was up to his waist in the water playing a very powerful fish at long range. He kept saying it was only a small one but knowing Steve of old, he never knows whether it's a tench or a carp until he's got it to the landing net. When he eventually did get it under his feet and we saw the flank of the fish and realised it was the big fully-scaled, it was panic stations for all three of us. This fish looked absolutely huge. We quickly reeled his other rod in and made sure we had some stones in case it got near the branches of the overhanging bushes and I waded in next to him with a landing net. It went into the landing net like a baby and he let out a cry across the lake, it was the big fully-scaled. On the scales 35lb 8oz, a truly remarkable fish.

Now it was only Phil who needed to catch. Everyone was willing him on but mainly myself. I'd had a really good week's fishing, Steve was very happy with his 35 pound fully-scaled and who wouldn't be? It was on the last day when his luck was to change, I'd taken a 17 pound common in the morning and was sitting in Phil's swim having a cup of tea, looking at his bow-string lines hitting the water just beyond the second bar. We were all fishing in the same gully - anyone could have caught those fish. Suddenly the rod tip bounced and Phil sprang up like a greyhound out of the traps. I've never seen an angler play a fish so hard in my life. He was so keen to get it in the net and prove that he could still catch something (only kidding Phil!). It was a fish of 27 pounds, one of the typical Harefield fish, lightly scaled with a high back. A good result. What a week's fishing we'd had! We couldn't complain.

It convinced me that this method of heavy baiting at short range accurately, tops of the bars in summer, gullies in the winter or colder weather was the most devastating method of fishing on

Harefield and certainly a method I would employ on future trips, providing I could get the swims.

I didn't have any more action and decided that I didn't really fancy the winter down on the lake, as I had caught the big one anyway. Yateley was always in the back of my mind, the Pad Lake. That fish had gone 43 pounds and that seemed like the best place for me to go and spend the winter. Little did I know what a horrible time I was about to have but what a good mate I was about to make, a friend who in years to come would net my biggest ever carp.

I'd done a few sessions down on the Pad Lake at Yateley when Longfield closed down. That winter was very productive for some people fishing the lake. Kevin Maddocks had taken a 25, Ritchie had taken several fish including the second biggest at 36 and two or three other fish had come out as well so the winter looked like a good idea. A little bit of action, good fish and plenty of choice of swims, at least that's how it was when Longfield closed down.

This year however, everybody seemed to have the same idea and this was even more so when in October Steve Newman took the second biggest fish, the same one that Ritchie had at 36, at 35lb 12oz. Everybody felt sure that the big fish, *The Forty*, would come out that winter. How wrong they were!

During the course of the winter I fished six weekend sessions and one full week session and during all that time there was not one single bite on the lake. This was mainly due to the fact that every swim was taken during that period of time. The lake was absolutely packed and these fish on this type of water just do not respond to heavy pressure from anglers in every swim, casting and baiting up. The most productive times in the history of the Pad Lake have always been when there are no more than two or three anglers fishing this very small water. However, certain very good anglers were very hungry to catch the big fish - Wayne Dunne and Dave Mallin, the Black Country duo were both down for a lot of time that winter. Many of the old Longfield anglers as well, Ginger Steve, Steve Nine/One, of course Steve Newman was full time. He'd just done three months on the Car Park Lake without a bite only to move over to the Pad Lake in October and catch the 35 on his first day. That's carp fishing for you! Everyone felt confident there would be a few more fish out that winter.

I tried every trick in the book, fishing in small corners, under bushes, any quiet or secluded place I could find to move away from

35lb 8oz 'Fully-Scaled'

Sunset over the 'Point', little did I know what was to come

the crowds. I even fished the highly productive *Pad* swim in pole position on several occasions, trying a variety of methods including sweetcorn, which had been a very good winter bait on Withy Pool. Nothing seemed to work, I tried heavy baiting with lots of free offerings, I tried peanuts, tigers, single hookbaits, slack lines, tight lines, railway lines but nothing. Absolutely nothing made any difference to that lake at all. Those fish were totally turned off, nobody had a take all winter. It was also one of those winters when the rain never seemed to stop and the mud got deeper and deeper. In the end, you were wading through a quagmire, bivvying up your groundsheet over a swamp. Winter fishing is bad enough: the lack of daylight, the cold throughout the day and the night, the dark nights coming in around four o'clock in the afternoon and the thought of all those hours sitting there were indicators motionless. To think that I once enjoyed winter fishing yet here I was, definitely not enjoying this sort of fishing. I was struggling to stay on there, I must be honest. It was only the thought of that fish being over forty pounds which kept me going back and the lake's previous history of fishing well in the colder months.

I don't intend to bore you with endless stories on sessions when no fish were caught but it certainly did get my mind wondering why these fish had so totally turned off. Surely they had to feed at some time during the winter? There were lots of different theories going round at the time as to why winter fishing had got so bad because it was not only the Pad Lake that was fishing badly, but waters all over the country. Darenth, which had previously fished quite well during the winter had turned off over the last few years and only one or two fish were coming out of the Tip Lake between December and the last couple of weeks of the season. Something was going on, people were beginning to talk. Could it be the fishmeals and the bulk oils putting on tremendous amounts of weight on the fish which enabled them to go through the winter, living off their fat reserves and not needing to pick up anglers baits? Could it be increased winter pressures on the waters? With so many anglers now fishing the winters and a lot less fish coming out during the colder months, there were fewer fish to go round between the anglers and of course the increased pressure could also put the fish off. It's probably something that we will never know, but winter fishing certainly has got harder and harder over the years. This question was a theory that was the subject of much debate in the

Big Carp magazine *Rotary Letter* where Kevin Maddocks, Rod Hutchinson, Steve Allcott, Zenon Bojko, Jim Gibbinson and myself had all experienced a decrease in winter action. I saw it out on the Pad Lake right through until 14th March when I packed up in disgust. It had been a terrible winter, I wasn't sure whether there was anything I could have done to catch a fish. I seemed totally helpless but it wasn't as though everyone else was catching fish and I wasn't. Nobody had caught anything.

So what had I learned from this season? It had started off very well for me, with *Nelson* on the opening day. My tactics and methods I thought could not be beaten, I was convinced this was the way to catch the Harefield carp. August and September of that year had shown me that I was totally wrong, Care Bear and Frogger with their method of fishing the close in bar, heavily baiting accurately had taken nearly twice as many fish as I had caught that year. To be fair, they did put more time in, living locally, they fished a lot of evenings during the week and it was during this time when the lake was not so busy that a lot of their fish were caught.

However, it was painfully obvious that this was a far better method and I made my mind up that if I was to fish Harefield next season this would be the type of fishing I would do. I'd seen some tremendous fish on the bank at Harefield that year, Peter Jones had taken *Nelson* during the summer at 37lb 8oz; Martin Clarke had taken a fully-scaled at 36, this really was a fish I'd like to catch but one of the best fish in the lake was the long linear that I'd seen at 31 pounds. I'd always had a passion for linears, a fantastic looking fish with striking huge scales running down its lateral line. I really would like to have caught this fish. I made my mind up that if I fished on there the next season, that would be one of the fish that I would be after.

The other Famous Five lads had struggled a bit. Dave had finished the season with only two fish and I think Steve Allcott had two as well, but of course they only fished weekends the same as myself. With full-time jobs, arriving at the lake Friday afternoon or Friday evening always left you with the last choice of swims, all the top swims had gone and many of the fish that had come out had already been out earlier in the week.

There are so many anglers that have a lot of time for fishing these days, those on the dole are encouraged to go for long periods of time and it wasn't unusual on Yateley at this time to see anglers that had been there for two or three months. I couldn't believe the difference in time that anglers now spend fishing.

Not only had my method of long-range single bait casting been out-fished by the short range multi-bait methods, but it was obvious that anywhere that you fished in the lake, if you could get extra bait out to that spot, you'd have a much better chance of catching fish. Harefield, because of its increased stocking, was turning out to be quite a hungry water and the fish certainly liked huge beds of baits. Any method that you could use to get bait further out into the lake was definitely a bonus.

I didn't intend doing a lot more time on Harefield but certainly when I did, I would try and fish swims where I could put out vast quantities of boilies. That was the summer, the winter was a disaster. Still, all winter fishing these days seems to be a disaster. There's always the close season to look forward to, friendly faces up at the Farlows bar. I certainly do enjoy myself when I'm fishing there and of course, the summer is only round the corner. June 16th would soon be with us again.

Chapter 7

CLOSE SEASON FISHING

Looking out from the bar at Farlows Lake in Buckinghamshire. This is the largest expanse of water on the lake and an excellent area throughout the year. I tend to fish this part of the lake during the winter and early part of the close season.

This 24lb 8oz mirror was taken in April, using a single pop-up fished on the bristle rig. It is during the close season that many of my experiments with baits, rigs and methods are carried out. Farlows has a large stock of fish which makes testing ideas and drawing conclusions much easier.

When I move onto venues such as Johnson's or Yateley, I want to have no doubt in my mind regarding my methods. These are definitely not waters on which to try out ideas as bites are so few and far between. This 20-plus common fell to a new fishmeal with which I was experimenting.

By microwaving a bait which already contains a polyball you can create a useful void in the centre of a rock-hard bait. If you drill into this void using a nut drill you can then inject Minamino, Ambio or milks into the centre of the bait. A useful method if you intend leaving the hookbait to sit for several days. This 21lb common liked it anyway.

Action of a different kind today. The police are investigating a murder in the area and frogmen search the lake for the body. I'm sure it was just an excuse to visit the excellent cafe and bar on site.

My good friend Steve Briggs now lives down at Farlows and I'm sure he would agree with me that experimenting with baits and rigs can be done very efficiently on this venue. Pop down this close season and check it out.

A typical, scaly Farlows mirror of 23lb taken from the island margins on the Herons Point on a single pop-up. Fished with no free offerings but cast accurately to a small gravel patch under an overhanging tree.

Chapter 8

BIG CARP ISSUES

As a historical record I thought it would be nice, to go briefly through some of the issues that we are facing at the beginning of the nineties, also to talk about some of the things that are going on in carp fishing at this time, and then to talk about carp waters around the country and what we may have to look forward to future years.

I wish I had done this when I wrote *Tiger Bay* and *Fox Pool* because it would have been nice to look at what was going on then and compare it to these days. The important issues of the time may mean nothing to us now and it would have been interesting, or even perhaps funny, to look back and see what we were all talking about ten or 15 years ago.

I don't know how many of you were actually fishing when the Carp Society was formed. It all came into place at the beginning of the eighties, and if you look through the first couple of Carp Fisher magazines, incredible statements were being made by some people. Waters like Yateley and Savay were referred to as the 'circus', and in those days anglers fishing the 'circus' or the 'circuit waters' were frowned upon by some of the anglers around the country.

Another major talking point of the time was the so-called 'north/south' divide. The 'circus' became embroiled in this controversy as well. In the early eighties most of the big fish waters were in the south and anglers were catching quite large numbers of 20 and the odd 30 pound carp. There were not the same number of big fish waters in the North, consequently the catches were not so spectacular. It seems that the forethought of fish farms in the South in developing such fish as the Leney strain was paying off. Savay in particular held a good stock of these big fish. Many of the Midland and Northern anglers have now taken the opportunity of fishing these renowned waters and have been very successful. I am pleased to say that this has certainly helped to bridge this so-called 'north/south' split.

In the early eighties when the Carp Society was first thought of, another major talking point was a thing called the 'numbers game' and this was the worst thing you could possibly do in carp fishing. The numbers game, for those of you who don't remember, consisted of anglers that went for targets - targets were another thing you weren't allowed to mention. You set yourself a target at the beginning of the season, this was a terrible thing to do and anglers would say they were going for ten twenties or 20 twenties or 100 doubles, and of course this was nigh-on impossible further north, where there were only a few waters that had the potential to do this. It was far easier in the South to set a target for yourself as there were far more decent venues to fish. From a southerner's viewpoint, it did seem that we were being slagged off by our northern colleagues for no reason. Nowadays, with people prepared to travel longer distances to fish different venues, the 'numbers game' can be participated in by anybody. It is not unusual for people to catch 20 twenties in a season, and with the advent of fishing abroad a great deal, a target of 50 thirties in a season is not impossible. It's strange that what was once the worst crime you could commit in the carp fishing world is now virtually ignored.

Again in the early to mid-eighties, there was a big fuss made about anglers drinking beer and eating curries, lots of people saying this was a terrible thing to do and that you ought to be ashamed of yourself. In fact my first book, *Tiger Bay*, came under great criticism from some of the leading anglers at the time. Few of them in my opinion were good anglers but they were trying to put themselves to the forefront by writing articles about bait and how proteins did this and that. People don't seem to write it these days, I think they realise that carp eat all sorts of things and not just the super-chemical creations. A lot of it is simply being in the right place at the right time with something that carp eat. They will eat the cheapest of baits to anything you care to put out there really, as long as it is edible. I don't think we have to go into the chemical equation theory like people thought we did at that time. So it was bad news to drink beer or eat a curry? With anglers having so much more time these days to go fishing, some on the dole and some self-employed (those that can take a fair bit of time off), people all over the country now like to enjoy the social side of fishing as well as the hard work side. It seems perfectly acceptable now to go and have a pint and have a curry afterwards if you want. There are still a couple of people who say: "It's disgusting, they're all pooing in the bushes the next day," but are these people trying to tell us that they don't go to the toilet when they're fishing? It seems quite amazing to me.

These were some of the issues that perhaps I should have written about when I wrote *Tiger Bay* or even *Fox Pool*. They were important then, but don't seem significant now.

I was saying briefly about foreign fish being easier to catch than

English fish. There are still people who say this is not true and they are just as difficult. The reason that big carp in this country are very difficult to catch is that they have had 30 years of fishing pressure, they have been pursued every day. *Bazil* alone has been 40 pounds for 12 or 13 years now and he has been fished for solidly all those years. I would doubt if there is a 40 pound carp in France that could boast that, despite there being thousands more than we have. The fish in France and Holland have just not had the constant angling pressure of years of carp fishing like the water have in this country. Some of the lakes in France have never even been fished, and there are lots of lakes out there that are just being discovered now which have loads of thirties and forties. The people going out there are just using things like sweetcorn or another simple bait and catching big bags of fish. That is not going to happen here, we would be very, very lucky to find a water that could do that. For the record, I'm against the introduction of big fish into this country.

Talking about waters which could be discovered with huge shoals of monster carp, we must mention the story of Martin Gay and his huge commons. A series of articles appeared in one of the glossy fishing magazines concerning a gentleman called Martin Gay. He caught an upper-forty common, and several big commons to go with it, on simple fishing techniques - stalking with sweetcorn. The angling world was alight with tales of these fish, and anglers such as Ritchie McDonald and Phil Harper searched high and low through Ordnance Survey maps, drove hundred of miles visiting different lakes around the country, looking for something that would give them a clue as to the whereabouts of this lake that Martin Gay was fishing. There was very little background in any of the pictures that were shown but people were looking for that particular type of shrub, and this type of grass, hoping upon hope that they would stumble across this magic water. Then, somebody put a spanner in the works and there were rumours going around that the fish were indeed caught but not from this country. People were suggesting all sorts of different places, Canada seemed to be the favourite and there was talk that perhaps these big commons had come from an unfished Canadian lake. This is a mystery which still has not been resolved because Martin completely clammed up and I don't blame him. He refused to name the water and despite people writing in to various magazines and saying that he should disclose the water he kept quiet. Fair play to him, if he *had* found

Foreign jumbos, do we want them?

a water in this country which contained a large number of huge, uncaught fish why shouldn't he keep it to himself? He threw a few clues, saying it was open for people to fish and they thought 'it must be that water down the road, I've never fished it but it's a pike fishery or it's a trout lake or whatever'. We still don't know for sure, there are lots of very good anglers who still believe that he caught the fish in this country. We've had articles and letters put in *Big Carp* magazine saying that we should believe Martin and that he had nothing to gain, no commercial interest in saying he'd caught such big fish or by saying it was in England. He would have gained great credibility from catching such wonderful fish from Canada anyway, if indeed that was where he caught them. So there are those who say that Martin has been very unfairly treated, there are others saying that he didn't catch them in this country, there couldn't be such a water and there isn't such a water and he should come clean and tell from where he did catch them.

For the record, I am honestly not sure one way or the other. He could have caught them from this country but he could have caught them from abroad. I am of the opinion that he had nothing to gain from saying he caught them in this country and I don't see why he should disclose it anyway. There is still a possibility that they were caught in home waters and what a marvellous venue that would be should we ever be lucky enough to fish it. I hope I'm bivvied up next to Martin one day - oh sorry he doesn't use bivvies, he stalks.

As I was saying earlier, there are a lot of people putting a lot of time into carp fishing at the moment. The economic climate in England in the early nineties has left many people unemployed, on the dole, whether by choice or just genuinely out of work, and there are many, many more people using this time for carp fishing. I remember ten years ago that going fishing for the whole of the weekend every weekend was thought to be very extreme. There weren't all that many people doing it, to be honest. In fact, I remember Savay in 1983, Roger Smith fishing all the week of his rota, which was one week every fortnight, and I thought this was an incredible amount of time for anyone to go fishing. I couldn't believe that anyone could actually do those sort of hours, I thought they must be mad or something. These days, at some of the waters I've been fishing, Yateley in particular, we've had a few anglers doing three or four months in one session. It's happening all over the country and people have got a lot more time and they seem to have the money as well. I don't really know where they are getting this from, but I don't think you could fish efficiently just on your week's dole money - there's not enough of it.

However, there are now full-time carp anglers with unlimited hours to spend and they now can get on the best waters, and of course they are also catching the big fish, so there are a lot more people catching big fish than there were ten years ago. If you look through the magazines and books of ten years ago, there was a hierarchy of carp anglers that were able to fish waters such as Savay and Redmire catching the big fish. In a list of big fish you were certain to find three or four names who were regular catchers of these fish over 35 pounds but these days everyone is catching fish, or at least it looks like everyone if you pick up the weekly angling papers. You always see 'young Tommy', 16-years-old with a 35 pound carp on his first trip. Of course there are thousands and thousands of anglers who are not catching this size of fish and the top anglers are still catching fish. Those that are still fishing in England are catching fish, still catching their good share still and those that have taken to fishing on the continent are doing very well. Those 'name' anglers don't stand out so much as they used to because so many people are catching good fish. There are so many people now with access to waters holding 30 and 40 pounders and even the best carp angler amongst us can't fish every water. Even if he fishes a lot of prolific waters, he can't be expected to catch the biggest ones all the time. Anglers are now able to walk into tackle shops and pick up the latest rig, bait and a book that tells them how to do it. They don't really have to think for themselves, they've only got to go and sit there for enough weeks and eventually something will come along, particularly if somebody else has been baiting it. Look at the Car Park Lake in 1993 - there were two or three anglers who baited heavily with hemp and tigers, and in the end fish became very keen on this combination of bait. To begin with there were only two or three doing it but in the end others could see that all you had to do was sit with a big bed of hemp and tigers and eventually a good fish would come along, lots of people cashed in on a couple of people's hard work. That is carp fishing, or at least carp fishing in the nineties.

It all sounds a bit 'doom and gloom' but there are also some very good things which have happened within the last few years. The Carp Society has gone from strength to strength and the old Carp

Anglers' Association (the CAA) is no more. I was a member of the CAA for quite a few years and also Regional Organiser of the CAA for Bedfordshire, Hertfordshire, Buckinghamshire and Oxford. I held regular meetings in Dunstable and really enjoyed my time with the CAA, but sadly that came to an end. I think everybody felt a little bit sorry that it finished. The Carp Society came along six or seven years after the CAA was formed and the people involved with the Carp Society knew that they had to do better than the CAA. They had a yardstick to measure by so they improved upon the magazines and conferences, they tried harder because they had to, they had competition, and now the competition has gone. I'm not saying that the Carp Society has stood still, it certainly hasn't, but I'm sure it would have progressed at a swifter rate, if it still had competition.

Some of the good things that the Carp Society have been doing within the last few years - purchasing Horseshoe Lake, an absolute brilliant idea by somebody. To buy this lake outright, take in a fee of about £300 each from a certain number of anglers which ran into hundreds of thousands of pounds. There were quite a few members obviously and I see an ever-increasing number of tickets up for sale within the swap-shop pages of the *Anglers Mail.* I wonder whether there are perhaps too many members now on the water or whether people are just trying to make a little profit out of their Horseshoe tickets just a year after buying them.

Anyway, it's 'well done' to the Carp Society and I'm sure that it won't be the last water they buy. In fact, as we know Redmire Pool came under the Carp Society flag within the last few years and it took over the running of the pool from Clive Dietrich and bravo to Les Bamford, one of the controllers of the pool, who is doing a fine job up there. They're getting their fish farm together, and moving the fish to other venues and these new fish are doing very well where they are being relocated.

So there are some good things that have been happening and hopefully when this book is read over and over in years to come, people will look back and say "Christ, it's ten years since the Carp Society took over Redmire and look, here's the new British record coming out - a fish that Les Bamford put in ten years ago." Maybe, who knows? I'm sure that Redmire Pool will do better under this management than its previous one, at least more people are getting the chance to fish Redmire should they wish to.

Another thing that's happened which is very good for carp fishing in the nineties was the release of *Big Carp* magazine. Our magazine, which is the first for the last 20 years or so, brings together the top writers and the top carp anglers of this era in one publication, airing their views in *Big Carp's* Rotary Letter, (the letter is a very exciting piece of writing which has been going on for a year or so now within the magazine). The magazine is bi-monthly and the contributors to *Big Carp* Rotary Letter are myself, Rod Hutchinson, Lee Jackson, Kevin Maddocks, Zen Bojko, Steve Allcott and Jim Gibbinson. It is a very exciting piece of writing, very controversial, very interesting, a little bit like this piece - it covers what's going on around the country and abroad, current news. The whole magazine brought about a big change in angling magazines, especially the carp fishing side of it. It was a new format and most of the big carp being caught in the country are featured in it. It's the first magazine to cover all the 40 pound fish that are caught, any sort of record braces and most of the top waters around the country. It has become a very popular magazine indeed and I'm sure it will go on for years. Every angler who's interested in carp fishing, even in a small way, should read it because most of the latest rigs and baits are being talked about long before being published in books like

The Carp Society, ten years old and already in control of several top carp fisheries

this.

Speaking of bait, the nineties were certainly the start of the bait wars. There have never been so many bait companies around, we will probably look back at this in the future and there will be ten times as many but at the moment, there are over 30 bait companies, most of them selling ready-made baits, ready-rolled in a machine. Of course a lot of these ready-rolled baits don't actually come from that source, they come from other companies which actually roll them. Richworth certainly had the market to themselves through the eighties, and still manufacture baits for a lot of the other companies, they are still doing very well indeed, but there are a lot more bait companies around now.

For the first time in the nineties, it was really the 'War of the T-shirts'. We'll probably look back at this and laugh but many anglers are now sporting bait company logos on their T-shirts and receive free bait or some other reward for doing so. Sponsorship - now we come onto something I'm sure will increase in the next few years. It's now just starting with carp fishing. Of course match fishing has always had heavy sponsorship by the big tackle companies such as Daiwa, Shimano and this type of company. These have always gone in big with match fishing and it's finally happening with carp fishing. Carp anglers are finally getting the recognition for the skill and the hard work involved in catching big carp. There is obviously a big market out there for tackle, rods and reels etc and some of the companies are now cashing in on the names.

It was in 1992 that Kevin Maddocks signed up with Shimano and also signed up with Fox. I was involved with Kevin Nash for three years and have now moved on to Mainline. Andy Little got involved with DAM and is doing very well as a consultant to them. There is obviously more money coming to successful carp anglers from these companies because it's plain to see through other sponsorship that it certainly works. Other anglers look and see what baits people are using and what type of tackle they prefer. It's obviously beneficial to the tackle companies to have a figurehead up there, using the gear, actually out on the banks being seen by other anglers doing the business.

We seem to have got on to money somehow and while we are on this subject, let's have a look at the price of tickets because this has escalated by monumental amounts over the last couple of years. We have to look at some of the syndicate waters around the country, the dearest one I know of is a lake called Broad Oak, in Surrey where the cost is £500 a year. That's a lot of money. It's probably a very good water - I don't know, it's a very secretive, low profile water. This does seem a little bit pointless, as there's no chance to get in there and most people couldn't afford it anyway.

Lakes like Withy Pool, Duncan Kay's Mid-Northants Carp Fishery and Harefield are all around the £300 mark. You've only to look back a few years when waters, including some of those already mentioned, were a lot cheaper. On the more exclusive waters prices have gone up and anglers are finding the money to do it. There's no shortage of people interested in getting onto Harefield and places like that. If anyone drops out there's soon somebody ready to take his place.

I would expect there to be a lot more TV coverage of angling within the next ten years. Here in 1993 we are just beginning to see the first TV programmes being made specifically on carp fishing and also on other types of angling. Chris Yates has done a series of angling programmes, one of them on Redmire Pool which, of course, features him carp fishing. Most of us saw this at the Carp Society conference at Dunstable but it's taken a couple of years to get on the telly. Channel Four are making programmes for a series later this year, I know they've already filmed Zen and several other anglers at Chigborough at the Junior Fish-In with the Carp Society. I believe Andy Little has done some filming somewhere, not too sure what he caught. I made a television programme for London Weekend television ten years ago, Kevin Maddocks, myself, Lee Jackson and a few others fished Walthamstow Reservoirs and of course the noddy didn't catch anything and I didn't feature in the film other than a couple of bits where I was trying to get in the picture, you know like you do, waving your hand, "hello mum, here I am". Since then there's really been nothing in ten years. Now I believe there's going to be more TV coverage of fishing, after all it's a very big, if not the biggest participant sport in the country and the video market shows that there is a big interest for programmes on the telly. I made the *Harefield Haulin'* videos in 1992 and they sold an incredible number, probably the most successful carp angling film ever made in this country because of the number and size of the fish that were caught. Of course this was down to Harefield being the exceptional water that it is and a little bit of hard work put in by myself and Stuart Gillham.

There you are - 1993, probably the start of the television era. John Wilson showed us the way a few years ago with his programmes on television, not specialising in carp except for one episode I believe, but I'm sure we'll see a lot more carp fishing on the television in various forms.

On to other subjects. The decline in action during the winter sessions is something which has been spoken about over the last few years. It wasn't so long ago that winter could be the best time of the year on many waters, there were certainly fewer anglers around and the fish were very responsive. It didn't seem to matter how cold it got, as long as the lake wasn't frozen up there was always a chance of a fish. Now it's not unheard of to hear about waters which don't produce a fish from November through to March. Yateley and most of the big fish waters, like Horton, producing well during the summer and going completely dead in the winter. This is something anglers countrywide have noticed and are discussing. There's one train of thought that there are a lot more anglers fishing in winter now and the pressure's a lot greater, the few fish that were caught in the winter are now split between a lot more people.

TV coverage, is it just beginning?

Another view is that the high fat-content baits have something to do with it, because in the bait scene a certain change that occurred in the nineties was the introduction of bulk oils in high concentrations, very 'liquid baits' were being used. Fishmeals combined with a very successful Premier Nodd Oil and various other fish feed-inducing oils. Some people have put an unnecessary amount of fish oil in the bait in my opinion, up to half of the bait being made up these days. Now, it is possible, although I'm no scientist and I couldn't say for certain, that these fish can put on reserves of fat, layers of fat, and live off them during the colder weather. Ten years ago it was quite common to see carp at their best-ever weights during the autumn and early winter, it was also

Tackle advances, the age of the mega-reel

quite common to see fish at their lowest weights through June, July and August after they had spawned. It does seem to have reversed within the last few years, it's now not uncommon to have a fish at its biggest weight at the start of the season, whether through spawn or not. They do seem to be spawning later, but certainly most of the fish seem to be bigger in the summer and build up weight, if anything, through June, July and August and then start losing it for the autumn period. Not losing necessarily but staying constant and not putting on weight for the winter like they used to at this time. Perhaps these baits, which are very fatty, build up the weights so quickly that they are able to live off it for a long time. We have seen a jump in weights on waters like Darenth, where fish suddenly came across huge levels of these fatty fishmeal baits, of up to eight pounds in weight in a year due to these baits. It's obvious that they can't keep feeding for ever like that as they're going to explode. That's what has happened now with winter carp fishing, there's a lot less fish hooked and one train of thought is it's these fats which they feed off during the colder months.

One thing which is covered in the book is the very sad end of Longfield, Fox Pool, the Leisure Sport fishery down at Staines was closed down at the beginning of the nineties and at the moment is run as a pike syndicate through the Pike Anglers Club. Most of this is covered within my stories in the book, I shan't go into much detail here but the outcome was that the fish were all transferred, all but a couple of fish anyway, to Horton. The Longfield fishery was closed down to carp fishing and reopened for pike fishing, this left a very bitter taste in the mouths of the anglers that fished there for a few years, myself included. I was absolutely livid and upset and felt empty inside for quite a period of time, it was like losing a close friend. I loved my time down at Longfield, I loved the fishery. It is, or was, in my opinion the best water I have ever fished and I must admit to feeling great contempt for those who moved the fish to Horton. I was sceptical, I didn't think they'd do well I wasn't aware at the time that there were very good reasons for moving the fish, since then it has been explained to me and we've only to look at the results the fish and the weights at Horton over the last year or so to know that Leisure Sport did the right thing. Those fish are doing very, very well indeed and I have to admit they are thriving more than they would have in Longfield. Horton is now probably the top water in the country along with waters like North Harrow

Waltonians and the Cons/Fisheries, but it's not possible to join the other three. Horton is a very fairly-run syndicate and it's possible to get on a waiting list. I am hoping to get in there next season - a very good water, but a sad end to Longfield.

Well, these are some of the issues that we are facing today in 1993 with my opinions expressed in a few of them, I'm sure you all have your own views on everything I've mentioned. We may look back on these things and they may seem unimportant in a few years time but at the moment, issues like foreign fish being introduced are very much on the minds of English carp anglers.

Before I move on to carp and carp waters and what we have to look forward to in the future, I will take a quick look at our tackle, not everything that we use, because a lot hasn't changed, but if we make a note now of things which are coming into vogue in 1993, maybe in 2003 that'll give us something to compare it to.

The early nineties have certainly been 'the time of the rig'. I have never seen as many combinations of rigs as people are designing these days, I'm sure a lot of them cannot possibly know how a carp feeds or what the inside of a carp's mouth looks like. Some of these rigs will certainly never catch but we have a much greater choice of bits and pieces for making up rigs here in the nineties than there ever was ten years ago. There are an uncountable number of hooklink materials around, different sorts of braids and combinations of strands, different colours and breaking strains, some solid, some hollow; mind-blowing really. Hooks: there's a bigger choice of carp hooks now than there's ever been. An incredible number of carp hooks are available on the market whereas ten years ago there were probably only two or three which everyone used. Buzzers are another thing which seem to have exploded in the early nineties. For the last ten years there was really only the Optonic on the market, almost everybody who went fishing had those or nothing else. There were one or two conversions around but basically, they were just Optonics. Now, in the space of two years, there are a lot more buzzers to choose from, the Daiwa Sensitron, Fox Micron in its various forms, the new Delkim, Bitech Viper. The list goes on and on with probably at least another ten different buzzers available. Along came swingers as well in their various forms. These are just an adaptation of what people used for carp fishing years ago, a piece of cork with a hairclip pushed in it attached to a piece of string. Now we have them made out of stainless steel. There is a fantastic amount of stainless steel around now through various companies, whereas ten years ago it was only those who could get it made privately, or made it themselves who had stainless steel bits and pieces. Everybody used to have matt black landing net poles, buzzer bars and banksticks, now the whole set-up is as shiny as a new pin.

Swingers, springers, extreme-range rods, huge reels with huge spools, much larger leads, Baitrunners, £200 beds, bivvy domes; these are all things which have really come into fashion in the last two or three years. Along with these ultra-expensive pieces of tackle has come the inevitable thievery on the banks. Never has it been so rife as it is at the moment, cars being broken into in car parks, tackle being stolen from the bank. I've even heard stories of people being held prisoner whilst their tackle was stolen and they've left beaten up, lying on the ground in a pool of blood. I just hope that this plague gets better, not worse, within the next ten years for I'd hate to be writing a book in ten years time telling you about someone being held at gunpoint for their tackle - you never know - *"Come on punk make my day!"*

Last but not least on the tackle side of things, the care and

Buzzers and swingers - a boom in the early 90's

welfare of fish on the bank has never been more uppermost in our minds. There are not many anglers walking the bank that haven't an unhooking mat of some sort - and not before time. It was Romart, I think, who really got the ball rolling. Of course, those anglers that had fished the big fish waters had always had unhooking mats of some sort. Down at Yateley people used to, and still do, just get their sleeping bag out and lay the fish on that. You are only likely to catch one or two fish a year down there and a little bit of slime on your bag once a year is worth it. There is no greater protection for a fish than lying on the sleeping bag, but for those that don't wish to do that, or those who catch a lot of fish in a year, there are some excellent purpose-made unhooking mats now available to everyone, although most are too small!

So general fish care and conservation is something that we have certainly improved upon in the last couple of years. We've even got medicines inside our tackle boxes now, just in case the poor little fella's a bit sick when he comes in.

The prospects for the future are looking better and better, never

With today's advances in hooklinks and terminal tackle, you'd think I'd have a decent tackle box

have our fish been so big and never have our waters been in such good condition, due mainly to the work of the NRA and the controlling club's management of the waters. If we take a quick look around the country at some of the very well known big-fish waters, we can look at what's happening now and what we can expect from them in the future. Some of them are very promising, others I'm not so sure about.

Darenth was controlled by Leisure Sport Angling for a great many years, under the hand of Jack Ashford. In 1993 the Leisure Sport control was given over to a new owner, a leisure company with great plans for the fishery and the land around it. During its first season in 1993, I believe they found difficulty in filling all the places in the syndicate although this has probably been resolved by now. The Darenth fish as we know have featured heavily in papers, magazine articles and books over the years and I am afraid to say that some of the fish are now the worse for wear. There are certain fish in the complex now which purely through the number of times they've been caught, not even the number of times they've been handled badly but just the number of time they've been caught, are showing signs of torn mouths, ripped fins and lumps of tail missing. A very sad state of affairs indeed and it's a shame that this is the legacy that we will be leaving to our children to fish for. Certain mouths on some fish bear no resemblance to the beautiful mouth of an uncaught carp or even those on some waters where they are less frequently caught. It does seem as though some carp are just gluttons for bait and seem to be caught every week, posing for the camera most weeks in the *Angling Times* or the *Anglers' Mail*, but now they are suffering for their greed they look in a very sorry state indeed. Perhaps it's time to move some of these fish to pastures new, to release them into large rivers where they'll never see a hook or line again, or if they do they will make some match anglers day. Give them the peace the deserve.

It's very possible that the new leisure club holding Darenth will choose to stock the fishery with some new blood and this could turn it into a very good water for the future. My present opinion is that some of the fish in there have now reached their maximum weight and won't be going on to be over 40 pounds in weight. It may be time to bring in some new blood, otherwise we may be looking at just a handful of fish which have the possibility of reaching 40 pounds in the next few years. There have never been so many 40 pounders around as there are now in 1993, although a couple of the very well known big fish have died in the last couple of years. The famous *Pinkie* at Fennymere, a fish which was caught quite a number of times, up to mid-forties, finally died but we never did get to know the reason for its death, it was probably just old age. Other fish too have died - the big fish from the Car Park Lake; the Harrow forty (the original Lee Jackson fish), unfortunately that was put to death by an unthinking angler. It's quite a few years ago now and Harrow has gone on to produce many new forties and perhaps that's the next water that we should look at. In 1992, Harrow, for the first time, had five different carp over 40 pounds in it, which was absolutely unbelievable to anglers at the time, the biggest fish there was 48 pounds and it's possible that by the end of the 1993 season we may see a new British record from the venue. There is potential in three or four of its fish for one of them to grow very, very big and get over the 50 pound mark or even over Chris Yates' Redmire record. I am sure that once we see that record broken, we will see it broken several times in a short space of time.

Yateley in 1993 has two 40 pounders on the complex, *Bazil* on the North Lake and *Heather* in the Car Park Lake. Jock White's forty from the Pad Lake has slipped back to 37 pounds and has been this weight for the last couple of years, but having two 40 pounders in such close proximity does mean that if one fish comes out, you can move onto the other lake. Withy Pool had its second forty in 1993. Savay continues to produce big fish over the last few years, Albert Romp and Max Cottis both took 40 pounders a few years ago and Bruce Ashby took another 40 pounder which happened to be *The Beast* in 1992. Not too sure where Savay's going to go in the future, but I'm sure that it will have some very big fish in it within the next few years and it wouldn't surprise me to see four or five fish going over the 40 pound mark.

Harefield Lake produced *Nelson* at 40lb 4oz in the nineties, it's very possible that this fishery will have three or four more fish over 40 pounds within the next five years. This inevitably leads to the two jewels in the crown - both Leisure Sport fisheries, Horton and Wraysbury. Horton, well we've talked about Horton, I think it speaks for itself, lots of big carp and it won't be long before there are probably eight forties in the water. Wraysbury went syndicate for the first time in 1993, it produced a fifty and 49 to Dave Cumpstone at the end of the 1992 season. This is another water that could well do the record. Who knows what'll come from the banks of Wraysbury? There are still fish in there, I'm certain, that haven't been caught for a number of years which should be well up there should they come out.

So that's about it. That's what we've been doing in 1992, those are the fish we've been catching. Let's just see what the next few years of carp angling has in store for us. I'm sure the mind would boggle if only we could look into the crystal ball.

Chapter 9

HAREFIELD HAULIN'

During the close season, as normal, I spent my time down at Farlows. As the close season is not really part of your normal fishing, people say that close season captures don't count, I suppose they *don't* really count as part of what you catch, but it's still very enjoyable to try out different methods, different rigs and certainly to try out the baits that you intend to use for the start of the season. Of course every water isn't like Farlows, but at least you can get an idea of whether the fish will pick up the bait or not.

At the start of the close season I spoke to John Stent about doing a video down at Harefield. He, for one, felt that it was very good promotion for Boyer Leisure if I did a video there and had no reservations about me doing it, he suggested that I fished the start of the season which seemed like a good idea to me and the plan I had in mind anyway. He said I could have the choice of swims, this I wasn't at all sure about, we normally had a draw and I didn't think it was fair on the other anglers that I should know where I was fishing and be able to prebait it for much longer than them. I wanted it to be a very natural fishing session and to have no advantages over the other anglers. But of course I wanted the film to be a success and thought to myself that I'd need to catch probably two or three 20 pound-plus fish over the week-long period to make the film a viable proposition.

Big changes were to take place within Boyer Leisure that year and John Stent was to leave by the middle of the close season. This left me in a very awkward position as I wasn't too sure who the new fishery managers would be. As it turned out my good friend Dougal Gray, was to be one them, who turned up with Ben Tucker, a fellow that I'd heard of before but didn't really know. As it turned out Ben was a very nice guy and we sat down on a couple of occasions and sorted out exactly what we'd do.

They both agreed that I should do the video and I promised to offer Ben and Dougal any free advertising that they wanted within the magazine as payment for them allowing me to do the video there for the first two weeks of the season. They changed the rules quite a bit that year and the rota system was brought into effect, this meant that most anglers, other than bailiffs, could now only fish every other week - the one exception to this rule was Stuart Gillham. Now Stuart and I had met many times in the Horse and Barge, he had been very, very successful on Harefield and has in fact done his own piece on his fishing there within this book.

It was agreed that Stuart and I should both fish on *The Point* at the start of the season. Stuart had the choice of swims, I would double up with him, therefore not having an advantage over anyone else. The only advantage I did have was, of course, that I could put bait in during the close season and this was to be used to great effect.

I was a bait and tackle consultant to Kevin Nash at the time and I sat down and formulated a bait that I intended to use during those two weeks at Harefield. Kevin had just brought out a new range of bait and a new range of palatants and it was combination of these ingredients that I would use. I decided to use a 50/50 split of his Amber Birdseed Mix and the Monster Pursuit Fishmeal. This gave me the best of both worlds, creating a bait which was fairly buoyant, quite hard and had a nice taste and smell to it, combined with this I would use the Nash Liver Palatant and a few other little bits and pieces of my own added in just for good measure. I had these rolled at the Catchum factory and one month before the start of the season I began my mass-baiting campaign. I was in a very fortunate position because the bait was free, not many people fishing the lake could get their hands on so much bait.

The September session that I'd done at Harefield the previous year had left me in good stead for the start of the season. I knew some of the best areas and I had taken the three 29 pound commons from a couple of these same spots. The bait was very similar to that which I had used the year before, so I knew that they would readily accept it.

The bait was made and I decided that I'd do one trip per week for the month before the start of the season with a Kevin Nash rucksack full of bait. I'm not sure how much is in there, but there's a lot and it certainly makes your bloody arm ache having to put all that lot out. It was quite a nice feeling actually going down there, knowing that I was the only angler, well Stuart and I were the only anglers, that were able to do this. It was an advantage and probably an unfair one over the other anglers but they would know where they were fishing in a couple of weeks time and would have another two weeks to do the same thing, should they wish to.

As it happened, I decided to do only three of these baiting-up sessions and went down three times with a Nash rucksack full of bait and baited the whole area out in front of *The Hump* swim. Now Stuart had gone to a lot more trouble than I thought he would to be successful in the video. He had markers at about six different places in his swim and he had put plenty of hemp, tiger nuts and Richworth Condensed Milk boilies all around these places, two or three times a week for that period. He certainly didn't want to be outdone in the video and who could blame him? He had the same chance as I did and it was every man for himself.

I arrived at Harefield on the lunchtime of the 15th, went in the pub and ordered myself the biggest steak they'd got with chips and all the trimmings and a nice bottle of wine and sat outside at one of the patio tables. This was to be my last cooked meal, except on the bank, for the next ten days and I was certainly going to enjoy it. It was great sitting there actually thinking about what was ahead. I've got to admit there was a lot of pressure on me to do well for this video, I was laying out quite a lot of money and it could have been a disaster if neither of us caught any fish and of course, I would still have to pay out the money. I sat outside the pub and I could see cars going up and down the road, the Colne Valley truly is a marvellous place with so many waters down there. There were people off to the Cons, down to the Fisheries, fishing on Savay for the first week and the exciting North Harrow Waltonians with a

The Guardian reporters slept all night with their heads in a camera bag

The film begins

chance of a new British record. Anglers going here, there and everywhere to their different waters, each of them stopping at the pub for a chat and a pint before they left. Chris Ball came down to see me on his way down to Wraysbury, wished me luck for the video and bought me a beer, this was a first and something that I shall never forget. I had a fair bit of tackle with me so I only stayed for a couple of drinks and then made my way over to Harefield. Two or three trips back to the car and I got everything loaded up onto *The Hump*, bivvied up, rods ready, plenty of bait. I was there to do the business...

Unfortunately, the fish weren't. Dave Whibley had drawn the workings end of the lake, down where I'd caught *Nelson* the year before. There were loads of fish out there in front of him. It was quite flat calm at the time, very hot and this is where the fish were holed up in the shallow water down by the workings.

Len Gurd (of the Original Video Company), had agreed to do the video for me and he was to stay with me over the ten-day period down at Harefield. Len and I have been good friends for years and we knew we'd have a good laugh down there together and of course with Stuart as company as well, what more could you want? We were really looking forward to the session, Len had got one of the expensive Beta Cam video cameras and it really is a professional camera, as used by the BBC I believe. The production quality that you can get from using a camera like this far exceeds the home video type that you see on the market today. After three or four trips down to the car, with a wheelbarrow to help Len bring the generator, camera, various tripods, lenses, boxes of films, a bivvy and bed, finally we were both ready. Then Stuart arrived and it was more trips to the car park. I was ready for a ten-day sleep let alone ten days fishing by the time we got all three of us set up.

A funny thing happened that night. *The Guardian* newspaper Sports Department sent two of their reporters down to Harefield to do a feature on carp fishing at the start of the season. I think they looked upon us as eccentric idiots, sat out there in our little green tents but certainly by the end of the first night it wasn't us that looked the idiots. The two reporters sat outside my bivvy on the mud waiting for the off, we hadn't gone up the pub or anything, we were far too excited for all that. Len had got his camera ready on the tripod in case we should have any action in the morning. We weren't allowed to sack any fish, so any we caught at night would have to be photographed and then shown on the video using flash. As it happened, not a single fish was caught at night which was quite a result for myself and for Len.

Eleven o'clock, 11.30, the time was ticking away. We had a last cup of tea and I asked *The Guardian* reporters what they intended to do for the night as they didn't seem to have any bedding, or even coats for that matter, all they had was a bag with a camera in it. "Oh, we're used to being out all night, we do stories here, there and everywhere and don't bed down for the night, we're going to stay up all night - what about you?" I said: "At 12 o'clock I'm going to cast out and then I'm getting straight in that bed and going to sleep, I've got a long session ahead of me." "Oh, we'll sit out here and wait."

Well, that night the weather changed completely, the wind began to blow - luckily up towards me, and the temperature dropped. At 12 o'clock Les Bamford let off an almighty rocket from the top bank which signified the start of the season and you could hear a hail of four ounce leads going out into the water. I thought to myself 'it'll be a few hours before there are any bites'. I said goodnight to the two *Guardian* reporters, zipped up my tent, got in the bag and must have been asleep by about five past 12.

At four o'clock in the morning, it was just getting light and I decided to have a look at the lake. I opened my eyes and there to my amazement lying on the mud, out in front of my bivvy, were the two *Guardian* reporters, shivering, frozen and covered in dew and the funniest thing of all was that one of them had put his head inside the camera bag to try and keep his head warm in the night. So much for being out all night in all weathers! I chuckled to myself, woke them up and made them a nice cup of tea, they were well pleased with that.

'Kodak' (from A1 Photos) had already taken a fish off the road bank. They went round there to see if they could get some pictures for their story. When they returned I was telling them about the magazine and suddenly the left hand rod roared off. I was into my first fish of the session, Len was quickly on the camera and I played in the first fish which luckily, tipped the scales just over twenty. A nice common and a good start for the video. *The Guardian* reporters were well pleased and took a few pictures of me with the fish and then they went through all my tackle, listing it all so that they could do their story on these eccentric carp anglers that spend a lot of their lives living by a pond. Off they went and it wasn't long

Classic Harefield common

'Big Carp' Man

before I was into another fish. This fish, a mirror, was just over twenty - so on the opening morning things were looking good.

It turned out to be a marvellous session as most of you that have seen the *Harefield Haulin'* videos will know. They are probably, no I'll be big-headed and say definitely, the best English carp videos ever made. We had a tremendous amount of fish and I ended up with 24, 17 of them over 20 pounds, two of them over 30 pounds and as a bonus I had the very long common that I'd caught the previous September, this time down slightly on his previous weight at 28 pounds.

Anyway for the record and for those of you that haven't seen the video, here's how the session went...

I have never felt so much pressure in all of my angling career as I felt the night before I made these videos. In fact the whole week before was completely nerve-wracking, but the night before in particular, when everything was going through my head - had I done my homework right? Was the bait going to work? Were the fish going to be up there at the start of the season? There were so many variables going through my mind. Harefield is a difficult lake at the best of times, we had certainly got an excellent choice of swims, we had put enough bait out between the two of us, but there are so many other things that could go wrong, these fish really did move around and we could end up fishing out there for a couple of weeks without catching. This wouldn't be the first time that people had done two weeks on there and hadn't had any action at all, you have only to look at the start of the season the year before when Knacker and Dave Whibley fished on *The Point* yet only landed one fish, I know it was a 31 pound common but really I could do with more than one fish to make a successful video.

I sat chatting with Dave Whibley the night before the start, and I think Dave realised that I was under pressure and he tried to make things as easy for me as he could. At the time Dave had a lot of the fish down in front of him, it's funny when you fish waters like this you know everyone that's fishing there and some want you to succeed, unfortunately there are some that don't and take great delight in you blanking. That's the way carp fishing is I'm afraid, you always get a few jealous people and even after I made the films, there were still some people that made snide accusations that I had used more rods than I should have done, baited up in the close season which was an unfair advantage etc, etc, but I didn't break any rules, I certainly didn't use any more rods than two and I just feel sorry for these people really.

Anyway come opening morning I had two fish straight away - a 20 pound common and a 20 pound mirror, and it did seem as though at last I could relax. I was certain that those wouldn't be the last fish of the session, but even if they were, we could still put together a video of 45 minutes with myself showing some rigs and some baits, a bit of plumbing, a bit of floater fishing, so it wasn't a complete washout. With two fish like that, so quickly, it did seem to me as though they were not going to be the last ones.

I decided to fish two separate areas. The right hand rod was fished straight out directly in front of the swim, there were about five bars stretching across the 130 yards of water in front of me and at approximately half way across, the central bar had a coot's nest on it and a small island on the end. It was the perfect marker and the bar at this point was very shallow, but deepened off quite quickly either side of the coot's nest, so it was possible to fish on the bar as long as you were away from the high point. There was another of these high points, which was above the water owing to low water levels so I could fish on the bar or drop down into the gully in front of the coot's nest, where the water was in the region of six feet deep.

Most of the swim was between four and six feet deep, perfect for warm-water fishing. I concentrated half of the bait in this area in front of the coot's nest, the other half I put out to my left on a strange shaped bar which has come to be known as the *whalebone* because of it's shape, it drops down as it comes towards me and forms a plateau under the water where the depth is about two feet. Going away from me towards the centre of the lake this deepens to around three feet and then comes up sharply when it meets the bar running from the *Someone's Coming* island across to the road bank island. The water over the top of this bar is a maximum of 18 inches. You *can* cast over this bar into the main part of the lake, but it is very risky and I wouldn't recommend it, only if there is no chance of catching fish your side of the bar and if you have very abrasion-resistant line. During the video, you will see that for 99 per cent of my fishing I was this side of that bar and only on rare occasions did I venture to the other side.

The plateau and whalebone bar area was the first to produce fish for me. I plumbed this very carefully in the close season and found

Maurice, thirty at last!

Clipped up tight

that where the whalebone island joins the water there is a very small channel where fish can move undetected close to the island. It was the mouth of this channel that I positioned my left hand bait, so that anything moving across the plateau either from the road bank island or from *Someone's Coming* direction could well come down this channel once they had crossed the plateau. It was an excellent interception point and the first couple of fish came from this area, although I did find later on in the session that the fish became a lot more wary and unwilling to come across the whalebone island. Instead they hugged the bar close to the *Someone's Coming* island down to the road bank island. The right hand rod which was fished across to the coot's nest was unproductive to begin with and turned out to be a very spasmodic area, there was always action on the left hand area, most days fish could be seen or some sort of bite occurred; whereas the right hand rod in the third bar/second bar gully was often unproductive and action came in fits and starts. I took four fish there one day and then went several days with nothing. Anyway two 20 pounders were under my belt so I was happy. In the morning *The Guardian* sports reporters had got their story and left it to me and Stuart to get down and make the video and with those two fish we both felt a lot more comfortable, at least now we could relax.

I haven't, as yet, told you much about the nature of Harefield or it's history, but it's a fantastic fishery of around 35 acres in size. There is a large open expanse of water near the workings, the old gravel workings, which are no longer used for digging gravel, but are now used as a refinery and washing plant. There is talk that these gravel workings will be wound up over the next couple of years and what's left of the land that the gravel workings are based on will be dug out back to the road, thus creating about another ten swims on the lake. Then there will be no more work carried out on Harefield at all, it will be very nice over there when that's done, to be honest the gravel workings are a bit of an eyesore and they occasionally have barges moving up and down, although not as many as in years gone by.

The open expanse is around 400 yards wide, but most of it is around 350 yards wide. It does mean that there is some water in the centre of the lake that can't be cast to at the moment with the tackle we are using, there may be developments in the next couple of years which will enable us to cast in excess of 200 yards, but at the moment the best casters are hitting around about the 150-yard mark with a reasonable thickness of line to enable you to get a fish back if you should hook one, of course you can cast beyond that distance with three pound line, but it's not even worth considering doing. I certainly will not go beneath ten pounds main line with 15, 20 or 30 pounds depending on the size of the lead that I'm using. As you move up the lake away from the workings the lake narrows slightly to around 200-yards across and there are some bays, islands and a lot more interesting areas of the lake at this end, although due to the heavy pressure placed upon the carp they don't tend to be in these bays very often, but prefer to be out in the open expanse of water out of harm's way as it were. If you can get them up the top end of the lake, off *The Point*, or in the bays, or around the islands they are a lot more catchable. You are then able to put out bait accurately and do not to have too far to bring the fish in once they are hooked. This is an obvious advantage because when you are fishing out across into the main part of the lake at around 150/160 yards you have probably got half a dozen very dangerous gravel bars to bring the fish over, some reaching up to within a foot or so of the surface which makes landing fish extremely difficult.

It is a typical gravel pit probably with more than its share of gravel bars due to inefficient working of the pit when it was originally dug after the war. This left quite large bars and although the gravel people have had a few goes at the bars since then and skimmed a couple of feet off the top it hasn't made the fishing much easier. However the water level has risen over the years and now there are not so many fish lost at Harefield as there were five or six years ago when the new fish went in. Ten or 15 years ago Harefield only had a handful of fish in it and it was being fished by many of today's well known anglers - Rod Hutchinson, Peter Springate, Kenny Hodder, Paul Gummer and Curly Hatchman.

John Stent's forward thinking, when he was fishery manager in charge at Boyers, led to the closure and netting of two of their best lakes (Willow Pool and Rodney Meadow) and the fish, over a period of time were transferred to Harefield Lake bringing the fish stock up from a handful to several hundred, many over 20 pounds with probably 20 or so over 30 pounds. Harefield has produced a forty on one occasion and there are two or three fish now hovering around that size so it won't be long before Harefield has its second forty. Rod Hutchinson, Pete Springate have moved on to different

Awesome Haulin'

Mid-twenty common

waters but Harefield is still fished by many of the top carp anglers around today and I think it still will be for years to come, as it is certainly one of the finest fisheries in the country.

I must admit that when later that day I bent into my third twenty of the day I was starting to buzz, I mean *really* starting to buzz, if you have ever seen the 'A Team' Hannibal says 'don't you just love it when a plan comes together' or something like that anyway, and the plan was coming together, big style. I was buzzing, and I mean buzzing, a big hit was on the cards, I just couldn't put a foot wrong, I kept whacking the bait in and made sure that the tackle was 100 per cent by changing the hooklinks regularly and making sure the hooks were sharp.

There were only five other fish caught opening morning on the whole lake, so I had done alright. Thus far into the season none of the big ones had been caught so they were all there for the taking. It was just looking better and better with the wind now hacking down our end, without doubt bringing the majority of the fish in Harefield Lake out in front of Stuart and I. This wasn't *haulin'* this was going to be *trawlin'*.

Stuart and Len were excellent company and we really had the crack, plenty to eat, loads of drink, real good fun. I couldn't wait for Stuart to catch something, we really needed us both to be catching the fish to make the video a success. To be fair, Stuart would have caught a lot more than he did in the ten-day session if he hadn't been doing his bailiff duties. Stuart Gillham is head bailiff at Harefield, or was at the time, and of course he had various problems to sort out during the first week of the season. However, on the second day Stuart's CV safety rig combined with his Richworth Condensed Milk boilie ripped off and he landed his first fish of the season, a nice 22 pound common, we were both dead chuffed. Stuart also brought his little puppy down with him which turned out to be great company, when it wasn't peeing all over my tackle!

We weren't getting any problems with tufties or seagulls on this trip, but we were getting problems for the first time with the Canadian geese, there seemed to be hundreds on the lake this particular season, they were coming past in their dozens. As soon as you picked up a throwing stick and began to put a few baits out, they would all speed up and get down there as soon as they could, hitting the baits before they got to the bottom.

I had a bit of a strange occurrence on day three of the session,

I'd been clipping up very tight but I changed over to the Baitrunner facility on my Shimanos in the hope of getting an instant indication as soon as the bait was picked up. It took quite a lot to pull the line out of the clip and I was worried that the tight line pulling over the top of the sharp gravel bars at short range might cause cut-offs, so I changed over to Baitrunner fairly tight, but not tight enough to cut on the top of the bars. I had three aborted takes that morning where the line was absolutely charging off the spool. I picked the rods up but there was nothing there, in fact I felt something on the second take, but on takes one and three I didn't feel anything at all. I sat there trying to think it out but I couldn't quite figure out what was happening, why should I be getting these takes and finding nothing there? I had been picking up quite a lot of silkweed on the bend of the hook, in fact the tops of the bars were covered and I think this was what was happening. As I was pulling back up onto the bars I was gathering up a thick mass of the silkweed on the bend of the hook and when the fish were picking up the bait on the Baitrunner, it was fairly free running and they could pull off with the hook point just barely nicked into the skin. As I was pulling, the change of direction was causing the hook to pull out or tear out through the soft fleshy membrane that it was hooked into. Once I changed back to clipped-up tight with the carbon clips at the butt end, the rod was taking on its battle curve in the rod rests before it was flying out of the clip and this increased pressure put on by the clip was enough to push the hook point home and I didn't have that trouble any more.

Going hard back in the clip certainly paid off and the next take that day was an absolute flyer. Once again as soon as I picked the rod up I knew it was a heavier fish than the low twenties I'd been catching. Having got the fish under the rod tip I thought at one time that it was *Nelson*, it had a very broad back and deep body, but then I saw that old telltale smile on it's mouth and knew that it was my old mate *Maurice* the mirror that I'd caught on my opening session down here twice. He had come back to join me for the video and it was nice to have him on there, particularly as he had gone over thirty for the first time at 30lb 2oz, a nice result. *Maurice* came out another five times that season up to 30lb 12oz, but never dropping below 30 pounds so there we had a new thirty on the banks of Harefield.

The action didn't stop there, I took another three fish in a short

'Always a thirty', but not this time

period of time. The next one another mirror just under 30 pounds at 29lb 4oz, then a common of 25lb 8oz and then a 23lb 12oz mirror. The session was getting better and better, we didn't seem to be able to do anything wrong and it was obvious that these weren't going to be the last fish either. It was the coot's nest area that paid off with these four fish. I kept putting the bait out even though I wasn't getting any action at all from that area. A lot of people may have worried that they were building up a lot of excess bait on the bottom, but I was certain that everything I was putting out was being eaten, not necessarily by the carp, certainly not by the ducks because there weren't any, but by bream. I actually caught two bream over seven pounds and lost another one. There are actually a few bream in Harefield, it's very difficult to get away from them when they are this size. Even with very big or very hard baits you still catch them, but at least you know that the old softening bait that's been out there for a day or so laying on the bottom is being cleared up and that the new fresh, hard stuff that you are putting out is there ready should any carp come along fancying a bit of supper. *Maurice* had a bit of a sorry old mouth on him and I have to admit, having recently seen a picture in one of the angling papers of a fish from Darenth with hardly any tail and no mouth to speak of, I do feel a bit sorry for these fish and it would be nice if somehow we could turn around and release them into some wild venue like, say for instance, the River Thames or River Medway or somewhere and just say 'thanks very much' we are sorry for what's

Centre Stage

been done to you, but thanks for the pleasure that you have given us over the last 20 years, now it's your turn to retire. Some of these fish are in a very bad way and I am pleased to say that the Harefield fish aren't like that and although *Maurice* has got a badly misshapen mouth the rest of him is perfect, but if he keeps on getting caught five or six times a year, maybe we will have to return him to somewhere like Broadwater and say cheerio mate, thanks very much, see you when you're 50 pounds.

Stuart was the perfect gentleman for all these captures, but I could see by the expression on his face that he wished that he was getting a bit of the action and so did I, I knew that it wouldn't be long before he cashed in on the huge beds of hemp that he'd been putting out. Geoff Bowers from Premier happened to walk round from the other side and was standing with Stuart having a cup of tea, probably slagging me off for catching all the fish and willing Stuart to catch a bigger one than me, when suddenly Stuart's left hand rod tore off and he was into his second fish of the session. I fished with Geoff down at Longfield over one season and found him excellent company and a very nice fellow to be with, you could always have a laugh with him and those of you that have seen the video know what I mean. It was a nice 26lb 8oz mirror for Stuart. The fish was a typical Harefield strain, short deep-bellied with high shoulders, a nice one and I couldn't have been more pleased for Stuart. Len had been carefully keeping notes of everything that had happened throughout the video. It turned out that by the end of the ten days he was to take almost 40 hours of video tape and by sequencing with numbers and times he was able to keep track of everything that was happening during the session. About five days in however disaster was to strike - a gust of wind was to take the notes from the video out into the lake, quick as a flash, never wasting an opportunity to get his clothes off, Stuart was in the lake and swimming out, he collected up all the papers, luckily for Len and I, otherwise I don't know how we would have sorted everything out once he got it back to the studios.

It was all beginning to look a little bit easy on the video and it would be hard for people watching it to realise that we were fishing a difficult lake, but putting it into perspective, there were over 50 anglers on the lake that day and only one other fish was caught, a fish of eight pounds! We were making it look easy. Another thing also became evident and that was we were going to have an awful lot of footage and a terrific number of fish and that there was a possibility that not one, but two videos could be done. This was something we hadn't even thought of doing, I'm not a greedy angler and certainly hoped that everyone else would also have their fair share of the fish.

The weather so far had been sunny although chilly, with the strong wind blowing up to our end. However towards the end of the week the weather changed completely, the heavens opened and I wondered if this would spoil our chances. The rain didn't seem to put the fish off and at nine o'clock that morning I had another 29 pounder and this one was an unknown big fish as far as I was concerned, although there were a lot of fish the season before in the 25 to 28 pound mark that were gradually creeping up towards the 30-pound mark.

The nights were very social occasions, but I don't think we had an evening on the lake with just the three of us present, more often than not several others came round and talked over the day's events and chipped in towards the BBQ and a few beers, it's really nice to have a BBQ on the lake, as I am sure you all know, there was no shortage of ribs, chops and steaks from the local butchers in Harefield.

I had a nice little break at the end of the first week as it was Fathers Day on the Sunday. I got up early in the morning and recast the baits as I wasn't too sure where they had landed the night before. I'd had a 19 the night before, first thing in the morning around the magical nine o'clock I had an 18lb 8oz, quickly followed up by a 21 pounder. Then it was over to the Horse and Barge to meet the family who I hadn't seen for nearly a week, I always miss them when I'm away from home and I was given my Fathers Day cards and presents, and then we had something to eat and a few drinks - it was a really nice little break midway through the session.

Coming back about five hours later having missed probably the most productive part of the day, not that I'm moaning of course, I quickly cast back in the same place and within half an hour a third 29 at 29lb 1oz, this fish has the unfortunate name of *The Turd* because of its snub nose, but if you ask me it's a beautiful fish. Dougal and his family popped down later in the afternoon and saw me catch the last fish of the day, a nice common about 18lb 8oz, we'd had another great day. This really was going to be some video!

At the end of the first week the fish were still up there with us, although they had moved out more in front of Stuart and he was getting a lot of bubbling over the hemp, line bites and general fish activity, so it came as no surprise when at five o'clock in the morning he had his first fish - 22lb 8oz - nice, almost fully-scaled,

'The Pink Linear'

Topping up the tan

very heavily scaled down the lateral lines. It was a beautiful morning, the lake was flat calm; then in a short space of time Stuart took another two fish, one of the original commons at 26lb 8oz which was a personal best common for him, he followed it up with one of the historic fish of Harefield: *The Orange Fish* at 33lb 8oz. It was ironic that this was the very fish that spurred him to fish here in the first place. This fish appeared in the Richworth Baits advert years ago with Ritchie McDonald holding it. Stuart was really a pike angler at the time, but one look at this superb fish in the arms of Ritchie McDonald made his mind up that he wanted to fish Harefield and it was a result for both of us catching it on the video for posterity. *The Orange Fish* sadly is no longer with us, it was dropped by an inexperienced angler, and even the most experienced do occasionally have accidents with fish, but it broke its tail and infection set in and some months later it died. Whether it was directly due to the tail breakage can't be certain, but it certainly didn't help.

The early morning wind sprang up, pushing hard north easterly and forcing the fish across the swim from my left out in front of Stuart to my right, on the video you can actually see huge patches of bubbles coming up over particles, I wondered if I was going to catch anything else and then at 11 o'clock in the morning the rod cast over that shallow bar that I was telling you about at the start of the chapter, the bar which runs between *Someone's Coming* island and the road bank island, absolutely leapt on the rest and the line purred from the reel. I was into a good fish, a fish that I have wanted to catch from the minute I stepped onto the banks of Harefield, this was turning out to be a red letter day for both Stuart and I. It was *The Pink Linear* at 30lb 12oz, an absolutely brilliant fish now almost 40 pounds in weight at it's '93 season high. It was certainly the biggest linear that I'd had the chance to fish for, the only one that I knew of bigger was the 38 pound fish in Wraysbury. I followed this up a little while later with another of the immaculate Harefield commons just under 26 pounds, I was amazed at the number of 20 pound commons that we were getting. Harefield's always known for its twenties, but to catch this many of this sort of size is almost unheard of - a beautiful common indeed.

Despite the fact that Stuart had the majority of fish in front of him I was still landing a few, although I couldn't believe it as all the fish we could see were feeding on Stuart's hemp. Later in the morning

I had another fish, 26lb 8oz, a typical Harefield mirror and then it all came right for Stuart. Once again the fish had got their heads down that evening just before dark, he had a 22lb 8oz common. Nothing that night, although fish were jumping all over his baits, we sat there in the darkness listening to the crashes like huge bodies out there in the darkness. Then at first light he was away again, his second thirty this session, *Spot* at 33 pounds. It was a fish I had never seen before on the bank, but a lovely fish indeed. Stuart was over the moon, two thirties apiece, we'd had a result, we were *Haulin'*.

Weather conditions had changed, the wind dropped completely, the sun came out and the forecast was for 90 degrees over the next few days, although I felt fairly confident of picking up a few fish from the tops of the bars I decided for the sake of the video to spend the next couple of days surface fishing as it would make an interesting change on the film and it's always been one of my favourite forms of fishing. I had been baiting several of the bays with mixers every opportunity I'd had, but so far had not had a chance to fish on the top.

Dougal came around the next day, late morning, and told me that there were two fish in the bay behind, and both looked around 20 pounds. I moved round to have a go there, it was nice that Len could film me across the bay, I began feeding the mixers in slowly and gradually I got the interest of the two fish. By this time several of my friends, from other waters, had come down to see me. Ritchie, Steve Newman, Ginger Steve and Steve Nine/One, who had all been on Yateley for the start. They came down with news of Little Ritchie taking *Heather the Leather* at 43 pounds and various other captures that had happened over the country. They had all heard about my results at Harefield and knew that the video was going to be a success. They sat down behind me, I didn't think this was a very good opportunity to catch one off the top as there were so many people there, also in the swim I was fishing I had lost a fish previously as there was a long bush protruding out into the water only a couple of yards to my left, if I did hook a fish I would have to keep it away from there at any cost if it was to be hooked and held.

The fish got more and more interested, but as yet I hadn't even cast out, Ritchie asked me if I was ever going to cast out because I think he was beginning to get a bit impatient at the time the fishing

'Arfur Tail' at 26lb 8oz

Hook and hold for this floater-caught 26-plus

was taking. "Not until they're ready my son," I said. When I thought the time was right I flicked some mixers out in front of the biggest of the two fish, it turned immediately and sucked it down. I was up on my feet calling across to Len, I wound down tight and pulled the fish in towards me, within two seconds the fish was in the net - 26lb 8oz. Ritchie looked at me in amazement, I don't think he realised that the snag was as dangerous as it was. "I like to play with my fish a little bit. I like to tire them out before I net them," he said. The fish was thrashing around in the net, he wasn't tired at all, I was well pleased with the fish anyway. I moved off around the bays and caught a couple more double figure commons just for the sake of the video. I was itching to get back, I knew a method that would certainly catch these fish in the hot weather from the tops of the bars, the method that I tried at the North Harrow Waltonians many years before when they were spawning and moving close to the surface on shallow bars in the hot weather. It's a simple rig, pop-up straight from the lead fished ten to 12 inches off a heavy fixed lead. A small brightly coloured bait fished on the swimmer rig placed in their path right on the top of the bar, irresistible to the fish moving along these pathways, they either had to swim around it or eat it and nine times out of ten they ate it.

I was actually filming the plumbing sequence on the lake when one of these rigs took off. I'd seen several fish out there earlier in the day feeding on one of the shallow points on the bar. The fish were also getting a little bit spawny and although they had spawned on May 8th, I felt as though they were about ready to do it again and I have scruples about this sort of thing, I don't like to fish while they are actually going through the motions. We decided to stay on for another day anyway just to see how it went, but in the evening of that day we were proved right when the fish did begin to spawn. Anyway, as I was saying, I was just doing a plumbing sequence on the film when the right hand rod, a small Crustacean dip pop-up, ten inches off the bottom, straight off the lead, ripped off and I knew immediately that I was into a very fast-moving fish. I couldn't make my mind up whether it was big or small to begin with, all I knew was that it was a very powerful fish, it weeded me several times, and when I finally got it to the net I recognised it as the very long common that I'd taken in the September before, slightly down on the scales at 28 pounds but truly one of the jewels of Harefield, an immaculate fish. Second time around for this one - an old mate.

This action came on the right hand rod fished on the bar straight out in front of me. I saw about six fish move along this bar and I swear that not one of them looked under 30 pounds, perhaps I was foolish in not bringing the other rod into this area, but I carried on fishing the gap between the islands with the left hand rod, taking two doubles, at 15 and 12 pounds. However, the right hand rod was certainly in the area of the big fish. Later that day I lost an absolute beast which may well have been *Nelson*, it certainly belted off on one of those powerful runs like it did the first time I caught it. The left hand rod was busy with the next fish, a 19 pound heavily scaled mirror and then I lost two. Stuart was also in with a bit of action, he took two double-figure commons but the fish were beginning to spawn, so we decided to call it a day earlier than we wanted to leave, but we couldn't risk hurting any of these beautiful fish. Just before we packed up my right hand rod tore off again and I was into another very powerful fish - I couldn't believe my luck - it was yet another 29 pounder, one of the old originals, *Split-Tail* - a beautiful fish. It was a fish that I'd seen Hampshire Chris with some years before, an original that never used to drop below 32 pounds, obviously spawned out through its recent activities.

We left the Harefield carp spawning on the islands, charging up and down, thrashing the water as they went, we could see some beautiful fish moving out in front of us, we probably could have stayed and caught more but we'd had fantastic results. I'd had 42 takes in ten days, almost unheard of on Harefield; 26 fish landed, 17 over twenty, two thirties. What a start to the season! This had certainly put me in good stead for a quiet summer down on the North Lake. Who knows what the summer would have in store for me, would *Bazil* grace my net? That would all be in the stars, all I knew was I was going down to have a try.

I left Harefield at the end of that ten-day session wondering if I'd ever fish there seriously again. I'd had some good results out of Harefield, I loved the water very much and there are still some big fish in there for me to catch, but there are other waters to fish, new horizons to be conquered, new fish to meet, friends to make; I had made some good friends there, both fellow anglers and some of the fish who had graced my net more than once. So I took my leave of Harefield, off down to Surrey in search of the big boys. I didn't know what was in store for me and how hard the fishing was going to be compared to Harefield but that's carp fishing, you never know

Ritchie with 'Heatber' at 43lb-plus

what's just around the corner.

It was in the summer of 1984 that one of the North Lake's inhabitants, *Bazil* as it came to be known, was made famous by one of the top carp anglers in this country, Ritchie McDonald. Ritchie and myself were fishing Savay and the North Harrow Waltonians at the time and I remember talking to him before he came down to fish the North Lake. He was telling us at the cafe down at Savay that morning that he had seen some pictures of this 40 pound fish, one that he had heard of lots of times before. It had been caught several times over 40 pounds by Chris Ridington and Jan Wenzcka to name but two of the several other good anglers of the era and also fished hard for by Kevin Maddocks for one. Ritchie hadn't fancied having a go for the fish until he saw these photos and thought what a

The long common again, but 'only' 28 this time

beautiful fish it was. Striking in its length and a nice scale pattern down by it's tail. However, it wasn't just the look of the fish, it was the lake he fancied fishing as well as it had always been known as a very hard lake and Ritchie had always been one for a challenge. So he left us that summer and headed down to Surrey to have a try for *Bazil.* I must admit at that time I couldn't quite understand the fascination with this fish as the Harrow fish was also to come out about the same time to Keith O'Connor and at its record weight of 43lb 12oz. In fact, for those of you that can remember the *Angling Times* in October of that year, Keith O'Connor was on the front with the North Harrow Waltonians fish at 43lb 12oz, but sprawled across it in big letters were the words "and an even bigger one inside". I always felt that this was a bit of a shame for Keith, he had caught an absolutely remarkable fish, a fish that was very difficult to catch and his moment of glory was stolen by a headline. In fact in the *Angling Times* that week there were three forties because the North Harrow Waltonians forty came out twice in two days. Now I just said that it was a very difficult fish to catch and this makes it look very easy, but on the Saturday and Sunday of that weekend Keith O'Connor and Zenon Bojko were both to take that fish, and those captures were the last ever captures of that particular carp.

Ritchie did very well this summer at Yateley and ended up with three fish off the North Lake; *The Thirty* at 28 pounds, another fish at 20 pounds and of course the now famous *Bazil* which he caught in *The Point* swim. This fish was to feature heavily in every angling publication at the time and was used as a great advertising carrier for ranges of bait, catapults and assorted bits of tackle, it really did bring Ritchie to the forefront in angling. This is, of course, the time that Ritchie should have brought out his book *Ritchie on Carp.* Ritchie was *the* angler at that time and if he could only have timed his book to come out then I am sure he would have made a killing in the marketplace. Unfortunately when his book was published, although it sold very well, as well as any carp books sell these days, the moment of glory was in the memory of a lot of people. Of course this was also before he caught the two forties at the end of the season from the other two lakes in the complex. His book is excellent but was badly timed and I am sure he would have done a lot better with it, had he brought it out to coincide with either of those two remarkable captures.

Carp anglers from far and wide headed down to the complex in search of this fish and it was to come out quite a few times in the next few years. I carried on fishing down at the North Harrow Waltonians and for those of you that have read the other two books *Tiger Bay* and *Fox Pool* will know that it was the next capture of the fish which really spurred me into wanting to try and catch it. I happened to be in The Fisheries, the pub that most of the anglers used at the time, this was before the Horse and Barge was done up. I was standing there with Phil Harper and he was telling me about a strange weekend that Kerry and he'd had down at the Yateley complex. They fished in *The Point* swim just where Ritchie had caught *Bazil* in the previous October and Kerry had caught *The Forty* at 42 pounds and Phil had caught *The Thirty* at 27 pounds, they'd caught the two biggest fish in the lake in a single weekend. They moved on to the Car Park Lake for the last day of their session and Phil lost a very big fish in there. This all sounded too good to be true to me, big fish and easy to catch and that's really what made me want to have a go down there. I got *The Forty* bug, the North Harrow Waltonians fish was to be killed shortly after and that left me with no alternative but to move on to the North Lake and have a go for the fish. I thought it was going to be a lot easier than it turned out to be. That may sound big-headed, but having seen two anglers that I knew very well catch the fish without too much trouble, though obviously they knew exactly what they were doing, in the right place at the right time etc. They caught the fish, that was the main thing. It was catchable and I thought that I would catch it, so when I fished the North Lake for the first time, I didn't really take the place too seriously, I must admit I went down there a bit cocky if you like, thinking that I'd soon knock a fish out and before too long I'd have *Bazil*. I didn't put a great amount of time in on the North Lake, did a couple of weekends in 1985, a few in 1986, probably a few more in 1987 and carried on right through until now, 1993, and I am still here trying for *Bazil*.

As you may have gathered by now, we have actually come almost up to date and I wrote this whole book as it happened. You have read about the *Johnson's Leather* written the day, or the week that I caught that fish, the same with the one from Fox Pool and all the other fish, there is no better way to capture the moment as I found through experience, but actually writing about the capture the day that it happens, then you get the feeling, the mood and the facts.

For those of you who don't know the complex down at Yateley,

'Split-Tail', one of the originals, just a fraction under thirty

'The Turd', yet another 29-plus

there are about a dozen lakes. None of them are very large, the Match Lake is about the biggest and I would guess that from 20 acres the other lakes decrease in size, some being smaller than an acre. Coming from the south end of the complex and moving north, the first lake that you come to is the Copse Lake. I fished that in the winter of 1986 for about four or five weekends and was fortunate to catch my first Yateley carp from this quite difficult small water which is very weedy and only a few acres, containing about three or four 30 pound fish. The largest fish in the water these days is one called *The Rudder*, which comes out around the 36 pound mark, although it does tend to fluctuate. You've got *Crinkle-Tail, Slate Grey* and *Split-Tail* each of these are in the low thirties. It was in that winter of 1986 that I was to catch *Crinkle-Tail* at 30lb 4oz - this story appears in *Fox Pool* and those of you that have read it will know the story well I am sure.

Moving northwards, you have the Nursery Lake, a lake full of snags, islands and trees, a little bit of an unknown quantity. There are a couple of 30 pound fish that have been caught from the water, but not many people fish this lake as the other lakes on the complex have fish that are far more well known. Some people say that they have seen a very dark, large fish in there but up to now it has not been caught and I believe the lake record stands at about 32 pounds.

You then come to the Match Lake, probably the most well-stocked lake on the complex with upwards of 50 carp, many of these are over 20 pounds, with a couple of thirties for good measure. This is probably the most hard-fished water on the complex, there are not many days during the season when there are not at least a handful of anglers on there and early season, especially at weekends, the lake is packed, but it does produce the goods. There are not many weekends go by without quite a few twenties being caught. This seems to be the starting lake for most anglers that come down to the complex. It's nice to go on there, catch one or two Yateley fish and then perhaps move on to one of the more difficult waters.

I will ignore a lot of the lesser known lakes on the complex such as the Pump House, the South Lake and Lake Ten. These, of course, all hold carp but none of the big ones that we're after. We have to cross the road to come to the next three lakes which are of interest to us. The Pad Lake, the smallest on this side of the road, has one fish of 40 pounds, two fish at 30 pounds and two 20 pounders; that makes five carp in total in a water of two or three acres.

Just across the path, you will find probably the best lake on the complex for big fish: the Car Park Lake. A bit deeper than most of the other lakes on the complex and a bit weedier. This lake contains the well known *Heather*, a huge leather carp which has come out four or five times over 40 pounds. It's a very difficult fish to catch and normally only comes out once per season, the few people who catch it are very lucky indeed. Other fish in the 'Car Park' include *Half-a-Tail,* which varies between 32 and 38 pounds, *Single Scale* which normally comes out around the 37 pound mark, *Chunky* 32 to 34 pounds, *The Dustbin* 31 to 33 pounds and *The Big Orange,* another low thirty. There are 11 fish in total in this lake, the others with the exception of one, *the small common*, are all over 20 pounds but any fish from this lake is hard earned, believe you me!

Then of course we have the North Lake. In here there are seven carp: there is *Bazil,* who normally comes out around the 45 pound mark, there's the *North Lake Thirty* which comes out around 34 pounds; there are three known as *the 30 pound mirrors*, one of these is normally around the 25 pound mark and there are two commons, one at 20 and one a double; so you can see the lakes are very low in stocks but the rewards are great should you hook into one of the big ones.

Now let us not forget the other lake on this side of the road, the Split Lake. Leisure Sport Angling, who control all the fishing on this venue, have taken it upon themselves to stock this lake over the last couple of years and intend turning it into a first-class fishery. I believe there are upwards of 20 carp in there up to 28 pounds, mirrors to 26 and the big one, the common, 28lb 8oz. These fish were all taken from Thorpe Park.

The Car Park Lake and the North Lake are about the same size at about ten acres. My assessment of the size of these waters may be slightly inaccurate for those purists amongst you who are reading this but to me it looks around about ten acres and that's good enough!

The Car Park Lake is quite an open fishery, there's one snag tree in the corner which is out of bounds and you're not allowed to fish there. Quite a few fish have been damaged or killed by anglers trying to bully them through the snags. The rest of the lake is a typical gravel pit with some huge gravel bars and plateaux which are easily visible, these do not normally tend to weed up. The rest of the lake however is usually choked with Canadian Pondweed.

The North Lake is a different proposition, there are many small islands and channels on this lake and lots of trees overhanging the water. The fish in this lake can hide away and not be seen for months. There is also now an abundance of weed, both Canadian and some other stuff that looks a bit like grass but is fairly soft to pull through should you hook a fish.

Bazil has been forty for over ten years, probably the oldest living forty in the country, or at least a fish that had been forty pounds for the longest period in this country. *Bazil* originally came from Leisure Sports Sutton Lake many years ago and was stocked into the North Lake at 20 pounds. Since then it has been caught by many famous anglers and for those of you that have read any of the old angling books, you may well have seen Kevin Clifford and Peter Springate with the fish at 31 and 26 pounds respectively.

Pizza, due the big one (33lb)

Jock and the last of 'the big three' at 44lb 4oz

After my success at Harefield and my comparatively bad luck in catching a forty for all the years that I have been fishing waters containing them, I really felt I needed to make a concerted effort on this water. We were into July when I first set foot on the lake, there had been one fish caught and two fish lost during the opening two weeks. I was to meet quite a character during the first session on this water, a young fellow who I'd never seen on Yateley before. He wore skin-tight blue tracksuit bottoms, his privates sticking out like a bag of walnuts and he soon gained the nickname the 'Ballet Dancer' because of his strange attire.

The Ballet Dancer was to do exceptionally well this summer on the water and ended up by the end of September catching five fish, two twenties and three small fish. These small fish are known as the Tells - *William, Aquatell* and *Little Tell* and had been stocked into the water from somebody's fish tank. Not something that I agree with or would recommend but they were put in at a few ounces and have now got up to six or seven pounds in size. They haven't seemed to have affected the other fish in the lake so I suppose we can be thankful and think ourselves fortunate that we had three other fish in the lake that perhaps one day would grow to record proportions.

I chatted to this Ballet Dancer chap as soon as I arrived at the water. He'd caught the only fish so far, that was opening night, a fish known as *the long twenty*, just over 20 pounds. He was a nice fellow and was enjoying the attention he was getting from having caught that fish. He did however come out with a remark which astounded everyone on the water when he told us that he'd caught *Bazil* the season before at 46lb 12oz. Now, *Bazil* had indeed come out the season before within the first couple of weeks of the season to Don Orriss at 46lb 1oz. It was then to come out twice in August at 43 pounds, once the first week of August and once the third week in August. Wayne Dunne and Terry Pethybridge, the two captors.

Now the Ballet Dancer reckoned he'd caught it the second week of August at 46lb 12oz and this had people wondering whether it was the truth. I must admit that I always give people the benefit of the doubt and the Ballet Dancer did say that he had photos of the fish at home. Now some of the anglers fishing the water became a little bit annoyed when he didn't bring the photos down. In fact one of the bailiffs asked him if he would care to produce one of the photos for the Leisure Sport records as a photo was being kept of each capture of this fish throughout its history. The Ballet Dancer never turned up with the photos and later that year he stopped fishing the water, which I felt was a bit of a shame. I think he had been bullied a little bit by some of the people and nobody knew for sure whether he'd caught it. Although logically, if the fish had come out three times in three weeks, twice at 43, it seems doubtful that it's middle capture would have been almost four pounds bigger. So that was the end of the Ballet Dancer, however he left his mark on the water by bringing a friend of his down for a weekend session in the August of this year. I'll tell you that story as we go through my first proper season on the North Lake.

There was no weed in the main part of the lake. The only weed that could be found in the North Lake was in the back channel behind the point. This area had been a favourite haunt of *Bazil's* for many years and I believed that the weed also was a contributing factor to that fish and many of the others spending so much time in the bay. In fact by the end of September this particular year, there was not a single fish caught out of the main part of the lake and every fish that had been landed had been caught in the bay. This made life a lot simpler as long as you could get a swim in the bay, but of course with so many anglers spending so much time on the water, it was very difficult to get one of the hot swims.

At the end of the bay on the opposite bank which you cannot fish is a huge bush hanging over the water. This bush became known as *Bazil's Bush*, *Bazil* having been caught there a couple of times prior to this season, but during this season it was to come out twice, once to Jock White and once to Micky Gray, both times at 44 pounds-plus. This was obviously a holding and feeding area for this fish.

I spent the whole of August and September down on the North Lake that year fishing three or maybe four days a week. This was more fishing in a short space of time than I'd ever done in my angling career before, I was desperate for this fish. It hadn't come out in June or July and the feeling of expectancy fishing down there in August left you full of awe. Nobody knew how big this fish would be, some people had seen it, I had not, and those that had said that it was enormous.

It had come out at the start of the previous season at 46 pounds and all sorts of figures were going through peoples' minds. Nobody knew how big *Bazil* would be on its first time out and I must admit to having ideas of 47 or 48 pounds in my head.

Jock White, of the Yateley Ya-Hoo Crew, had already done one and a half seasons on the water and had been quite successful, having caught *The Thirty* on two occasions at 34 and 36lb 12oz. He was a Premier Fishmeal man and had done well on all the lakes on the complex using this combination of bait. Everyone felt as though he would be favourite to catch the fish as he had arrived a few days before the start of the season and by mid-August he had not yet gone home, putting in over nine weeks fishing in a continual session after this fish with not a single bite from a carp, but his confidence was still high.

At the beginning of August Jock moved into *Bazil's Bush*. The Ballet Dancer had already taken two or three fish from this area and Jock felt it was his best opportunity of intercepting *Bazil* if it moved into the bay and of course, he was right. Feeding in a combination of peanuts, tigers and fishmeal boilies, Jock caught the fish on August 13th. I was fishing about three swims to his right, heard the take and came running in to his swim.

The calmness that I saw in that man's face will stay with me for ever. He was into a fish the size of which nobody knew for certain, but definitely between 40 and 50 pounds, and all he could say was that he wanted the video camera on and for Pinky to take a film of him playing it and he was turning round, looking over his shoulder telling Pinky how to turn it on and how to focus the camera properly. Not watching the fish at all but gently pulling the fish across the lake out in front of him. The first time it swirled, it looked like a twenty to me, it was deep down in the weed and I must admit never for once, at the beginning of the fight, did I think it was a forty but Jock had no doubts in his mind.

As soon as it rolled, he turned round to me and said: "Is that what I think it is?" And it was then that it came home to me, Jock had got *Bazil*. On the bank, although it was the second time I'd seen the fish, I was absolutely astounded by the size of it. Laying on his unhooking mat, it was like a huge hippo, its fat belly bulging down to its anal fin. I still didn't have a clue how big it was going to be, but on the scales it registered 44lb 4oz. Jock punched the sky - he was *the man* and the following piece that I put in the magazine did Jock justice for the time, the effort and the continued pressure that he'd put on the North Lake and in particular that fish. Well done Jock, you deserved it!

In previous years, once *Bazil* had been caught, the North Lake was almost empty of anglers. After all, with so few fish and only one thirty, it was hardly worth most people staying on, especially with the Car Park Lake only next door with five or six thirties in it and a forty which hadn't often come out. This year was to be different, the Ballet Dancer stayed on and as I was telling you earlier, brought down one of his friends, Leroy.

Leroy had done a little bit of carp fishing before but to be fair to him, and I think he would admit this, he was still very green. The

Car Park Lake bonus. My first from this side of the road

story that was told to me was that the Ballet Dancer gave him his bait, tied his rig and told him where to cast out, I believe it was the Ballet Dancer that told me this so it may not be entirely true. But sure enough, just over a week later in the opposite corner of the lake Leroy latches into *Bazil*. Leroy's biggest fish was a double and there he was, middle of August, with a 44lb 8oz mirror. Where do you go from here I asked myself? Now this was a shock to everyone fishing the water, never had the fish reappeared as quickly as this. It had normally been several weeks or even months before the fish came out again. Only once before when Wayne and Terry Pethybridge had caught it over a two or three week period had it been captured so quickly. People didn't know whether to stay on or move. It had now come out twice, surely it couldn't come out again?

I missed the capture when Leroy had it but came down a week or so later and fished, no sign of anything. I went home for a week, lo and behold *Bazil* was to come out again, this time off the bush. A remarkable set of events led to this capture by Micky Gray, an angler who'd fished on the complex for many years. That week, no fewer than five anglers had fished in *Bazil's Bush* for short periods of time, in fact Dave Mallin, one of the Black Country duo from Wolverhampton, was actually fishing in the bush that day and packed up at five o'clock in the evening. Micky Gray moved into the bush at six o'clock, cast out a single bait and before he had the chance to put any free offerings around it, about seven o'clock in the evening it tore off and *Bazil* was once more on the bank - this time at 44 pounds exactly.

Three times in about four weeks! This was too much to handle. I really didn't know whether I was on my arse or my elbow. I didn't know whether to stay, to go, it could come out the next day, it could come out in the next five minutes or it may not come out for the rest of that season, nobody knew for certain what to do. The only thing that you could do was hang on in there.

I came down for two more three-day sessions at the beginning of September and fished in the bush area, or as near to it as I could. I was sure that this fish must get in the bush again, it seemed to love it in there. Pizza had fished on the North Lake for two seasons, he'd done exceptionally well on a couple of the other lakes on the complex, having taken *The Parrot* in the Copse Lake some years before and several of the big fish from the Car Park Lake including *Heather* at 39 pounds, *Single Scale* at 36 pounds and *The Dustbin* at

32 pounds, now he was after *Bazil.*

He caught *The Thirty* the winter before but was determined that he would stay on the North Lake no matter what. He hadn't had a bite so far that season but he was sure that everything he was doing was right. It was the corral area that he chose for his baiting campaign and during September he was to take no fewer than three fish, two of the twenties, the 25 and the long mirror at 20 pounds and a few ounces and then later that month *Bazil* again. Its fourth capture, this time at 43 pounds and a few ounces but Pizza had done it, he had achieved his goal and caught *Bazil.*

Despite all the time that I put in on the North Lake, it was only Jock's capture that I'd seen, I'd missed the other three. It seemed as though every time I went home, the fish was being caught, the North Lake was working against me and everything I tried ended in failure. All I could catch was tench and bream. I knew that I'd have to change my bait next season and move onto a fishmeal-type bait as it was beyond doubt that this lake and its inhabitants preferred fishmeal to any of the other base mixes.

Pizza moved on to the Pad Lake directly after catching *The Forty,* and being the good angler that he is, caught *The Thirty* at 36lb 12oz the following week. What a good season Pizza had.

Now with four catches of *Bazil* by the end of September, it did strike me that this would probably be the last capture, although it was possible that the fish could come out at the end of the season. So although defeated, I made my mind up that I would leave the water and maybe come back at the end of the season but I needed to go somewhere and catch some fish. This was the first time that I had ever done anything like this, the water had beaten me. I felt absolutely rock-bottom confidence-wise.

I had been fortunate though at the end of September to catch one fish from the Car Park Lake, a consolation prize if you like. I took the small common at about 18 pounds off the surface on Chum Mixers, but surely this was not enough reward for the great number of hours that I'd put in at the complex that summer. I didn't fancy going back to Harefield for the winter. Winters on there had been as hard as anywhere but I'm a carp angler and I have to be carp fishing and I do like to see the indicators move so I decided that I'd do a winter down on Farlows in the hope of catching one of the big fish from there.

There were now three or four thirty pound-plus fish in the water.

So far I'd been unlucky and not caught any of them although I had caught them at just 25 pounds. Going down to Farlows was like a breath of fresh air and confidence was soon sky high, I caught loads of fish that winter and carried on fishing it right through the close season. Fishing around the Herons Point area, off the front in winter and down in the islands once the warmer weather of the close season came around. The biggest fish was a 22 pound common, so I still haven't caught one of the big ones out there but when you're catching 12 to 15 double-figure fish at a weekend, after a blank summer on the North Lake, each fish you catch is such a pleasure.

I made my mind up however that I would fish the last two weeks of the season back on the North Lake and spent four or five days getting everything ready for this two week period. I was going to take some hemp, some tigers, some fishmeal boilies that I'd be rolling myself, plenty of bait, lots of rigs tied, new line, nothing would be left to chance.

I packed the car the night before the session, it had been quite cold at the end of the season and I know that a couple of the lakes over there had frozen up on two or three occasions. I decided that I'd better phone Pinky just to make sure that the North Lake was free of ice, although I was certain it would be. When I phoned him that night, he wasn't in so I left a message on his answerphone, asking if he could get back to me sometime and tell me if the lake was free of ice and if anything had happened. He phoned me later that night with the worst possible news: *Bazil* had been caught that day off the point at 42lb 8oz. So much for my end of season two weeks, the North Lake had kicked me in the nuts once more.

I had however gained a wealth of experience from that summer down on the North Lake. I didn't know of course whether it would do me any good or not but I'd learned some good spots, I'd seen other anglers and how they fished, the rigs they used, the areas they fished. Those that had done well and those that hadn't had all gone through my mind and I was sure that I'd stand a better chance of catching at least *a* fish out of the North Lake, even if not the big one, the following season. To be honest, the way I felt about the North Lake, I'd be grateful for anything.

Chapter 10

BAZIL

After my dismal results on the North Lake the previous season, I had to make my mind up in the close season was I really going for *Bazil* or not this season? If I was, it was going to demand 100 per cent effort, tunnel vision and sacrificing everything else in my life over a period of time which was undecided.

It had become painfully obvious that there were only two methods of succeeding on this type of water. The first was by luck and this had happened many times for people in the past, their first time on the water, they dropped in the right place at the right time and knocked out *Bazil* or one of the other fish. The other way was by hard work. This how that most people caught the fish. It did seem from looking at the history of anglers that had tried to catch *Bazil* that those who really wanted to succeed, had triumphed in the end, even though it may have taken them several years to reach their goal.

Of course there are anglers that had been on there for quite a few years now, fishing for this particular specimen who still haven't caught it and I could quite easily see myself in that category. Although I have always caught more than my fair share of fish, it's not always possible to single out the largest individual in the lake. One thing for certain was that I was going to try and avoid getting in the position I had the previous year. Going on for a few days and then pulling off for a week or so, because this had meant disaster for me the previous season. It seemed every time I went home, the fish were being caught.

Not only is the North Lake geographically a very difficult lake to fish due to its size, the number of bays and islands, and the small head of fish, but also the class of anglers that you find on this venue is generally very high and everyone there, without exception, is after *Bazil*. Nobody goes onto lakes like these to fish for a twenty or a thirty pounder. The people that are there go to catch a forty pound carp. That makes your job a lot more difficult because even if these anglers aren't of a high quality, they are still taking up swims, and usually for quite long periods of time.

Last season had seen the disappearance of Jock White and Pizza, two very good anglers who had been on the lake for several years after *Bazil*. This of course meant that my job would be easier because those two very good, long session anglers were now off the water. However, they weren't the only good, long session anglers to be fishing the North Lake this season and I realised that some of the anglers would be putting in as much or more time than I.

I am in a very fortunate position with running *Big Carp* magazine; a lot of the work I do can be carried out actually on the bank, if I'm writing water reports, answering letters or receiving information for some of the columns such as Carp Slyme or Carp Casualties, this can all be carried out in the bivvy and then dropped off at the Post Office or at my printers Dave Watson of Print Solutions. So time for the 1993/1994 season was not going to be too much of a problem to me. However, I did have plans other than just catching *Bazil* but I was determined not to let these plans, however important they were, interfere with my fishing on the North Lake this season. It was tunnel vision for me, *Bazil* at almost any cost.

Because you are not allowed to prebait or even walk around Yateley during the close season without express permission, it's very difficult to draw any conclusions as to where the fish might be at the start of the season. However, you are allowed on the venue a week or so before the start, so I decided to make use of this small period of time before the start of the season. I had a few walks round during this time but did not see *Bazil* at all on my travels. The only two fish I did see were the North Lake *Thirty* which I estimated to be around 34 pounds, and the small common, which I estimated at around 18 pounds.

The actual stock of the North Lake has already been described in previous chapters but as a quick check, there is one forty, one thirty, four twenties and four smaller fish, so you can see you are not going to clock up large numbers of fish by tackling venues such as this. The most that people are looking for is one or two bites per season and many do not receive even this.

I knew that competition on the lake for swims would be very fierce again this season, as several anglers had told me that they intended to do large amounts of time on the venue. These anglers were Bernard Loftus and Sandy from the north, Dave Mallin from the Midlands, Kevin from Lowestoft, Alan Taylor and local anglers, Jeff Pink, Bucks Fizz and Stuttering Steve. Add to that the infrequent anglers, the anglers who come down for a week's holiday or a long weekend and it was obvious that most weeks would see upwards of eight to ten people on this very small water.

Previous indications had shown that large numbers of anglers which created a great deal of pressure did not equal large quantities

Early season success for Bernard Loftus with 'Arfur' at 32lb from the Car Park Lake

of fish coming to the bank. I realised that the competition was going to be very difficult and that not only was I going to have trouble in locating and finding *Bazil*, but locating or finding a swim would be equally difficult.

I arrived at Yateley two days before the start of the season and found myself in very good company in the car park. There were anglers from the other lakes on the complex who had the same idea as me. To get down a couple of days early, have a good look round and maybe trickle in a few baits in some likely looking spaces. The knowledge I had gained from last season just could not be ignored. The bay area behind the point and in particular *Bazil's Bush* had to be one of the places from where *Bazil* would be caught on a number of occasions this season. It always had in previous years and last year, it became obvious to all who fished there that *Bazil* was spending a large amount of time in this bay, as were the other fish.

This was due, we thought, to the large amount of Canadian Pondweed which could be found in this area. Something happened to the North Lake over a three or four week period before the start of the season which was to alter the nature of the lake completely

The Car Park Lake

from any year that I had ever fished on there. An outlet from the Split Lake into the North Lake had recently been opened out. The Split Lake had always been known for large quantities of weed whereas the North Lake never had any weed, not a strand, other than in the small bay around *Bazil's Bush*. This I think was due to a small inlet from the Car Park Lake at this point.

The opening of this new inlet into the North Lake allowed seeds and spoors from the weed in the Split Lake to enter the North Lake, and the weed in the North Lake was to flourish once the warmer weather arrived. In fact, by mid-July, the North Lake was virtually unfishable due to the huge amounts of weed growing in the water, which has an average depth of around about seven feet. The weed was growing from top to bottom all over the lake, except for the back bay. The area around *Bazil's Bush* seemed to be the most weed-free area of the lake this year. However at the start of the season I did not know this was going to happen so on arriving two days before the start, and having several walks round, I decided that I would move into *Bazil's Bush* for the start of the season.

I must admit to being a bit obsessed about the *Bush* but the results from the previous season had left me in no doubt that eventually *Bazil* would visit the *Bush*. I would be waiting for him and when he got there, I would catch him.

The two days before the start of the season in the car park passed very slowly. On the 15th of June, Ray Varndell, the area co-ordinator, drove into the car park and informed us that we were now allowed to move onto the lake and asked us if everyone had sorted out where they were fishing. This had all been sorted out the day before. In fact the North Lake was not going to be as busy as it had been in previous years. I believe there were about 12 anglers who intended to fish the first week of the season, whereas the season before I believe there were 18 anglers, that's just about every swim taken on the lake.

After making several trips from the car park up to *Bazil's Bush* with my tackle, I put the bivvy up, set the rods up, arranged my tackle and by midday on 15th June I was set up, ready in ambush for *Bazil*. My confidence was sky high, I'd joined Mainline Baits in the close season of this year and Zen had told me about a new bait that they had been formulating at the end of the season and during the close season, which had shown outstanding results on every water that had been fished. They called the bait the Grange Bait as it had taken the forty from the Small Grange in Essex on several occasions.

I decided that I would go in on this bait. In all the years that I've been fishing, with all the bait and tackle companies that I've been involved with, I have always formulated my own baits and I had always known exactly what the make-up and ingredients were. This was the first time that I did not. But I relied upon the merits which Zen and others told me about this bait. This bait was to be the most attractive ever put into the North Lake and *Bazil* was soon going to be mine.

During the afternoon of the 15th, most of the anglers on the lake were installed. There were still several swims free and everyone was walking around, chatting, looking in likely areas hoping to see the fish. Obviously they were keeping well down, having not seen this much activity on the banks for a number of months. Once the evening came around, several of us decided that we'd go to the pub for a couple of hours, have a couple of pints and something to eat and toast the new season.

There was to be a strange twist of fate for one angler from the West Country. I remember quite plainly standing at the bar talking to one of the bailiffs, Rob McGill, about the anglers that were now installed on the North Lake and saying that the *Corral* swim was still empty, and how incredible this was, as it had been one of the most productive swims on Yateley for a number of years.

Around this time, two anglers who had arrived from the West Country made their way up to the pub to find out what swims were left on the lake. One of these anglers was Bill Fowler. We told them what swims were empty, including *The Corral* and the swim next door, and he and his friend decided they would move in to this area. I remember thinking what a very good chance they had of catching a fish, but not *Bazil*. I thought they couldn't possibly catch *Bazil*. *Bazil* was going to be in *Bazil's Bush*.

At midnight that night, after a number of disasters, which included smashing one of the sides of my bedchair and burning down the front of my bivvy door and floor, but that's another story, I managed to get two baits out next to the bush. The method that I use for fishing close up to islands or trees, when you have to make the cast after dark, is by first making the cast as close to the bush as possible, tightening up the line and clipping the line behind the small half-moon shape clip on the spool of the reel. The bail-arm is then shut and the retrieve is made as normal. When you then want to cast this bait out accurately, up against trees or islands, you simply cast, giving an exaggerated force and when the lead pulls the line against the clip, it drops in under the bush. This does not damage the line in any way, it's very safe and I can recommend it fully as accurate casts can be made, even if you have been in the pub all evening, which of course is something that I would never do!

At first light it began to rain quite heavily so, putting on my waterproofs, I walked up to speak to the anglers that were along the bank from me. Everybody was complaining about the weed and how they had never experienced anything like it on the North Lake. Little did they know that the weed hadn't even come up properly yet.

Spike with 'Single-Scale' at 36lb. Car Park Lake - August '93

We had not seen anything in the bay or along the works bank area but, on the other side of the lake, some exciting events were taking place. Bill Fowler and his friend had walked down into *The Pipe* swim in the corner of the islands, 50 to 70 yards down from where they were fishing. The pipe was the outflow from the Split Lake into the North and the water was pouring through at a rate of knots, obviously creating quite a lot of oxygen in this small bay area. As they stood there looking into the bay, three fish appeared from the islands, one was *Bazil*, one was a 20 pound mirror and the other was the small common which on its last capture was 17 pounds.

Bill quickly went back to his swim to get a rod and dropped in a freelined, hair-rigged boilie amongst the three fish and a few free offerings. All three fish were seen to be feeding. In the confusion of the three bodies moving across the bait, Bill assumed that the bait had gone. It's still possible that the 20 pound mirror had in fact taken the bait and that Bill had struck the bait from it's mouth but when he did strike, he spooked the three fish. He may have even pricked the 20 pound mirror but that was the last they saw of *Bazil* and the small common, for an hour at least anyway!

North Lake - 'Works Bank' looking across to the 'Corral'

Going back to their swims and casting out, Bill's friend had a run in the early hours of the afternoon. According to him, he thought it was a coot when he first struck, and on seeing the line kite away from the island, he realised he'd got a carp. He shouted down to Bill who came down to help him with the netting. It was the small common, its weight slightly up at 19 pounds. They decided to photograph it there and then, even though it was raining but just as they were unpacking the video camera, one of Bill's rods screamed off. It was the rod which had been cast towards the island on the left hand side of *The Corral*, baited with Premier Fish Base and Peach Melba flavour which Bill had purchased on his way to the lake, knowing that this bait had been used a great deal on the North Lake. An unspectacular fight resulted in one of the biggest carp in the country sitting in Bill's net. It was *Bazil* at 45lb 12oz. At times like this, anglers have mixed emotions. You are obviously pleased for the angler successful involved and of course, it's quite natural to be disappointed yourself that it's not you that's caught the fish. I was very disappointed that it had not been me who caught *Bazil*. I didn't resent Bill his capture, he told me that he'd done some other fishing on the North Lake in previous years but I did know he was not one of the anglers who had worked for the fish as some others had done in the past.

When I spoke to Jeff Pink, later than afternoon as he was packing up, this being the end of his one week's holiday, he told me that he'd walked round to see Bill early in the morning and informed him of the spot where Jock White had taken the thirty on two occasions, a hot spot in *The Corral* with your rods cast down to the left towards the island. At this time, Bill had not been fishing this area and had chosen to fish out into the lake. On Pinky's recommendation, Bill had cast down there and an hour or so later, *Bazil* was in the net.

"So what can we do now?" I said to Jeff. Well Jeff was off to Elstow, he'd gained a season ticket in the Elstow syndicate for the year and intended fishing the rest of his week's holiday there. Although I hadn't caught any of the other fish in the North Lake, including *The Thirty*, I had set my stall out to try and catch a forty pound fish this season. If it wasn't going to be *Bazil*, then it would have to be *Heather*, *Heather* being the only other forty now on the complex. There were several swims now available on the Car Park Lake so I decided that a short move along the works bank to a swim next to Steve Nine/One could well be the order of the day.

During that day, I slowly packed up my tackle and thought about my recurring nightmare, which was happening yet again on the North Lake. When would *Bazil* come out again? Would *Bazil* come out again? Where would *Bazil* come out next? These were the very same questions that I was asking myself the previous year and now *Bazil* had been caught and it had all started again. I was very dubious about whether *Bazil* would ever come to my net.

I moved onto the Car Park Lake but didn't really have my heart in it. I intended doing a week on the Car Park Lake and then to move back on the North Lake, hopefully back in *Bazil's Bush*. Somebody in the meantime had moved into *Bazil's Bush*, a very dark fellow known as Rasta Andy. Andy was down for one week and decided to move into the *Bush* for whatever came along, carp, tench, bream anything. In fact, he had an array of rods ranging from swing-tip rods to roach poles, and of course a couple of carp rods as well, and seemed to spend an hour using each rod in rotation. However, he was enjoying himself and that's all that mattered.

I must admit that I wasn't really enjoying myself and after a couple of days I decided to pack up. I made arrangements to come back down in a week's time when Andy had gone and move back into *Bazil's Bush*. I was still convinced that *Bazil's Bush* was to be the place.

I said at the beginning of this story that I was intending to do things other than try and catch *Bazil*. Other quite major things... I suppose the biggest of these was trying to sell my house and the offices of Bountyhunter Publications and find myself a new place and new offices. Now this was obviously going to be fairly difficult when I was fishing on a lake 80 miles from where I lived. I decided to make full use of the next week by arranging mortgages, solicitors etc., all in Yateley, so that I could visit them quite easily from the lake and have everything carried out from my bivvy, rather than being at home. Other than selling my house and the Bountyhunter Publication offices, I, of course, had magazines to get out so all in all, I had quite a lot on my plate and my bivvy resembled my office more than a place that I used for fishing.

I moved back in the *Bush* a week later and started to put out my new Mainline bait in large quantities. There was quite a lot of activity around the *Bush*, with a large shoal of bream which made its way up and down the bay during the course of the day, and tench could be seen every now and then rolling just short of the tree line. I didn't know it at the time but the tench were really going to like this new bait. Over the next three weeks that I spent in *Bazil's Bush*, I was to catch over 50 tench from the *Bush* area, most of these fish being five pounds-plus. I also had several of the lake's bream but so far no carp action.

I was very concerned that the bait was being eaten as soon as I put it out there and that any chance I had of having a bit of bait there ready for *Bazil* when he came in for his dinner, was highly unlikely because of the tench.

Three weeks into the season, I received my first carp take on the North Lake. It was 5.30 in the afternoon, I was fishing quite tight, bait run up against the right hand side of the *Bush* when suddenly the whole lot just took off. Most of the takes I'd had from the tench had been small drop back bites but this was no way a tench. As I picked the rod up, the fish sped along the margins, moving to the right, heading out of the bay. It went under several overhanging trees and I could see quite clearly the wake the fish was making in the shallower water in the opposite margins.

I called down the bank for some assistance, no way did I want to

The 'OK Corral'

lose this, my first North Lake fish. Suddenly the line fell slack, and retrieving my tackle I found that the hook had totally straightened. I was certain that I hadn't applied that much pressure to the tackle, even though I was using 16 pound line with a 25 pound hooklink, but with only two pound test curve rods, it would have been very difficult for me to straighten that hook out on such a long line. Seventy yards of line has a fair amount of stretch in it as I am sure you will agree.

It occurred to me that I had perhaps opened the hook out by pulling back against the gravel, or that the hook point had not fully penetrated the fish's mouth, enabling the hook to open out. However, my first North Lake fish had disappeared. The worse thing was I didn't know which one it was, but in my heart of hearts I felt it wasn't *Bazil*.

I began to see a few fish in the bay around this time, and Dave Mallin had found two of the *Little Tells* caught in one of the corners in about 18 inches of water. Later that day, the small common was up there with them. I saw the small common on a number of occasions over my next session and it was on this next session that I received my next bite on the venue. My next carp bite that was.

Alan Taylor with 'The Thirty' at 34lb 4oz

Of course I was still catching tench, upwards of 12 a night.

My next bite came from the front of the *Bush,* but even though I was locked up and screwed down tight, the fish still made the sanctuary of the branches. Luckily for me, Kevin West was fishing the main *Works Bank* swim and, after a little bit of persuading, he agreed to swim out for me and see if he could free the fish. Kevin is a very strong swimmer and dived down under the branches. When he came up, he was shaking his head. He told me that it was very, very snaggy indeed under there, which of course I knew, but he had no chance of getting the line back. Everything was stuck solid and he couldn't see the fish anyway.

In the end, Kevin pulled for a break for me and everything was lost. Yateley North Lake two, Rob Maylin nil. I was getting very fed up at this time with the amount of tench that I was taking. It seemed to me that there was no bait being left by the morning and it was the morning I was sure, from experience of previous seasons, that *Bazil* would be caught. So I decided to have a word with Steve Morgan at Mainline about making me up a different bait which might be a little less attractive to the tench.

The bait I decided to use was basically a fishmeal and Robin Red boilie with a Plum flavour. A bait which I felt was very effective, knowing the taste that these fish on the North Lake preferred. I struck up a new friendship at this time with a fellow called Alan Taylor, not the Alan Taylor that makes the Kevin Maddocks videos, but another Alan Taylor, from Guildford. Alan had fished the lakes for a couple of seasons and was just as determined to catch *Bazil* as me.

A month or so into the season Alan had done no time on the water at all, having been fishing another water in the area, but decided that he would come down on the North Lake now the pressure of the start of the season was beginning to decrease and there were fewer anglers on the venue. Alan came down and had a chat with me and then had a walk round. I was fishing in the bay and *Bazil's Bush* as normal with Dave Mallin to my right in the next swim down.

As Alan came round the corner, he told us that he had seen two fish up in one of the top corners, a twenty and a common. He then informed us that he was going to fish on *The Point* at the other end of the lake. Off he went and Dave Mallin came round for a cup of tea. "He's a nice fellow, that Alan Taylor", he said to me. "Yes, he is",

I replied. Then Dave said: "Do you think he's a good angler?" "Yes, I think he's a good angler" I replied "why do you ask?" "Well it seems a bit strange that somebody who sees two fish in the top corner goes down and fishes *The Point* at the other end of the lake." "Yes, I suppose so." At seven o'clock the next morning, Alan was to have a take on *The Point* which turned out to be the second biggest fish in the lake, *The Thirty* and its weight was 34lb 4oz.

Alan was delighted, as we were for him. A splendid achievement on this difficult water and the third fish out from the venue.

Whilst I'd been fishing the *Bush*, I'd been keeping an eye on the top corner of the Car Park Lake. I knew that the fish in the Car Park Lake would take a floater and every now and then I'd sneak over with a pocket full of dog biscuits and my catapult and put some bait out around the bars, hoping that something would come up and take them. I'd done this on many, many occasions. In the previous season I'd taken the small common and had had one more chance at a fish. This season however, until now no fish had come up. In July this was to change, and over a two-week period I was to have three very good chances of taking fish off the surface. The main problem was the Canadian geese which moved into the swim to eat the mixers as soon as they heard the sound of the catapult. This was very annoying and if I could have caught a goose at this time I hate to think what I'd have done to it. They are such greedy, stupid animals, they just do not understand that the biscuits are not for them!

One Tuesday morning when returning from the cafe along the works bank, I noticed a fish of about 30 pounds mouthing the surface at some floating leaves half way along that bank. I quickly made my way back to *Bazil's Bush* to get my floater rod and some floaters. It was then that I realised that I'd left all my mixers in the car. Alan Taylor was fishing next to me at the time, I told him of my predicament and he said that he'd a bag of mixers that had been in his bag a long time. I quickly dropped in a few teaspoonfuls of one of Zen's Peach Melba Ultra Marine Oils and swilled them around in the bag and then moved back over on the Car Park, taking Alan with me.

The fish wasn't where it had been the first time I saw it, in fact it had moved round to the causeway between the Car Park Lake and the North Lake. I dared not fire out any mixers because I knew that this meant the end of any chance of the fish. There were around 40 Canadian geese on the lake at the time and if I fired out half a dozen mixers, 40 of them would be in my swim within two minutes and the fish would be gone.

It was a very difficult cast from under the trees on this causeway bank swim but after several attempts, and much swearing and retackling, I managed to get my float out at about the right distance that the fish was moving. The fish was way to my left at this time. I could see my float quite clearly sitting out there and my mixer a couple of feet away from it. It was textbook stuff really. Alan and I both saw the fish moving in from the left hand side. I turned to him and said "it's going straight for it" and Alan looked at me and said "it knows it's there". It went straight up to the mixer and swam straight past it. My heart was in my mouth. I turned to Alan but before I could say anything, he said "it'll be back" and with that, we both looked out, saw the fish turn round 180 degrees, swim back towards the float and the head came out of the water. In a second, the mixer had gone, the float disappeared and the line tightened up and I was in. Literally in, because I ran straight into the lake to get past the first weedbed while Alan ran back to get my unhooking mat and landing net from *Bazil's Bush*, some 20 feet away. I saw the fish roll after about five minutes, it was putting up a tremendous fight.

The captor returns

First blood, the incredible 'Dustbin' at 32lb 6oz

I definitely saw scales on its shoulder but the next time I saw it and it's leathery side, I wondered to myself could it be *Heather?* I seemed to have forgotten totally that I'd seen scales only a few seconds before. Anyway into the net it went and how pleased I was. I cannot tell you *how* pleased I was to finally land a fish from Yateley this season.

It was the fish known as *The Dustbin* and it's weight was 32lb 6oz. A beautiful fish and I was well pleased. This season wasn't turning out to be too bad after all!

The next fish to come out of the North Lake was a fish called the *Twenty Five* which came out at 26lb 8oz from the islands. The fish were spending an awful lot of time in the islands and although I liked fishing amongst islands, I try to reduce any chance of losing a big fish by fishing away from snags. I think the worst thing would be to hook a very big fish only to lose it because you fished in an impossible position to land it.

On my next trip down with my new fishmeal and Robin Red bait, I decided to fish *The Corral.* It was the first time I'd fished it this season, having put in an incredible number of nights in *Bazil's Bush.* Ironically the week that I moved out of the *Bush,* one of the *Tells* was caught from there and it had put on weight. It's new weight, 12lb 4oz. I did feel a bit of a wally at the time, all that time I'd fished in the *Bush* and I hadn't caught anything. Was something wrong, were the baits no good? Were the rigs a failure? I didn't think so, I'd caught well on these baits and rigs before and I'm sure that it was just pure chance that no fish happened to be there at that time.

Anyway, I wasn't going to let that spoil my next session on the water. I was in *The Corral,* a new swim and a new horizon. *The Corral* has to be the nicest looking swim on the lake, it sits centrally along the far bank and has a wide variety of features and areas that you can fish. To the right, you have the main islands. To the left you have probably the largest island in the lake at around 50 yards range, and out in front of you, a large open expanse of water which, this season, was totally choked with Canadian Pondweed.

I made several casts out into the main area of the lake but found it too solid with weed and decided that I would fish towards the large island to my left, the area where *Bazil* had been caught on opening day. I put out about 200 baits in two spots along the side of the island and was pleased that on the first night, I did not receive any bream or tench. I was sitting there at 8.30 the next morning, putting together some notes for this book actually, when the left hand rod suddenly screamed and the line pulled from the reel.

Bernard Loftus was fishing next to me and he heard me shout when I picked up the rod and found that a carp was indeed attached to the other end. Unfortunately, this fish had made the snags and, even though I was fishing with 20 pound line, I did not want to risk losing the fish in these bushes. I had already made up my mind that, should it get through the snags, I would undo the bail-arm and go out and try and free the fish from the branches. Bernard came down and offered to swim out whilst I held the rod. He would hopefully free the line, allowing me to play the fish from the bank using the rod.

When Bernard got out there, he found there was a massive spider's web of branches and lines close to the island and that the fish had zig-zagged through these snags. However, the line had gone right through the snags and out the other side. He informed me that there was no chance of me pulling it back by the rod, and that I should get out there with the net to him as we may have to bring the line in by hand and net the fish just on the line. Of course, I did not really want to do this but under the circumstances I had no option. Bernard informed me that he had now seen the fish and it wasn't *Bazil,* and although it was a relief that it wasn't *Bazil,* because I could well lose this fish, I was still very disappointed. Disappointed in one way but pleased in another. This was to be my first North Lake carp, it was the big common at 24lb 4oz. The first time that this fish had been landed in three years, a very long, old fish, but it made me very happy indeed and a celebration was definitely in order.

August slipped slowly by, there were no fish caught at all. In fact the water seemed totally devoid of life. I spent many hours walking around the pit on the sessions that I had down there. My actual number of nights were now clocking up to between 40 and 50 on the lake. I'd managed to sell my house, purchase a new one and the Bountyhunter offices. This did mean one day away from the lake, when I went home to help my wife move. How lucky I am to have someone so understanding. My wife, Karen, knew how much I wanted this fish and she was 100 per cent behind me. In fact, on a number of occasions, she brought the children down to the lake to spend the day with me because she knew how much I was missing her and the children, having spent almost all of the summer down at Yateley.

I'd been baiting the River Blackwater with particles over the space of a couple of weeks because Alan Taylor and I had seen several carp in amongst the streamer weed. Alan and I actually cleared a swim out because there are no swims on that stretch, nobody fishes the river, everybody goes there to fish the lakes. By continual baiting we soon attracted a large number of small carp into the area. These fish seemed to be between four and eight pounds, the majority being mirrors.

On one of the trips when my wife brought the children down, I decided to have our first go at fishing the river, and my daughter Natasha who is only eight, was delighted to catch her first carp - a little mirror of five pounds which made her very pleased indeed and her dad very proud! Not to be outdone, my son Ashleigh caught a chub of a pound and a half, a great achievement as Ashleigh is only six, and they did it all on their own.

I must admit to being quite interested in fishing the river. In fact, I was so bored fishing the North Lake that I became more interested

Bazil's Bush

in fishing the river than the lake. During the next few weeks, I caught 12 different carp from the river, none of them very big but all very exciting fishing. I shared my fishing with Steve Nine/One and Alan Taylor and in the end, we had 16 different carp from the river. These were all returned to the river and may well grow into doubles in years to come.

Towards the end of August, Dave Mallin and I were sitting in the *Bush* swim when a fellow who we'd seen walking round on a number of occasions informed us that he'd seen *Bazil* and *The Thirty*, and several other fish up in the top corner of the lake. Dave and I quickly reeled in and made our way up to this corner. Indeed, there they were, *Bazil* and *The Thirty*. On climbing the trees, we could see there were not just a few of the fish, but all ten and some bream were basking up in this top corner.

Dave and I tried every method we knew, floaters, free-line baits, float fishing - everything, but nothing would make these fish feed. As it turned out, Dave Mallin had to go home that afternoon so I moved into the top corner as quietly as possible and hoped that the fish would stay there. I decided not to put a bivvy up but to lay my bedchair out flat and to lay on it out in the moonlight. I had my rods

Looking down the bay from the 'Bush'

as close to hand as possible, positioned the baits under those hanging branches in the corner and went to sleep full of anticipation.

There were no anglers on the North Lake that particular night, which was unbelievable, considering there had been more than a dozen most nights of the season. I had the place to myself and I was on the fish. I was very confident. This had been the second or third time where I'd actually been on the fish this season. At three o'clock in the morning, laying there fast asleep on the path, I suddenly felt a pair of hands pushing down on my chest, I jumped out of my skin as you can well imagine, only to find that Bernard Loftus, walking round with his tackle, had stumbled across my bedchair and fallen on top of me.

If I could have got my arms out of my sleeping bag, I would have definitely knocked him out, but I was thrashing around like a lunatic in a straight-jacket, trying to get this fellow off the top of me. Bernard apologised profusely, this was the sort of time that he always turned up, doing his shift on the buses and then driving for three hours to the North Lake. You have to admire him for his determination.

The next time I came close to catching *Bazil*, we found him in an area known as the *Thirty, Forty* swim. This swim was in the heart of the islands, a swim where a number of years ago a chap named Ray Fuller had caught *The Thirty* and *The Forty* in a single morning. There's a large bush to the left hand side of the swim and in this bush, four fish could be seen clearly; one was *The Forty*, the other three were twenties.

Dave Mallin was first to move and went quickly into the *Thirty, Forty* swim. I moved to his left into the *Pipe* swim where the fish had been pricked on opening day. Both Dave and I were confident that something would happen but although we fished there for three days, we didn't see a single fish after we'd moved in.

There have been a number of lines lost around the lake by people fishing in the snags and *Bazil's Bush* had become almost unfishable due to the amount of tackle that had been lost in there this season. Personally, I had lost three lots of line which had obviously caused other people to lose their tackle. I got permission from Ray to go out in the boat and get the snags and line out of the bush. Whilst I was out there, I had a good look around. The bush area just didn't look right, the weed had completely died off in the bay and it looked very barren under the bush.

Whilst rowing back to my swim in *The Corral*, I had a quick look around the *Corral Island* and found two clear gravel areas up against the island margins. This I thought would stand me in good stead for future sessions. Over the next few days, I moved swims several times and on the advice of Glyn, the cartoonist for *Big Carp* magazine, who had seen a fish jump on the works bank. I moved round there for a four-day session in the most torrential rain and worst conditions I think I've ever fished in. My confidence was at rock bottom, conditions didn't look good, the fish just weren't showing but I knew that I must keep the pressure on, keep going down there at all costs and in the end, surely *Bazil* would be mine.

When I moved off the works bank, Bernard Loftus and his friend Corky had moved into the *Corral* and the next one down from the *Corral* for a four-day session. I intended going home for three or four days but hoped to get back before they left. However, due to work commitments and a very enjoyable time at home with my family, I stayed an extra day and missed Bernard and Corky. When I went back to the North Lake, no-one had seen anything but Wayne Dunne, who was fishing the Car Park Lake, told me that Bernard had seen a fish to the right of the *Corral*.

The *Corral* area had always been good around September/ October. This had been the time when Pizza had caught his fish the year before, and also when Jock had caught the two thirties in the two previous years. So I moved my tackle in the *Corral* with the intention of doing a ten-day session. I really was putting in a tremendous amount of time, but for the most part, I was enjoying it. Kevin from Lowestoft moved into the swim to my left which fishes the back edge of the island. I don't really like anyone fishing this area while I'm in the *Corral* because it does seem to cut your chances down of any fish moving from the far side of the island to your side, getting to you without being intercepted by other baits.

There were several of us along this bank, we all felt as though this was the area to be in, and at four o'clock the next morning Kevin came down with the good news that he had indeed caught a fish. His first from Yateley complex in three years fishing, it was the *Twenty Five* again at 26 pounds exactly. I knew that I was definitely in the right area and I made my mind up that I'd keep putting the bait in and stay in the *Corral*.

The two areas that I fished were down towards the channel, and one of the clear spots up against the island that I'd found when I was out there in the boat. I found this area virtually impossible to bait because of the ducks. The water here was only two feet deep, the gravel totally clean and as soon as I put any bait out, the ducks were diving down on it and causing me untold problems. The left hand bait in the channel however, stayed virtually untouched. One week into the session I'd seen no fish at all but still felt very confident that I was in the right area. I baited up very heavily down towards the channel with crumbed boilies, I was sure that this would be the area where I'd catch a fish. The water here is about six feet deep and the ducks weren't diving down, they were more interested in picking up the baits on the right hand rod which was in the much shallower water.

At ten o'clock on Wednesday 22nd September, I was sitting behind my rods, looking out at the lake when I had a bleep on the left hand rod. I was fishing the Baitrunners totally locked up so that the fish could pull no line from the reel whatsoever. The idea was that I would stop them reaching those snags which had almost cost me the common. I had a brand new 20 pound line on with a 25 pound Kryston Silkworm hooklink and a size four hook. I certainly had the tackle to keep anything away from those trees.

I hit the rod on the single bleep and the rod arched over. A fellow called Nick who'd been fishing the Pad Lake was standing next to me at the time (he'd recently caught the Pad Lake fish at 38 pounds). The rod bent over and I immediately turned to him and said that it was definitely a carp. I bent the rod to maximum test curve to hold the fish away from the snags and it surfaced up against the branches no more than six inches from the dangerous snags. This was a tight line, the fish kited along the front of the island and travelled along a section of the island for about 15 feet. We could see the back of the fish quite clearly, light brown with a pinkish hue.

Both of us realised that I'd hooked a very big fish indeed. Nick turned to me and said "that looks like *The Thirty.*" I wasn't convinced - it was a very long powerful fish, and regardless of how much pressure I was putting on with the rod, it was holding its ground. Still, I'd moved it away from the snags, surely it was going to be mine now? Suddenly the line cracked like a gun shot, the line had parted - a brand new 20 pound line. It had cut on the close-in bar. I was absolutely devastated. I threw the rod down into the lake and my arms fell by my side and I felt the blood drain from my body

Natasha and Ashleigh

as shivers ran up my spine.

I left the swim and walked up to see Dave Mallin, I met him coming my way with a carp. "I've balls'd it up Dave," I said. "Oh no what have you done?" he replied. I said: "I've lost one of the big two." Dave interrogated me like the SS for the next half an hour, he too wanted to know if I thought that it was *The Forty*. If it had been there was little point in either of us staying on. Nick and I were both convinced that it had to be *The Thirty*, it couldn't be *The Forty*. *The Forty* was gun metal blue on the back, this was a very light brown-pinky fish. It had to be *The Thirty*. I convinced myself that I hadn't hooked *Bazil* and I was still in with a chance.

Everybody that turned up over the next few days was told the same story and by the end of the week, I was certain that it was *The Thirty,* and that *The Forty* was still well on the cards. On Friday 24th September, Peter the Painter, Nanu, and Steve Newman turned up to fish and moved in to the two swims to my right. These two fellows are excellent company. I'd first fished with Steve down on the Pad Lake several years before and we'd struck up a strong friendship. I couldn't think of two people whose company I'd prefer, although I've got some very good friends down on the North Lake, most of those weren't fishing over this period.

On Saturday 25th September, at ten o'clock in the morning, I was sitting in Nanu's swim looking out across to the works bank which is directly opposite the *Corral* where I was fishing. There had been someone in the *Works Bank* all week and he hadn't caught anything. Pinky, who was fishing on the point, was sure that a fish had jumped out in front of the works bank on the Friday. As I sat there (at ten o'clock, Saturday morning) looking out across to the angler's bivvy, I saw *Bazil* jump three feet from the water. I cried out "*Bazil* " and Pete the Painter and Nanu both stared into the lake. The ripple had taken away the splash where the fish had landed but they had a rough idea of where it had jumped. I ran down to my swim and looked across to pinpoint the position. It was roughly in front of the works bank, straight across from me at 80 yards range.

I cursed my luck that someone was on the works bank as I would have liked to move round immediately. Half an hour later Pete the Painter told me that the fellow was going home at 12 o'clock, somebody was coming down to pick him up. Now I had a decision to make, was I going to move round or was I going to cast from the *Corral*, a long distance into the weed?

Of all the days that I'd fished the North Lake during the season, I had never made any appointments there was nothing I needed to do. Every day was my own, but, on this particular Saturday evening I had made arrangements to have dinner with my wife, brother-in-law and sister-in-law. Of all the days in all the year to have to pack up and go out for dinner, it happened to be the one day that I had seen *Bazil* jump out in my swim. Unbelievable! I just couldn't believe it. What a strange twist of fate.

At 12 o'clock the fellow in the *Works Bank* swim packed up and left. I wound both my rods in and cast out to where I'd seen *Bazil* jump. The weed was very, very thick. Pulling back, I found a couple of areas that weren't clean but the weed was sparse and I decided to leave my baits there for the four hours I had left before I had to pack up at four o'clock in the afternoon. I put out 30 baits, roughly in that area and stood behind my rods willing *Bazil* to take the bait.

During those four hours, I saw *Bazil* on three more occasions. Twice just his head popped up, and on the last occasion, at five minutes to four in the afternoon, *Bazil* leapt clear of the water again. One of the most amazing sights I've ever seen in carp fishing. This huge fish, black, red and blue leaping clear of the water and crashing back on top of my baits. Nanu knew that I had to go at four o'clock and Pete the Painter was already packing up to go. "There's nothing else for it mate," I said "I've got to go." So, packing everything up, I made my way back to the car park, praying that no-one would go in the *Works Bank* swim before I returned after having taken the wife out.

I'd arranged to meet my wife at her mother-in-law's in London, as it was in London that we were going for the meal. When I saw her, the first words I said were: "*Bazil* and the others (I exaggerated slightly) are jumping out in my swim." She turned to me and said "you should have stayed." I couldn't believe it. Yes I should have stayed, but I'd made arrangements to go out and I had to stick by them. My wife had been very good to me over the course of the season, one of the very few occasions that I'd taken her out, I could not break the date.

We went out and had a wonderful meal, and at about 1.00am I drove her back to my mother-in-law. At this time it was not *Bazil* that I had on my mind, I must admit, but as I was told there was no chance of 'that' I made up my mind that I would go back and set up again in the *Corral*. I drove back from London and arrived back in

The big North Lake common

the car park at quarter past two on Sunday morning, quickly got changed and made my way up for the hundredth, thousandth time through all the mud and crap on the long haul up to the North Lake slipping and sliding through the puddles, up to my knees in mud. I was tired, it was 2.30am, what the hell was I doing back up here?

I decided as I reached the North Lake that I wasn't going to be the only one awake. I'd go round and see Nanu, get him to make me a cup of tea and tell me if he'd seen anything. I woke Steve up and he said that he'd been asleep since about seven o'clock that evening and was glad to be woken up for a smoke and a cup of tea. We sat and talked and had a couple of cups. Steve said he'd seen one fish out in the area.

At 3am on Sunday 26th September, I retackled my rods, put on fresh bait and cast back roughly in the area where I'd seen *Bazil*

"YEEEEES!"

jump on Saturday afternoon. I was so tired I could hardly be bothered to zip my sleeping bag up, but as it was so cold and I was out in the early morning air, I fastened it right to the top and snuggled down for a good night's sleep.

At 8am the left rod was off. I was totally in a daze, I couldn't seem to get my eyes focused. I remember waking up, facing away from the lake and wondering where the hell I was. I tried to pull the zip down on the sleeping bag but I couldn't, so I swung my legs off the bed, stood up in all the mud just outside my bivvy, still in the sleeping bag, grabbed the left hand rod, tightened up and then fell back into the bivvy, sitting on the edge of my bedchair with the rod poking out of the doorway. Nanu was then at my side. His first words were: "what is it mate?" I was into the fish and felt the head knock, that telltale knock when you know exactly what you've got on the end. "It's a carp" I said, "it's definitely a carp." "Yes," he said, but I was 80 yards out in an absolute jungle of weed. Still, I had a 20 pound line on, I'd got a very good chance just pulling it in.

I began to haul, pumping, hauling, pumping, hauling... a huge weedbed at 80 yards range came into view. Any second I was waiting for the line to snap again as it had done on the 35. Slowly the weedbed came towards me, not once had I felt the fish in the whole fight. The weedbed that came towards me was the size of a dining room table. There must have been about 500 pounds of weed sliding across the surface. "Is it still on?" Nanu said. "I don't know mate, I'm not even sure what it is. I'm certain it must be a carp. Net the whole lot," I said to him. Nanu sank the net down into the water and I dragged the weedbed into the net.

We stared down into the weed. At first nothing moved and then in the left hand corner of the net, we saw a piece of brown tail the size of a postage stamp. "It's a carp, it's a carp!" We shouted across the lake and both of us jumped up and down like school kids. The next minute, we were indeed like two school kids opening Christmas presents on Christmas morning, ripping into the weed to see what was in the net. "It's got to be a twenty" I said, but more weed was moved and the size of the fish grew: "Oh my God, it's got to be *The Thirty.*" Another clump of weed came out of the net. Nanu turned to me: "You've got *Bazil* mate, you've got him, you've got *Bazil.*"

I was stunned, totally and utterly lost for words. Well for about five seconds anyway, because after five seconds, they heard me in

Birmingham. I just screamed the place down, left Nanu with the fish in the net and ran a victory lap around the North Lake, jumping as high as I could in the air every five steps and screaming "*Bazil*" at the top of my voice. An absolute raving lunatic... but I'd done it.

All the hard work, all those nights. It was tunnel vision. The pressure, the achievement, I'd done it, I'd caught *Bazil*. Jeff Pink came round with his mobile phone and I phoned my wife, she came on the phone and I said: "I've got the bastard!"

I was too nervous and uncontrolled to be able to weigh the fish so I left the weighing to Nanu and George, one of the other anglers on the lake. They weighed the fish for me and informed me that it was 45lb 6oz.

"Yeeeeeessssss," I punched the sky again. I phoned my good friend Dave Watson, who helps me with the magazine, and he came down with his camera to take some pictures. It was a very emotional time, I was smiling so much that I'd almost swallowed my ears during the pictures. I did a series of photos on the bank, holding *Bazil*, telling *Bazil* that it was alright, she'd soon be back in the water, not to worry, I wasn't going to hurt her. Then taking hold of the sack, I climbed into the lake with *Bazil* and held her in my arms and stroked her sides because I didn't want to let her go.

I'd fished an incredible amount of time, gone through heartaches, lost fish, jealousy on three occasions when other people had caught *Bazil* and I'd been left disappointed. Now for this brief moment I had *Bazil*. I just held her in the water and felt her breathe and felt her gill covers going in and out against my hand. I looked into her glassy eye and she looked at me, definitely. Perhaps she was thinking 'at last I've got Rob Maylin and he's going to be off the lake'.

And that was it! That was *Bazil*! It's funny but I looked in the *Anglers Mail* the week after I caught *Bazil* and there were about four forty pounders caught. I mean there were four forty pounders in there that week, they weren't all caught that week, they were caught over a number of weeks, but all featured that week. I just thought to myself 'well I'm not even going to put her in the paper' I caught her for me, not for anyone else, not to endorse a bait or endorse some tackle. I caught *Bazil* for me and I think I'm something like the twenty-fourth person to catch it, but that doesn't matter. Loads of forties everywhere, there's only one *Bazil*. She's in the North Lake and I've had her.